T0135724

Jan Olaf Blech

Certifying System Translations Using Higher Order Theorem Provers

Vom Fachbereich Informatik der Technischen Universität Kaiserslautern zur Verleihung des akademischen Grades Doktor der Naturwissenschaften (Dr. rer. nat.) genehmigte Dissertation.
Eingereicht: 19.4.2008; wissenschaftlichen Aussprache: 16.2.2009; Dekan: Prof. Dr. Karsten Berns; Vorsitzender der Prüfungskommission: Prof. Dr. Stefan Deßloch; erster Berichterstatter: Prof. Dr. Arnd Poetzsch-Heffter; zweiter Berichterstatter: Prof. Dr. Markus Müller-Olm.

Bibliografische Information der Deutschen Nationalbibliothek

Die Deutsche Nationalbibliothek verzeichnet diese Publikation in der
Deutschen Nationalbibliografie; detaillierte bibliografische Daten sind
im Internet über http://dnb.d-nb.de abrufbar.

ISBN 978-3-8325-2211-7

Logos Verlag Berlin GmbH
Comeniushof, Gubener Str. 47,
10243 Berlin
Tel.: +49 030 42 85 10 90
Fax: +49 030 42 85 10 92
INTERNET: http://www.logos-verlag.de

Abstract

In this thesis, we present certifying system translations. This is a technique to guarantee the correctness of system translations. When conducting a translation of a system we compare for each translation the original and translated systems and decide whether the translation has been carried out correctly. This decision is based on a certificate generated during the translation process. Thus, we guarantee correctness of translations by verifying each translation run instead of the translation algorithm and its implementation.

The notion of correctness for system translations is formalized in a higher order theorem prover and based on distinct formalized operational semantics of the involved systems. Our systems are deterministic. Certificates are proof scripts. In this thesis we present a general methodology for certifying translations. Our primary focus is on a certifying compiler back end. A secondary case study is the translation of transition systems to reduce size for use by a model checker.

It has turned out that checking the certificates is the actual bottleneck of certifying translations. We compare the theorem provers Isabelle and Coq for their ability to serve as certificate checkers. We present solutions to problems arising in the context of this bottleneck. Finally, we discuss an implementation that has overcome this bottleneck thereby demonstrating the feasibility of certifying system translations.

To our knowledge, we are the first to present a certifying translations approach comprising automatically generated proof scripts as certificates and an explicitly formalized notion of correctness.

Kurzfassung

Diese Arbeit behandelt zertifizierende Systemtransformationen. Dies ist eine Technik, um die Korrektheit von Systemtransformationen zu garantieren. Nach dem Transformieren eines Systems vergleichen wir das Original- mit dem transformierten System und entscheiden, ob die Transformation korrekt durchgeführt wurde. Diese Entscheidung wird mit Hilfe eines Zertifikates getroffen, das während der Transformation erzeugt wurde. Wir garantieren also die Korrektheit der Transformationen, indem wir uns jeden Transformationsvorgang ansehen. Dies steht im Gegensatz zu Methoden, die Transformationskorrektheit garantieren, indem sie den Transformationsalgorithmus und dessen Implementierung ein für alle mal als korrekt nachweisen.

Unser Begriff der Korrektheit ist in einem Theorembeweiser formalisiert. Unsere Systeme sind deterministisch und zeichnen sich durch eine operationale Semantik aus, die auch im Theorembeweiser formalisiert ist. Zertifikate sind Beweise für den Theorembeweiser. Wir präsentieren eine allgemeine Methodik für zertifizierende Systemtransformationen. Unser primärer Fokus liegt jedoch auf der Codegenerierungsphase eines Übersetzers für Programmiersprachen. Eine zweite Fallstudie präsentiert zertifizierende Transformationen auf Zustandsübergangssystemen. Hier reduzieren die Transformationen die Größe der Systeme.

Die Zeit, die gebraucht wird, um Zertifikate zu überprüfen, ist der "Flaschenhals" bei der Verwendung zertifizierender Systemtransformationen. Wir präsentieren Lösungen, um das Überprüfen schneller zu machen.

Nach unserem Wissensstand sind wir die Ersten, die zertifizierende Systemtransformationen mit automatisch generierten Beweisen und einem explizit definierten Korrektheitsbegriff vorstellen.

Contents

List of Figures

1 Introduction

An important precondition for correct software development is the availability of compilers that can be trusted. Consider a compiler producing target code from a piece of source code. If the target code does not exactly perform as specified by the source code the compiler is not working correctly. Errors occurring due to such an incorrect translation can be very hard to trace.

This thesis is about guaranteeing that compilers and related translations work correctly. We present a methodology to achieve this goal: *certifying system translations*. The main contribution of this thesis is its application to compiler code generation.

The keyword *certifying* in certifying system translations describes the approach we use to guarantee correctness: We compare for each distinct translation run the original and translated systems. We use a tool that decides whether the translation run has been carried out correctly. The tool uses a *certificate* generated during the translation process. With our methodology we guarantee correctness of translations by verifying each translation run instead of verifying the translation algorithm and its implementation. *Systems* in our terminology comprise classical notions of state transition systems as well as programs given in some kind of programming language. *Translations*, in this terminology, comprise all kinds of transformations carried out on the structural elements of the involved systems.

The tool used for verifying the correctness of translations by checking the certificates is a higher-order theorem prover. We use an explicitly formalized notion of translation correctness for systems within our theorem prover. We base the decision whether a concrete system translation may be regarded as correct on these notions and distinct formalized operational semantics of the involved systems. Our notion of translation correctness is based on the execution traces of the systems. This captures the run-time behavior of systems adequately. Certificates are proof scripts for use by the theorem prover.

Apart from certifying compiler code generation we regard correctness of translations on transition systems as a second case study. These translations are conducted in order to reduce their size for use by a model checker. The results are used in a larger project for guaranteeing correctness of automotive systems.

The greatest challenge addressed in this thesis is the checking of the certificates. Checking them with the higher-order theorem prover has turned out to be the bottleneck of certifying translations. The task is especially time consuming. We show theoretical investigations and present techniques to solve the problems arising from this bottleneck. Among these techniques are checker predicates. These are predicates formalized in an executable way in a theorem prover to speed distinct subtasks of certificate checking up. Furthermore, we discuss implementations that have overcome the speed bottleneck.

To our knowledge we are the first to present a practical working methodology for automatically verifying translation runs based on generated proof scripts and an explicitly formalized semantics framework.

1.1 Motivation

The need to guarantee correctness of system translations arises in various areas throughout computer science. The two exemplary application areas of our methodology: code generation – a compiler transformation – and system abstractions are chosen carefully to demonstrate the feasibility of our methodology.

1.1.1 Code Generation

A guarantee for correctness of code generation is a prerequisite to achieve trusted software. It is especially valuable since today's software systems are developed using high-level model or programming languages even in safety-critical embedded systems. The systems' run-time behavior, however, is controlled by the compiled code. Results achieved from static analysis and formal methods on the source code level have often to be considered worthless if the formalization chain from high-level formal methods to the machine-code level is not closed. For this reason, the need for trusted compilation is more pressing than ever.

A small motivating example comprising a piece of source code and two pieces of machine code is shown in Figure 1.1. This example demonstrates two important aspects: we present the task of code generation and its characteristics. Moreover, we motivate our notion of translation correctness based on the run-time behavior of programs.

The source code program assigns the constant zero to a variable i. In a while loop the value of i is increased until it reaches 1000. During each execution of the loop the value of i is printed to some output device. Finally, after the loop the value of i is returned (and might eventually be given to some output device, too). Two possible machine code programs are shown. The first one returns the final value of the code piece – the value of i: 1000. The printing of the value of i during the execution is ignored. If one is only interested in the fact that a final value is computed correctly, this machine program may be regarded as a correct translation. A lot of classical verification work has been done using such functional notions of correctness. With verification facing the challenge to guarantee correct code for reactive systems the need arised for a more comprehensive notion of correctness. Such a notion takes the whole behavior of a program during its run-time into account. This is addressed in the second machine program. The second machine program is a direct translation of the source code. The constant zero is stored in a register. The increment operation and the printing of the value of i – corresponding to the register r1 – can be seen. The while loop is realized using two instructions: a comparison comparing the value of r1 to the constant 1000 storing the result in a second register r2 and a branch depending on this result. Finally, the value of the register r1 is returned. This second alternative captures the run-time behavior of the source code adequately with respect to the ideas underlying this thesis. Apart from the necessity of

Source Code
```
i = 0;
while i < 1000
        i = i + 1;
        print i;
return i;
```
Machine Code (alt. 1)
```
1: RETURN 1000
```

Machine Code (alt. 2)
```
l1: MOVE r1 <- 0
l2: ADD_CONSTANT r1 <- r1 1
l3: PRINT_CONSTANT r1
l4: LESS_THAN r2 <- r1 1000
l5: BRANCH r2 l2
l6: RETURN r1
```

Figure 1.1: Code Generation Example

regarding the whole run-time behavior of programs, several other characteristics can be seen from this example:

- There is a correspondence between variables and registers.

- A source code statement may be realized using several machine language instructions.

- Certain values may be computed in the machine code (the contents of register r2) that do not explicitly appear in the source language.

The techniques presented in this thesis crucially depend on the fact that certain parts of source code have corresponding parts in the machine code.

1.1.2 System Abstractions

Verifying system abstractions has gained importance in recent time. A huge amount of research has addressed the verification of large, complex or infinite-state systems using model checking. However, due to inherent limitations model checkers are unable to deal with such systems directly. So research concentrated on finding abstractions to reduce the state space sufficiently while preserving necessary precision. Since abstractions are getting more complex, it is not always clear if they are valid, i.e. that properties verified for the abstract system also hold in the concrete system. In our work on system abstractions we are bridging this gap: We apply our certifying translations framework and achieve certifying system abstractions. This is used to guarantee correctness of large classes of system abstraction runs.

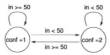

Figure 1.2: Example System Before Abstraction

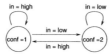

Figure 1.3: Example System After Abstraction

A simple running example for system abstractions and their verification is shown in Figure 1.2 and Figure 1.3. The first one shows a system before abstraction. Based on an input value a configuration (depicted as a circle) is chosen. If the input value is greater or equal than 50, the first configuration is encountered. If it is below 50, the second configuration is taken. Suppose, we want to modelcheck that the following very simple characterization:

input value below 50 *then second configuration is chosen*

of the system indeed always holds. If we model check the system in a naive way by examining each possible state, the state space explored gets very large, if the domain of the input value is large, e.g. there will be an infinite amount of possible state transitions if the domain of integers is chosen. Eventually it will get too large to perform the check that our simple characterization always holds. The solution of choice is to abstract the system using abstract values. In the case of the abstraction of the considered system the abstracted domain of the input value only comprises two values: low and high. This is enough to describe a system which behaves the same as the original one. The state space the model checker has to examine is reduced drastically: there are only four possible state transitions. One might, however, ask whether this abstraction has been conducted correctly. I.e. the question arises whether it is really sufficient to model check the abstract system to check a property of the original system.

A methodology stating conditions that guarantee that the checking of the abstract system is sufficient is presented in this thesis. Based on these conditions we present a framework and an implementation that does correctness of abstraction checks automatically. Thus, we are able to prove the correctness of an abstraction for a given property and then model check the abstract system for the property instead of the original one.

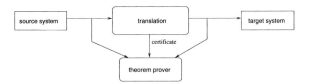

Figure 1.4: Certifying Translations

1.2 Our Approach: Certifying Translations

The certifying translations approach promoted in this thesis has been elaborated by us during the last years [BPH07, PHG05, GBPH06, Ble07]. It is best classified by comparing it to the classical approach to guarantee correctness of system translations: certified translations. We follow in this thesis the notions given by Xavier Leroy in 2006 [Ler06b] for compilers and adapt them for general translations. According to Xavier Leroy the two general approaches to guarantee translation correctness are characterized as follows:

- To achieve *Certified Translators* one proves in a first step that the translation algorithms work correctly for all given well-formed input systems. This is called algorithm correctness. In a second step one proves that the algorithms are correctly implemented on a given machine. This is called implementation correctness.

- *Certifying Translators* (cp. Figure 1.4) provide a proof (called *certificate*) that a concrete target system is a correct translation of a concrete source system. Such a proof is done whenever such a certifying translation from a source into a target system is performed. It is important to notice that these proofs do not make a statement about a translation algorithm or its implementation, but only about the relation of the two systems. In the case of a less complicated translation one does not always provide an explicit proof script. Nevertheless, if we prove the correct conduction of the translation after each run, we still call it a certifying translation.

Both approaches have already been studied in the context of compilation correctness for several decades.

Compared to translator certification, the technique of translators certifying their results has four main advantages:

- The issue of implementation correctness can be completely avoided. We do not have to trust the implementation of the translation algorithms on a hardware system or prove it correct.

- Similar to the proof carrying code approach ([Nec98, Nec97, App01]), the technique provides a clear interface between the translator and its users. In the certified translator approach users need access to the translator correctness proof to assure themselves of the correctness. For this reason, the manufacturer of the translator has to reveal the internal details of the translator, whereas the translation certificates can be independent of translator implementation details.

- The abstraction from implementation details frees us from reverifying the translator once an aspect of implementation changes slightly.

- Generating a proof script guaranteeing a correct translation run is often easier than verifying a complete translation algorithm. This is due to the fact that we do not have to consider very unlikely input systems for which a translation might be very hard to verify. We rather assume that the translation of such an unlikely system is always done incorrectly. Thus, in certifying translations we can give up completeness to make the proofs easier.

The disadvantages of the certifying translator approach is that a certificate has to be generated and checked for each (critical) translation. For larger systems, the checking of a certificate may be very time consuming.

The Trusted Computing Base of Certifying Translations

An important notion when reasoning about software correctness is the trusted computing base (TCB) of a computer system. The TCB is defined comprising all parts of a computer system we do not verify but have to trust in order to be convinced that our verification work indeed guarantees correctness.

In our work the TCB comprises the following items:

- The hardware and the operating system on which the checking is done.

- The parts of the theorem prover that check whether a proof script indeed provides a valid correctness proof.

- Sometimes, it is necessary to represent systems in a way that theorem provers can handle them. This involves some – usually simple – transformations. These transformations (and the hardware and operating system of the machine on which they are conducted) are part of the TCB, too.

Not part of the TCB is the piece of code that does the actual system translation. Moreover, the tool that generates the certificates is not part of the TCB. Certificates serve as an oracle to the theorem prover. They tell the theorem prover how to prove something correct, but only if it is indeed correct. Even if incorrect certificates are delivered the theorem prover will not be able to prove an incorrect translation run correct!

Regarding the formalizations that we fit into the theorem prover, we have to trust our semantics and correctness of translation formalizations. In some of our publications [GBPH06, GBPH06, BPH07] we have subsumed these trusted formalizations as *translation contract*.

1.3 Contributions

The contributions achieved in this thesis range from formalizing semantics of systems and the definition of translation correctness to practical engineering problems arising in our case studies like the application of theorem provers to large scale systems.

In our opinion the most important contribution is the establishment of techniques for certifying system translations that allow the use of notions of correctness and the representation of systems in a higher-order theorem prover while achieving time efficient certificate checking. This section summarizes this feature and other features presented in this thesis.

1.3.1 General Methodology

We have developed a methodology for certifying system translations and a semantics framework. It comprises the following features:

- We regard systems for which a deterministic small step operational semantics does either already exist or is defined by us.

- We formalize a generic notion of correctness that is based on states and state transitions. It is trace based and takes run-time behavior into account. It is formalized using simulation between the systems. Our notion can be instantiated for different application areas to ensure particular correctness issues that are not needed in every application domain.

- Our presented semantics and correctness criteria are formalized using higher-order theorem provers. Higher-order formalizations are well suited for providing an easily understandable basis to guarantee correctness with respect to formal verification.

- We discuss the relation of our notion of translation correctness and its relation to notions used in other works. Furthermore, we investigate how the need to formalize notions of correctness in a theorem prover effects the process of choosing such a notion.

- We present methods useful to improve the process of proving that two systems fulfill a correctness criterion.

Our methodology is aimed to prove distinct translation runs automatically correct with respect to the semantics and the correctness criterion. To our knowledge we are the first to use higher-order theorem provers and a distinct semantic framework in a certifying translations approach using proof scripts as certificates.

1.3.2 Certifying Code Generation

Apart from the features of our general methodology our compiler code generation phase has the following key characteristics:

- We have formalized syntax and semantics of intermediate language and MIPS target machine code. Moreover, we have instantiated our correctness criterion from our general framework resulting in a distinct correctness criterion for code generation.

- We regard a transformation from an intermediate language featuring arithmetic operations, array accesses, conditional and unconditional jumps as well as procedure invocation into MIPS machine code.

- Our code generation phase features several passes over the intermediate representation. It generates one or more MIPS instructions for one intermediate language statement.

- We present a compiler that is extended with a generator for automatically generating the proof scripts. These scripts are able to prove a distinct code generation run correct within our theorem provers.

- We present a theorem proving infrastructure that is able to automatically check generated proofs in adequate time. Furthermore, we analyze it with respect to time complexity issues.

- Executable checker predicates are used to further speed up the proving process. They may be regarded as little programs that check that a certain aspect in a proof script has been done correctly. We prove them correct and gain powerful tools that work much faster than traditional theorem proving for distinct problems. We present a general strategy for using checker predicates and some application areas in our infrastructure.

- One of our checker predicates makes use of specialized semantics definitions for the intermediate and MIPS language in order to achieve further speed gains. To prove this checker predicate correct, we first prove the specialized semantics correct with respect to the original semantics definitions.

To our knowledge executable checker predicates have not been studied with use in generated proof scripts before.

1.3.3 Certifying System Abstractions

Our system abstraction case studies include the following key items:

- We have developed a formal framework to apply well known theorems stating conditions under which properties of systems are preserved during abstractions to our case studies. This enables us to use simulation based correctness criteria from our framework. Thus we can apply our methodology used for compilers in this case study as well.

- We use a shallow embedding of the semantics for representing our systems.

- We present an implementation and show that abstraction case studies originating from a larger project can be verified in acceptable time.

- Our investigated abstractions comprise omitting parts of system descriptions and the abstractions of variable domains.

1.3.4 Evaluation

We present an evaluation of our implementations featuring the following issues:

- We compare our different checking infrastructures with respect to their overall design and concrete implementations.

- We investigate bottlenecks in the certificate checking process. We state time and time improvements achieved for our different techniques aimed at overcoming these bottlenecks.

  Since most bottlenecks appeared during certifying code generation the evaluation part puts its focus on it.

- We compare the theorem provers used in this thesis: Isabelle/HOL and Coq with respect to their ability to solve typical problems that have appeared during the context of this work.

1.3.5 Restrictions

Our methodology puts one major requirement and restriction on the systems we deal with.

- Our framework requires non-determinism to be mapped to deterministic constructs. For instance, a non-deterministic choice due to a user interaction is mapped to a deterministic consumption of an element of a universally quantified stream of user interactions. We do, however, present solutions that allow us to formalize non-deterministic systems within our framework.

Furthermore, we like to mention that apart from some use in the verification of the checker predicates from the certifying code generation, verification of translation algorithms is not part of this thesis.

1.4 Overview of the Thesis

Figure 1.5 shows a graph depicting the dependencies between the chapters of this thesis. After starting with this introduction comparable approaches to the certifying system translations approach are discussed as related work in Chapter 2. This chapter emphasizes on a comparison between different approaches on a very general level. It does not logically depend in any other chapter. More specialized related work is mentioned throughout this thesis and discussed in the appropriate chapters. We recommend reading

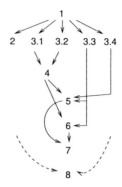

Figure 1.5: Inter Chapter Dependencies

the prerequisites. These are discussed in Chapter 3. They comprise sections introducing various mathematical notions (Sections 3.1 and 3.2) as well as a brief introduction to the theorem provers Isabelle/HOL (Section 3.3) and Coq (Section 3.4). We introduce our general framework for certifying translations in Chapter 4. We present and discuss our general notion of correct translation and its relation to other notions of correctness. This chapter is independent of a concrete theorem prover. A major part of this thesis is dedicated to the construction of our certifying code generation phase. The application of our framework as well as further issues in correctness of code generation are described in Chapter 5. We present our checker predicates in this chapter, too. The other application area of the framework is our system abstraction case study. It is presented in Chapter 6. In Chapter 7, we present the evaluation of our framework and our implementations. The focus of this chapter is on evaluating the code generation implementation. Apart from this a comparison between the theorem provers used throughout this thesis is given. Summarizing the achievements of this thesis, Chapter 8 features a conclusion as well as the discussion of possibly interesting areas for future work.

Some Conventions

The presentation of this thesis features the following conventions:

- We use *italics* for defining notions throughout the text. In general we do not reuse italic printing for further appearances of a defined notion. However, if we think it helps to understand the text, e.g. because a defined notion consists of several words, we make an exception.

- The keyword **definition** is used for definitions that are well known in the literature or slight adaptations of them. Other definitions are presented as figures.

2 Related Work

In this chapter we discuss related work. While the more specialized work is discussed in the context of the chapter it is relevant to, this chapter focuses on presenting related approaches to our certifying translations in a more general manner. In Section 2.1 we begin with a short review of work related to our main notions of translation correctness used in our general framework description. Starting with an historic overview Section 2.2 discusses work related to compiler correctness. All approaches known to the author that are especially relevant to certifying translations are extensively discussed in Section 2.2.1. Work that is especially relevant to compiler correctness and not covered in Section 2.2.1 is discussed in Section 2.2.2. Most notably we discuss certified compiler approaches. Since the area of certified compilers is older than certifying compilers and far more people produced contributing work within this field we only present most important work or work that is exceptionally relevant to this thesis. Finally, work on correct system abstractions is discussed in Section 2.3.

2.1 Work on Behavioral Equivalence

Our notions for expressing correctness of translations are based on simulation: A notion to capture the run-time behavior of systems and to relate them with each other. Simulation for program correctness was originally introduced by Milner [Mil71] in 1971. Different kinds of simulation have evolved over time. Van Glabbeek gives a comprehensive compilation of simulation based notions used for stating semantic equivalence of systems ([Gla01] and [Gla93]). His work is aimed as basis for process algebras which – like in our work – use simulation based notions of system equivalence.

Our framework uses operational semantics which was made popular through Plotkin's work on structural operational semantics in 1981 [Plo81]. Operational semantics captures the state transition behavior of systems. We do, however, not restrict ourselves to continuation based semantics as proposed in his work.

2.2 Work on Compiler Correctness

A large body of research has been done on certified compilers during the last decades. A bibliography [Dav03] is available covering most work from 1967 up to 2003.

Painter's and McCarthy's work [MP67] from 1967 is widely regarded as the first correctness proof for a compilation algorithm. A compiler transforming arithmetic expression into an operand stack oriented (like in today's Java byte code) machine language is proved correct. Further early investigations on proving correctness of compilers comprises the work by Samet in the mid nineteen-seventies [Sam75, Sam76]. He already proposed a certifying compiler approach. Furthermore, he investigated techniques of symbolically executing code sequences.

A further step towards formal compiler verification was done by Moore [Moo89, Moo96] during the late nineteen-eighties and early nineties. To the author's knowledge this work is the first to use a theorem prover (ACL2 [KM]) to show compiler correctness.

2.2.1 Work Related to the Certifying Translations Approach

Despite Samet's early work on certifying compilers, the idea of programs that check other programs' work is generally attributed to Blum and Kannan. Their 1995 paper [BK95] presents the idea in a more explicit fashion. Nevertheless, they do not look at translations that transform some kind of semantic carrying system representation, but look at computation of matrix rank, sorting, and greatest common divisor of two integers. Some of the possible advantages of the certifying translations approach are already proclaimed in this paper. These comprise the fact that for computations that solve or approximate solutions for problems in NP it is easier to check a solution, than to compute it in a first place. This can be derived from the fact that solutions for problems that are in NP can be checked in polynomial time with the help of an appropriate oracle which can be a certificate.

Translation Validation

The first major port of the certifying translations idea into the compiler community is translation validation [PSS98, ZPFG02, ZPFG03, ZPG+05, BFG+05, RSW01] by Pnueli, Siegel, Singerman, Zuck et al. The first paper was published in 1998. In the translation validation approach the compiler is regarded as a black box with at most minor instrumentation. For each compiler run, source and target program are passed to a separate checking unit comprising an analyzer generating items that have to be proved correct (called verification conditions). These items are checked using an independent checker. This checker is realized as a small theorem prover. The trusted computing base of translation validation comprises the checking infrastructure. This includes the analyzer and the small theorem prover.

Translation validators for different compiler phases have been developed during the last decade. They comprise *voc-64* where verification conditions for optimizations in the SGI Pro-64 compiler are generated (cp. [ZPFG03] by Zuck, Pnueli, Fang, and Goldberg) and TVOC for (cp. [BFG+05] by Barrett, Fang, Goldberg, Hu, Pnueli, and Zuck) generating verification conditions for optimizations in Intel's Open Research Compiler [RSW01]. A translation validation approach and implementation for the GNU C compiler has been done by Necula [Nec00] in 2000.

Like in translation validation, we consider correctness for each single compiler run. The analyzer generating the proofs in translation validation corresponds to our certificate generator. In contrast to translation validation our approach is based on a general higher-order proof assistant as proof checker. We also have an explicitly formalized semantics and a formal criterion under which we regard a transformation as correct. Further on, we use (more) information to generate the proof scripts from the compiler. This results in a relatively small certificate generator.

Tristan and Leroy present the first translation validation checker (called validator) that has been formally verified in their 2008 paper [TL08]. Thus – like in our work – correctness is based on a formalized semantics. The validator is used for verifying instruction scheduling. It is generated out of a verified Coq specification. The applicability of the validator is demonstrated using a compiler test suite with programs comprising up to 1000 lines of code.

Credible Compilation

Credible compilation introduced by Rinard in 1999 [RM99, Rin99] is an approach for certifying compilers. Credible compilation largely uses instrumentation of the compiler to generate proof scripts. These are used to prove distinct compilation runs correct. Like translation validation and in contrast to our work credible compilation is not based on an explicitly formalized semantics.

Proof-Carrying Code

Proof-Carrying Code [Nec98] – introduced in Necula's PhD-thesis during the late nineteen-nineties – is a framework for guaranteeing that certain requirements or properties of a compiled program are met. Typical requirements are type safety and the absence of stack overflows. It is mostly used in a scenario where one wants to execute code from an untrusted source. Proof-Carrying Code can guarantee that the code fulfills certain safety policies. Two kinds of parties are distinguished: code producers and code receivers – or consumers. While the code receivers may establish some criteria that they want the code to fulfill, the code producers prove that their code fulfills these criteria. They send the proof along with the code to the code receivers. A code receiver uses a checker to validate – using the proof – that the code indeed fulfills the demanded requirements.

In 1998, Necula and Lee [NL98] described a certifying compiler for their approach guaranteeing that target programs are type and memory safe.

In the early 2000s other authors have taken up the idea of Proof-Carrying Code. Foundational Proof-Carrying Code by Appel [App01, App03] is a technique for keeping the trusted computing base small. Wildmoser and Nipkow [WN05] prove a generator generating verification conditions that the code receiver wants to be fulfilled correct and relatively complete using the Isabelle/HOL theorem prover.

Proof-Carrying Code is aimed at guaranteeing distinct necessary conditions that have to be fulfilled in a correctly compiled program.

Unlike in our work, translation validation and credible compilation the goal in Proof-Carrying Code is not to ensure a comprehensive notion of compilation correctness. If one would use proof carrying code to guarantee compilation correctness, the code receiver would have to specify the behavior of the complete program to be received. In contrast to our approach and like in translation validation and credible compilation, there is no formal definition of correctness required. The challenges addressed by Proof-Carrying code community are mostly based on the problem that code producer and code receiver are not the same and the code producer is potentially not to be trusted.

The clear separation between the compilation infrastructure and the checkable certificate is realized in our approach as well and was highly influential for us.

2.2.2 Work Related to Certified Compilers

In this section we give an overview of the most important work on certified compilers and work which is especially relevant to us.

Leroy proves in 2006 [Ler06b] algorithms for a sophisticated multi-phase compiler back-end correct using the Coq theorem prover. To achieve a trusted implementation of the algorithm, it is exported directly from the theorem prover to program code. The work features a comparison and classification of certifying compilers. These are differentiated from algorithm verification based certified compilers. For this thesis we have adapted some of his notions he has introduced in this paper.

A similar approach exporting an executable implementation out of a theorem prover specification based on Isabelle/HOL is presented by Klein and Nipkow [KN06] in 2006.

In the late nineteen-nineties and early 2000s further work on compiler correctness was done in the Isabelle/HOL community. A compiler translating a subset of Java into Java byte code is proved correct by Strecker using Isabelle/HOL [Str02]. A working compiler is extracted from this specification by Berghofer and Strecker [BS03] resulting in executable ML source code. Nipkow specifies and verifies an algorithm performing lexical analysis correct [Nip98]. The specification is extracted to ML code.

Before investigating certifying compilers I was involved in verification of compiler optimization algorithms. The one described in 2005 [BGG05] uses an explicit simulation proof scheme for showing semantic equivalence which was formalized in a very similar manner to the simulation scheme described in this thesis. The work was done using Isabelle/HOL.

An important step in the direction of automating the generation of correct program translation procedures is explained by Lerner and Millstein [LMRC05] in 2005. A specification language is described for writing program transformations and their soundness properties. The properties are verified by an automatic theorem prover.

Lacey et al. [LJWF02] present in 2002 a framework to prove compiler optimizations with respect to temporal logic properties correct. Hence – like in this thesis – they use a trace based correctness criterion. The frameworks feasibility is demonstrated by proving three optimizations correct.

Techniques and formalisms for compiler verification, compiler result checkers, decomposition of compilers, notions of semantic equivalence of source and target program as well as stack properties were developed during the nineteen-nineties in the Verifix project [GZ99, GDG+96, Zim06, GGZ04] and the ProCoS project [BBF+92, FMO94, MO97] by Goos, Langmaack, Müller-Olm, von Henke, Zimmermann et al. Some of the formalization and verification work in Verifix was done using the theorem prover

PVS [ORS92]. Some of the work uses a combination of algorithm verification and program checking to produce certified compilers. The main motivation of using program checking in Verifix is that proving the correctness of the checker programs is simpler than proving the correctness of the compilation phase. Semantics definitions of the involved languages comprise operational semantics defined via abstract state machines and are related via a simulation based notion of correctness.

The development of a formally verified compiler for a C subset by Leinenbach, Paul and Petrova [LPP05] is part of the Verisoft project focussing on pervasive formal verification of computer systems.

2.3 Work on Correct System Abstractions

Prior to us work on correctness of system abstractions concentrated on showing soundness for all possible systems an abstraction algorithm or a certain abstraction technique was going to handle. In this section we give an overview on such work. To our knowledge, we are the first to introduce a certifying translations approach to the verification of system abstractions.

Abstract Interpretation [CC77, CC79] by Cousot and Cousot is commonly used for abstractions of data domains. It is often used for abstractions in transition system based scenarios.

Property preservation by simulation has been studied for different fragments of the CTL* logic and the μ-calculus. These are used to guarantee correctness of system abstractions. Clarke, Grumberg, Peled [CGP99], Bensalem, Bouajjani, Loiseaux, Sifakis [BBLS93] as well as Dams, Gerth, Grumberg [DGG97] use Kripke structures as their underlying system model. Either states of a system in consideration are labeled with atomic propositions or atomic propositions are labelled with states. Simulation based techniques often require correspondence checks between different states of a system. Using atomic propositions to characterize states for comparing two systems reduces a property preservation proof to the checking that the labeling of states that should correspond to each other is the same. Nevertheless, doing so complicates the treatment of systems where states contain valuations of variables.

Clarke, Grumberg, and Long [CGL94] use a system model similar to the one we present in this thesis, but this work is restricted to data domain abstraction, while our technique can be applied for different abstraction mechanisms, such as omitting entire parts of systems, too. Abstract interpretation based simulations as used by Bensalem, Bouajjani, Loiseaux, and Sifakis [BBLS93], and Dams, Gerth, and Grumberg [DGG97] also focus on the abstractions of data domains.

A language for representing transition systems and its formalization in PVS is given by Shankar in 2000 [Sha00b, Sha00a]. Their language is used for various purposes including system abstractions and reasoning about properties of systems.

Related work on formalizing state transition systems (I/O automata) in Isabelle is done by Müller and Nipkow [MN95, Mül98]. Reasoning about combining model checking and theorem proving techniques is done [MN95]. A methodology is presented [Mül98] to prove abstractions correct with respect to preservation of formulas. They use a notion of correctness based on output trace inclusion equivalent to simulation for abstractions. Correctness with respect to trace inclusion is proved for a class of abstraction functions. In contrast to Müller and Nipkow's work, we provide a methodology to prove that concrete abstractions fall into a well established class of correct abstractions. Their work concentrates on establishing such a class.

Müller and Nipkow have also developed extensions for Isabelle's HOL with types making the representation of traces easier ([MN97] and [MNOS99] (with Oscar Slotosch)). They use their extension in their work on theorem proving techniques for proving abstractions correct. An extension of HOL with a logic for computable functions (HOLCF) is presented.

3 Prerequisites

In this chapter, we present some prerequisites comprising basic mathematical notions, transition systems, simulation, and an introduction to the theorem provers used in this thesis. We assume that the reader is familiar with basic notions of compiler construction and some logic. For this reason, an introduction to compiler construction and logic is not covered in this chapter.

Section 3.1 presents some basic mathematical notions. Transition systems and simulation are discussed in Section 3.2. Brief introductions to the theorem provers that we use are given in Section 3.3 – presenting Isabelle – and in Section 3.4 – presenting Coq. The section presenting Coq concludes with a short comparison between the two theorem provers.

3.1 Basic Mathematical Notions

We want to emphasize some basic mathematical notions. These are particularly important to the semantic framework introduced in this work: (partial) orders and lattices.

Definition 1 (Partially Ordered Set, Poset) *A partially ordered set is a binary relation R over a set P (denoted (P, R)) for which the following conditions hold (assuming $a, b, c \in P$):*

$$
\begin{array}{ll}
a \; R \; a & \text{(reflexivity)} \\
\text{if } a \; R \; b \text{ and } b \; R \; a \text{ then } a = b & \text{(antisymmetry)} \\
\text{if } a \; R \; b \text{ and } b \; R \; c \text{ then } a \; R \; c & \text{(transitivity)}
\end{array}
$$

Definition 2 (Lattice) *Consider a partially ordered set (L, B). (L,B) is a lattice, iff for all elements x and $y \in L$, the set $\{x,\ y\}$ has both a least upper bound in L (join, or supremum) and a greatest lower bound in L (meet, or infimum).*

3.2 Transition Systems and Simulation

In this section, we present definitions of formalisms for representing transition systems. Furthermore, we define relations between transition systems: simulation and its variations. These notions are extensively used in the next chapters of this thesis. Recall from the introduction (Chapter 1) that certifying system translations are always based on some kind of transition system.

Transition Systems

The simplest form of a transition system is given in the following definition:

Definition 3 (Transition System) *A transition system* $K = (S, R)$ *is defined by* S, *the set of states and* $R \subseteq S \times S$, *the transition relation.*

A system may encounter states which change during a state transition.

All systems and programs that are subject to this work may be regarded as transition systems with respect to some abstract view. Recall the motivating example in Section 1.1.2 for typical representations of transition systems.

Definition 4 (Transition System with Initial States) *A transition system with initial states* $K = (S, S_0, R)$ *is defined by* S, *the set of states,* $S_0 \subseteq S$, *the set of initial states, and* $R \subseteq S \times S$, *the transition relation.*

The case studies regarded in this thesis have a set of initial states which may be explicitly mentioned in the definition.

The transition relation may be enriched with labels associated with a state transition.

Definition 5 (Labeled Transition System (with Initial States)) *A labeled transition system* $K = (S, \Lambda, R)$ *(with initial states* $K = (S, S_0, \Lambda, R)$*) is defined by* S, *the set of states, (* $S_0 \subseteq S$, *the set of initial states,)* Λ *the set of labels, and* $R \subseteq S \times \Lambda \times S$, *the transition relation.*

Labels may be used to encode output occurring during a transition. No output is denoted by $\tau \in \Lambda$. A transition featuring τ as output is called a silent transition.

A subcase of transition systems are deterministic transition systems.

Definition 6 (Deterministic Transition System (with Initial States)) *A transition system* $K = (S, R)$ *(with initial states* (S, S_0, R)*) is a deterministic transition system iff*

1. $\forall s . s \in S \longrightarrow \exists s_1 . (s, s_1) \in R$

2. $\forall s \ s_1 \ s_1' \in S . (s, s_1) \in R \wedge (s, s_1') \in R \longrightarrow s_1 = s_1'$

Thus, a deterministic transition system has a transition relation where each state from S has exactly one succeeding state. The transition relation defines a successor function on states (denoted $next : S \to S$). Deterministic transition systems are a key concept to this work.

Our definition of deterministic state transition systems does not allow that there is no succeeding state to a state encountered during a system run. Thus, we have no way of dealing with terminating systems directly. To fit them into our deterministic state transition definition, we allow to emphasize some states as final. We require that the succeeding state to a state from the set of final states ($final$) is always a final state, which is :

$$\forall s \in final. \ \exists s' \in final. \ next(s) = s'$$

Definition 7 (Deterministic Labeled Transition System (with Initial States))
A labeled transition system $K = (S, \Lambda, R)$ (with initial states (S, S_0, Λ, R)) is a deterministic labeled transition system iff

1. $\forall s. s \in S \longrightarrow \exists s_1 \in S. \exists l \in \Lambda. (s, l, s_1) \in R$

2. $\forall s \; s_1 \; s_1' \in S. \forall l \; l' \in \Lambda. (s, l, s_1) \in R \land (s, l', s_1') \in R \longrightarrow l = l' \land s_1 = s_1'$

The transition relation defines a label function on states (denoted *nextlabel* $: S \to \Lambda$) mapping a state to the label encountered during the next state transition.

A transitive closure R^+ may be defined upon transition relations of labeled transition systems inductively in the following way:

$(s, l, s') \in R \longrightarrow (s, l, s') \in R^+$
$(s, \tau, s') \in R^+ \land (s', l, s'') \in R \longrightarrow (s, l, s'') \in R^+$
$(s, l, s') \in R^+ \land (s', \tau, s'') \in R \longrightarrow (s, l, s'') \in R^+$

It allows the "merging" of consecutive sequences of transitions containing at most one non-τ label. This allows to compare transition systems with labels appearing in the same order.

We use transitive closures on transition relations to define a kind of transition system which remembers the last label it encountered: Labeled transition systems with label memory. These transition systems save the last label encountered inside their states. It can be recalled by a special function *prevlabel*.

Definition 8 (Labeled Transition System with Label Memory) (and Initial States) *A labeled transition system $K = (S, \Lambda, R)$ (with initial states (S, S_0, Λ, R)) is a labeled transition system with label memory iff there exists a function prevlabel $: S \to \Lambda$ such that:*

1. $\forall (s', l', s'') \in R. \; \forall s \in S. \forall l \in \Lambda. (s, l, s'') \in R^+ \land l \neq \tau \longrightarrow prevlabel(s'') = l$

2. $\forall (s', l', s'') \in R. \; (\neg(\exists s \in S. \exists l \in \Lambda. \; (s, l, s'') \in R^+ \land l \neq \tau)) \longrightarrow prevlabel(s'') = \tau$

This definition is used to model systems which always remember parts of their execution history, as e.g. a system that writes values during its execution to an output buffer – and the buffer is modeled as part of the system's state. Note, that the label memory ensures that a distinct state must always have last encountered a unique label, even if it can be reached via different predecessor states. Thus, this definition puts constraints on the modeling of systems and states (some level of bookkeeping of execution history in the states is required).

Kripke Structures

Another kind of transition systems are Kripke structures. Using the definition from Clarke, Grumberg, and Peled [CGP99], we define Kripke structures as follows:

Definition 9 (Kripke Structure) *A Kripke structure* $K = (AP, S, S_0, R, L)$ *is defined as a five tuple where:*

1. *AP is the set of atomic propositions.*

2. *S is the set of states and S_0 the set of initial states.*

3. *$R \subseteq S \times S$ the transition relation.*

4. *$L : S \to \mathcal{P}(AP)$ the labeling function assigning sets of atomic propositions to states.*

Note, that unlike for labeled transition systems where labels are associated with transitions, in Kripke structures labels are associated with states.

(Bi-)Simulation Relations

Simulation and its derivatives relate two systems to each other by comparing possible initial states and the transition behavior.

A prerequisite to relate systems via simulation to each other is the establishment of a simulation relation. Simulation relations relate states from the systems in comparison to each other.

Definition 10 (Simulation Relation) for Unlabeled Transition Systems *Given two transition systems K and K', a relation on their states $H \subseteq S \times S'$ is a simulation relation between K and K', iff for all states $s \in S$ and $s' \in S'$ with $H(s, s')$ the following condition holds:*

- *For every state $s_1 \in S$ such that $R(s, s_1)$, there is a state $s_1' \in S'$ with the property that $R'(s', s_1')$ and $H(s_1, s_1')$ hold.*

For labeled transition systems, we require the labels encountered in both systems during a state transition to be the same (cp. e.g. [Gla93] on this).

Definition 11 (Simulation Relation) for Labeled Transition Systems *Given two transition systems K and K', a relation on their states $H \subseteq S \times S'$ is a simulation relation between K and K', iff for all states $s \in S$ and $s' \in S'$ with $H(s, s')$ the following condition holds:*

- *For every state $s_1 \in S$ and label $l \in \Lambda$ such that $R(s, l, s_1)$, there is a state $s_1' \in S'$ such that $R'(s', l, s_1')$ and $H(s_1, s_1')$ hold.*

For deterministic transition systems the last condition can be simplified to:

1. *$H(next(s), next'(s'))$ holds.*

2. *$nextlabel(s) = nextlabel'(s')$ holds.*

If we can prove that $H(s, s')$ or $H(next(s), next'(s'))$ implies $nextlabel(s) = nextlabel'(s')$ we can abandon the second item.

Simulation allows non-deterministic behavior in one system to relate to a deterministic version of the behavior in another system. If one wants to preserve all the non-determinism, bisimulation is the simulation derivative of choice.

Definition 12 (Bisimulation Relation) *Given two transition systems K and K', a relation $H \subseteq S \times S'$ is a bisimulation relation between K and K' iff for all states $s \in S$ and $s' \in S'$ with $H(s, s')$ the following conditions hold:*

1. *For every state $s_1 \in S$ (and label $l \in \Lambda$) such that $R(s, s_1)$ $(R(s, l, s_1))$, there is a state $s'_1 \in S'$ with the property that $R'(s', s'_1)$ $(R'(s', l, s'_1))$ and $H(s_1, s'_1)$ hold.*

2. *For every state $s'_1 \in S'$ (and label $l \in \Lambda$) such that $R'(s', s'_1)$ $(R'(s', l, s'_1))$, there is a state $s_1 \in S$ with the property that $R(s, s_1)$ $(R(s, l, s_1))$ and $H(s_1, s'_1)$ hold.*

For deterministic transition systems, simulation and bisimulation are the same.

Weak (Bi-)Simulation Relations

Sometimes, it is convenient to merge several transition steps and treat them like a single step. This is what a weak simulation relation does. With weak simulation, we can relate labeled systems where several transition steps in one system correspond to several steps in another system.

Definition 13 (Weak Simulation Relation) *Given two labeled transition systems K and K'. R^+ and R'^+ are the transitive closures on the transition relations of K and K' containing at most one non-silent transition. A relation $H \subseteq S \times S'$ is a weak simulation relation between K and K', iff for all states $s \in S$ and $s' \in S'$ with $H(s, s')$ the following condition holds:*

- *For every state $s_1 \in S$ and label $l \in \Lambda$ such that $R^+(s, l, s_1)$, there is a state $s'_1 \in S'$ with the property that $R'^+(s', l, s'_1)$ and $H(s_1, s'_1)$ hold.*

For deterministic labeled transition systems, the definition of weak simulation can be based on the *next* function if some bookkeeping of labels is done within the states. We can rewrite the weak simulation condition ($next^x(y)$ denoting that the function *next* is applied x times to the value y):

- For every state $s_1 \in S$ and natural numbers i such that $s_1 = next^i(s)$, the system in state $next^i(s)$ has encountered at most one non-silent transition $l \in \Lambda$ in the last i steps, there exists a state $s'_1 \in S'$ and natural number j such that $s'_1 = next'^j(s')$, the system in the state $next'^j(s')$ has encountered at most one non-silent transition l during the last j steps, and $H(s_1, s'_1)$ holds.

For deterministic labeled transition systems with label memory, we can write this in the following form:

- For every state $s_1 \in S$ and natural numbers i such that $s_1 = next^i(s)$ where $next^i(s)$ contains at most one non-silent transition,

  1. there exists a state $s'_1 \in S'$ and natural number j such that $s'_1 = next'^j(s')$, $next'^j(s')$ contains at most one non-silent transition,
  2. $H(s_1, s'_1)$ holds,
  3. $prevlabel(s_1) = prevlabel'(s'_1)$ holds.

A notion of weak bisimulation relation can also be defined. This ensures the preservation of non-determinism but allows the correspondence of several steps in one system to a couple of steps in another system.

Definition 14 (Weak Bisimulation Relation) *Given two labeled transition systems K and K'. R^+ and R'^+ are the transitive closures on the transition relations of K and K'. A relation $H \subseteq S \times S'$ is a weak bisimulation relation between K and K', iff for all states $s \in S$ and $s' \in S'$ with $H(s, s')$ the following conditions hold:*

1. *For every state $s_1 \in S$ and label $l \in \Lambda$ such that $R^+(s, l, s_1)$, there is a state $s'_1 \in S'$ with the property that $R'^+(s', l, s'_1)$ and $H(s_1, s'_1)$ hold.*

2. *For every state $s'_1 \in S'$ and label $l \in \Lambda$ such that $R'^+(s', l, s'_1)$, there is a state $s_1 \in S$ with the property that $R^+(s, l, s_1)$ and $H(s_1, s'_1)$ hold.*

For deterministic labeled transition systems, the definition of weak bisimulation can be written in the following form:

1. For every state s_1 and natural numbers i such that $s_1 = next^i(s)$, $next^i(s)$ contains at most one non-silent transition l,

   a) there exists a state s'_1 and natural number j such that $s'_1 = next'^j(s')$, $next'^j(s')$ contains at most one non-silent transition l, and
   b) $H(s_1, s'_1)$ holds.

2. For every state s'_1 and natural numbers j such that $s'_1 = next'^j(s')$, $next'^j(s')$ contains at most one non-silent transition l,

   a) there exists a state s_1 and natural number i such that $s_1 = next^i(s)$, $next^i(s)$ contains at most one non-silent transition l, and
   b) $H(s_1, s'_1)$ holds.

For deterministic labeled transition systems with label memory, we can write this in the following form:

1. For every state s_1 and natural numbers i such that $s_1 = next^i(s)$, $next^i(s)$ contains at most one non-silent transition,

   a) there exists a state s'_1 and natural number j such that $s'_1 = next'^j(s')$, $next'^j(s')$ contains at most one non-silent transition,
   b) $H(s_1, s'_1)$ holds,

c) $prevlabel(s_1) = prevlabel'(s_1')$ holds.

2. For every state s_1' and natural numbers j such that $s_1' = next'^j(s')$, $next'^j(s')$ contains at most one non-silent transition,

   a) there exists a state s_1 and natural number i such that $s_1 = next^i(s)$, $next^i(s)$ contains at most one non-silent transition,

   b) $H(s_1, s_1')$ holds,

   c) $prevlabel(s_1) = prevlabel'(s_1')$ holds.

Simulation and Kripke Structures

Similar as for transition systems, simulation relations can be defined for Kripke structures. We require the following:

Definition 15 (Simulation Relation on Kripke Structures) *Given two Kripke structures K and K' with $AP \supseteq AP'$, a relation $H \subseteq S \times S'$ is a simulation relation between K and K', iff for all states $s \in S$ and $s' \in S'$ with $H(s, s')$ the following conditions hold:*

1. $L(s) \cap AP' = L'(s')$.

2. *For every state $s_1 \in S$ such that $R(s, s_1)$, there is a state $s_1' \in S'$ with the property that $R'(s', s_1')$ and $H(s_1, s_1')$ hold.*

Note that with the first condition of our simulation requirements for Kripke structures we already put a requirement on the semantic nature of the simulation relation itself: property correspondence of states. Using labeling of states notions of weak simulation and bisimulation relations may be defined on Kripke structures as well.

Relating Systems via Simulation

Simulation of systems is defined using simulation relations and requires the initial states of systems to fulfill the simulation relation:

Definition 16 ((Weak) (Bi-)Simulation) (Of Transition Systems with Initial States and Kripke Structures) *Let K and K' be two transition systems with initial states (Kripke Structures). We say that K' (weakly) (bi-)simulates K for a set of pairs of initial states H_0, iff there exists a (weak) (bi-)simulation relation $H \subseteq S \times S'$ such that*

$$\forall\ s_0\ s_0'.\ (s_0, s_0') \in H_0 \longrightarrow H(s_0, s_0')$$

The fact that K' simulates K is denoted by $K \preceq K'$.

Deviant Simulation Definitions

The set of pairs of initial states H_0 in the definition of (weak) (bi-)simulation of transition systems allows grouping initial states from both systems pairwise. Many authors do not consider requirements on initial states at all. Clarke, Grumberg, and Peled [CGP99] put the following requirement on initial states for the bisimulation of Kripke structures instead of our definition:

1. for all $s_0 \in S_0$ there exists $s'_0 \in S'$ such that $H(s_0, s'_0)$.

2. for all $s'_0 \in S'_0$ there exists $s_0 \in S$ such that $H(s_0, s'_0)$.

The notion of simulation has been especially popular in the process algebra community and is used in the theoretical background of model checking. Especially the process algebra community works with systems that react with their environment by exchanging information during every step. This is so fundamental that there exists notions of simulation for systems with both, integrated input and output behavior during a state transition. As for labeled transition systems, steps without such a behavior are marked as silent.

The notion of (bi)simulation is commonly used by different communities whenever one wants to reason about trace equivalence. Different definitions with and without information exchange during a step are used. The adaptation to systems without explicit reaction to incoming or outgoing information is done on our own choice.

The definition of labeled transition systems with label memory is done on our own choice, too. It ensures that states do "remember" the last label encountered.

3.3 A Brief Introduction to Isabelle/HOL

One of the theorem provers we use to realize our certifying translations is Isabelle/HOL [NPW02, Pau94, Pau93]. Isabelle/HOL is the instantiation of the generic theorem prover Isabelle with Alonzo Church style higher-order logic [Chu40]. While the Isabelle framework provides a general meta logic for reasoning about proof objects, the HOL instantiation provides an object logic that allows the formalization of second-order logic formulas. Moreover, it features functional programming language elements that allow the specification of computable functions. Isabelle/HOL is one of the theorem provers used for formalizing our systems and our correctness criteria. It is also used as a certificate checker for our certifying transformations. In this section, we briefly give an overview about characteristics of Isabelle that are used in this thesis. We rather present simplifications at some points since a complete presentation of Isabelle's features would go far beyond the scope of this prerequisites chapter.

Isabelle works on documents called theories. These allow the definition of types and functions. Inductive datatypes are defined using the keyword datatype. An induction principle is generated automatically for such datatypes. Using the keyword primrec, we can define primitive recursive functions over such datatypes in a way very similar to the handling of datatypes and functions in the ML programming language (cp. [MTH90]). Non-primitive recursive functions require a termination proof.

Isabelle's type system is very close to the type system of the standard ML programming language [MTH90]. Primitive types like *bool* and *int* can be defined and composed to types again. E.g.

```
(int * int) => bool
```

is the type of a function taking a tuple of integers and returning a boolean value. Like ML Isabelle supports parametric types.

Lemmata and theorems can also be formulated in a theory. A lemma or a theorem is usually stated in a declarative way using predefined and previously defined logical artifacts such as functions. A lemma or a theorem may have a name and is followed by a proof script. This proof script may be regarded as a program that does the searching for a proof using HOL axioms and lemmata or theorems proved earlier in the document or in other Isabelle files. A proof script consists of applications of tactics. These tactics may be regarded as functions transforming the original lemmata into easier provable *proof goals*. Most commonly, tactics do a search for a proof or split a proof goal into sub-goals. Once the proof succeeds, it is finished with the keyword done. The finished proof now becomes itself available to ease conduction of further proofs. Isabelle theories can depend on existing theories. A simplified structure of an Isabelle theory is given in Figure 3.1. It is typical for the layout of Isabelle documents used in this thesis.

To get a look and feel for Isabelle's theory files, Figure 3.2 gives a very small example. We define our own datatype mynat representing natural numbers. Further-on, we define a function apply_n taking a function f that maps an argument of parametric type 'a to 'a. Moreover, the function apply_n takes an initial value s of type 'a, and a mynat number. apply_n applys the given function f a number specified by the mynat argument of times to the initial value s. Finally, we prove a lemma mylemma correct in the given theory. It states that if we apply a function adding a value a two times to 0 we end up with the value 2*a. Parameter a is implicitly universally quantified. In the lemma, we have to specify the type of the 0 to be an integer. The proof script consists of a call to Isabelle's auto tactic which can do the proof automatically. More complicated lemmata require much longer proof scripts. These consist of up to several hundreds of applys. Apart from heavily automated tactics, there exists a large number of tactics that perform a single transformation step on the proof goal. Most of them are defined to work on a meta level. Typical examples are tactics that rewrite terms by equivalent terms and the splitting of proof goals into sub-goals. These tactics are basic transformation rules. They are applied by matching the transformation rule against the proof goal via higher-order unification.

Isabelle/HOL especially, when using Isar [Nip03], is aimed at overcoming the boundaries between mathematics and the theorem prover language. In this work, however, it is sometimes necessary to explicitly differentiate between them. We have to emphasize that there are indeed two levels of abstractions and reasoning: the theorem prover level and the pure mathematical level.

```
theory  name imports Main  further existing theories
begin

   ...
   type definitions

   ...
   function definitions

   ...
lemma   name: " ... "
...
   proof script
...
done


   ...


theorem   name: " ... "
...
   proof script
...
done


   ...


end
```

Figure 3.1: Structure of an Isabelle Theorie

```
theory mynatex imports Main
begin

datatype mynat = N | S mynat

consts apply_n :: "('a => 'a) => 'a => mynat => 'a"
primrec
  "apply_n f s N = s"
  "apply_n f s (S n) = apply_n f (f s) n"

lemma mylemma: "apply_n (% x. x + a) (0::int) (S(S(N))) = 2*a"
apply auto
done

end
```

Figure 3.2: An Example Isabelle Theory

```
Require Import   an existing Coq file.
    ...
Require Import   further existing Coq file.
    ...
   type definitions
    ...
   function definitions
    ...


    ...

Lemma   name:  ... .
Proof.
    ...
   proof script
    ...
Qed.


    ...

end
```

Figure 3.3: Structure of a Coq File

The Isabelle work in this thesis is essentially build upon Isabelle 2005 – the stable version of Isabelle that was released in 2005.

3.4 A Brief Introduction to Coq

The other theorem prover used in this thesis is Coq [The07]. Coq builds on the Calculus of Inductive Constructions [Cas04]. Most constructs available in Isabelle have corresponding constructs in Coq and vice versa. The structure of Coq files is similar to Isabelle theory files (cp. Figure 3.3). Like Isabelle, Coq allows the definition of types, functions, and the stating of properties as lemmata. Like in Isabelle, the latter are usually followed by a proof script.

A corresponding Coq file realizing essentially the same as the Isabelle code in Figure 3.2 is shown in Figure 3.4. The correspondence between Isabelle's datatype construct and Coq's inductive definitions is easy to see: the different constructors N and S are followed by a type annotation that allow recursive datatype definitions in Coq. Note that in the Coq version the apply_n function has the type it operates on as an explicit argument. Moreover, the argument on which the induction is defined (the i) is explicitly specified via the struct construct. In the lemma, we need to give more type information. Z denotes a type of integers. Furthermore, every free variable needs to be explicitly quantified. The proof script needs the application of three tactics. The intro tactic eliminates the

27

Require Import ZArith.

Inductive mynat : Type :=
 | N : mynat
 | S : mynat − > mynat.

Fixpoint apply_n (A:Type) (f: A − > A) (s:A) (i:mynat) {struct i}: A :=
  match i with
   | N => s
   | S n => apply_n A f (f s) n
  end.

Lemma mylemma: forall a, apply_n Z (fun x => (x + a)%Z) 0%Z (S(S(N))) = (2 * a)%Z.
intro.
unfold apply_n.
auto with zarith.
Qed.

Figure 3.4: An Example Coq File

quantification. The unfold tactic unfolds the function definition and finally we can do
the rest of the proof using auto with its special instantiation for arithmetics.

As in the Isabelle version, most proof scripts used in this thesis are considerably longer
than the one presented in this example. Like Isabelle, Coq has meta logic features that
allow splitting a proof goal into several sub-goals and rewriting of terms by equivalent
terms.

The Coq work in this thesis is built upon Coq version 8.1 [The07].

Coq's and Isabelle's Design Goals and Differences

Isabelle/HOL and Coq provide similar features. It is relatively easy to convert formalizations between the two theorem provers. Nevertheless, the initial design goals were
different. Isabelle is designed as a generic theorem prover that can be instantiated using
many different logics. One characteristic of all versions of Coq – building on intuitionistic
logic realized by the Calculus of Inductive Constructions – is that proofs are regarded
as executable programs.

In Isabelle, proof scripts are executed to solve the proof goals or split them into
simpler proof goals. Once every proof goal is solved, the lemma or theorem to be proved
is regarded as correct. In Coq, proof scripts are compiled first into an Ocaml [Ler98]
program. This does the search for the actual proof and builds a so called proof term.
A proof term can itself be regarded as a program. During its execution it performs the
actual correctness proof and proves the considered lemma correct. Proof terms may be
given directly to Coq.

Coq sometimes provides different formalizations for the same logical artifacts. For
example, there are several formalizations of sets which are logical equivalent. The same

holds for different integer formalizations. The Z type denotes a binary encoding of integers, i.e. integers are essentially encoded using a list-like type of boolean values. Apart from Z, there is an int type which formalizes integers building on natural numbers formalized via a null constructor and a successor constructor. This is similar to our mynat definition in our example. Using and exchanging these formalizations is a little bit of an engineering task. Isabelle on the other hand feels more like a tool for a more mathematical oriented community. There is usually only one definition for one logical artifact.

Another difference is the handling of equality. In Coq, one defines for each inductive datatype its own equality predicate defined on the inductive structure of the type. Isabelle has a more generic notion of equality.

Coq allows that functions specified within the Coq theorem prover may be executed within its virtual machine (cp. [Gre03] on this elaborate technique). This is more native than an execution of a function by matching transition rules written in the theorem prover language against the function's definition. Isabelle 2005 in principle does execution of specified functions by matching the function definition against the argument using the higher-order logic unification of the theorem prover. To execute a recursively defined function, this has to be done over and over again. Moreover, since equality is usually a recursive function in Coq, it can be decided by program execution. In Isabelle, a more general term comparison mechanism is encountered.

However, features that were later added to Isabelle also allow a more native execution of functions specified within the theorem prover. In Isabelle 2007 [1] functions may be compiled into ML code and executed in the ML environment of the theorem prover. Coq features in version 8.1 a native handling of coinductive datatypes.

---

[1] available since the end of 2007

4 A Framework for Certifying Translations

In this chapter, we introduce our semantics framework for certifying translations and discuss general strategies for its application. Our framework is used to guarantee correctness of transformations: Having a description of a source system (e.g. a source program) and the result of its transformation (e.g. a piece of target code), we want to decide if the transformation has been carried out in a way acceptable to us. We restrict ourselves to deterministic systems.

We regard different transformations in this thesis. One of our goals is that the presented methodology shall be applicable to as many other application areas as possible. Therefore we pull as much as possible of the semantics and correctness principles that are shared among different transformations from the upcoming chapters and present them here in a unifying fashion.

The restriction to deterministic systems is done for the following reasons:

1. Deterministic systems are easier to handle and reasoning on them can be carried out faster in a theorem prover. It is easier to determine successors for given states. We can directly use the fact that there is only one successor for a given state whereas non-deterministic systems would require a case distinction. Furthermore, successors can be computed by applying a state transition function which is relatively fast.

2. Our applications – compiler code generation and system abstractions – use deterministic languages or systems.

The restriction to deterministic systems is not done in order to make the framework presented in this section significantly easier for humans to understand or more elegant. All the basic definitions (e.g. simulation) we base correctness upon have originally been established for non-deterministic systems.

We need some kind of criterion under which we accept a transformation's result. We use a predicate as our criterion that takes two concrete systems: the original system and its transformation. Based on the systems' semantics, it returns true if the transformation is acceptable to us. Otherwise, false is returned. Since we want to decide the correctness automatically in a theorem prover, we formalize our criterion in the theorem prover language.

We regard different transformations working on different kinds of systems possibly working with different notions of correctness. Thus, one design goal of our framework is to present one generic correctness criterion that can be instantiated for different purposes.

Regarding our work on certifying compilers, given a source program, it is not always easy to define when to accept a target program as a correct translation of the source. A transformation is only acceptable if the observable behavior specified in the source code is preserved in the target code. This means that the generated traces of outputs have to be the same. For this reason, we need a mechanism to compare the run-time behavior of the involved systems in our criterion. In our system abstraction case study, comparison of run-time behavior is also important. Hence, the framework presented in this chapter is aimed at establishing a correctness criterion that compares such behavior. We keep it as generic as possible and instantiate it for our case studies.

Overview

A generic correctness criterion and two derived criteria that can be instantiated for different notions of correctness are presented in Section 4.1.

In the second part of this chapter we show general principles of how to use our criteria in different scenarios. Section 4.2 discusses how to use deep and shallow embedded languages with them. In Section 4.3, we present notions that help conducting correctness proofs. Furthermore, in Section 4.4 we discuss our criteria with respect to different notions of correctness that are common in different communities of computer science.

Finally, in Section 4.5 we discuss issues on formalizing the notions developed in this section in a theorem prover. This is an important prerequisite for the following more theorem prover oriented chapters.

4.1 Our Semantic Framework

This section introduces our formal framework to ensure correct translations. A way of representing systems is introduced. Furthermore, we introduce our *Generic Correctness Criterion* in Subsection 4.1.1 and discuss its relation to weak bisimulation. It relates an original and a translated system to each other and states whether the latter is a correct translation of the first. Derived from the *Generic Correctness Criterion* two other correctness criteria are presented in Subsection 4.1.2. These are special cases of the *Generic Correctness Criterion*. They are used in our certifying code generation and system abstractions. The steps to establish certifying translations using the *Generic Correctness Criterion* are sketched in Subsection 4.1.3.

All introduced criteria are defined comparing the trace based run-time behavior of systems via an adapted notion of weak bisimulation. We introduce a notion of state correspondence and step correctness that allow to specify when states semantically correspond to each other and transitive steps may be treated as a single on a generic level.

Most of the notions introduced in this section are based on the prerequisites introduced in Section 3.2.

4.1.1 Framework Specification

Correctness is defined with respect to deterministic state transition systems with initial states (cp. Definition 6). The deterministic state transition systems are used in thesis for

Initial States (based on a given datatype state)
$$S_0 : \text{state set}$$
State Transition Function (based on a given datatype state)
$$next : \text{state} \Rightarrow \text{state}$$
System Definition (based on a given datatype state)
$$S = (S_0, next) : \text{state set} \times (\text{state} \Rightarrow \text{state})$$

Figure 4.1: Systems Considered in this Thesis

representing the semantics of programs and our systems from our system abstractions case study. They are specified through the following characteristics:

1. A system encounters states during its execution. Therefore we have to define a datatype to represent them.

2. A system has a set of initial states.

3. A system has a state transition function that maps a state to its successor.

Furthermore, there is usually a label associated with a state transition or state, as in Definition 5, or a set of labels with a state as in Kripke structures. Labels are e.g. used to encode output that occurs during state transitions. Since, we only deal with deterministic systems, we encode the labels as part of the states. For this reason, we can in many cases omit to explicitly mention the label function since it is just a projection returning a part of a state. Some of our application scenarios require access to old labels, which may be kept in the state, too (cp. Definition 8 : labeled transition systems with label memory).

Thus, the considered state transition systems can be formally represented as a tuple as defined in Figure 4.1. This definition is generic in the sense that it does not put any restrictions on the type state. In comparison to the definition of labeled state transition systems in Definition 7, we encode the labels encountered during a state transition in the states – like in Kripke structures. Furthermore, we do not explicitly mention the set of states, but rather give a type state that may represent possible states. As mentioned in Section 3.2, we do not have a way to represent terminating systems directly. We rather allow to mark states as final and require that each final state is mapped to a final state again by a state transition function.

We can group different deterministic state transition systems into *classes of systems*. These are characterized by the types of their states.

When comparing an original and a translated system for correctness of the translation, our framework requires the preparation of the following items (types and signatures for these items are shown in Figure 4.2):

1. We have to group the initial states of two systems in comparison into a set of pairs of initial states. Each pair consists of an initial state from the original and a corresponding initial state from the translated system. We assume that when

The Set of Corresponding Initial States
$$H_0 = (s_0^1, s_0'^1), ..., (s_0^n, ..., s_0'^m) : (state \times state') \ set$$
The Two State Transition Functions
$$next : state \Rightarrow state$$
$$next' : state' \Rightarrow state'$$
State Correspondence Predicates
$$C : (state \times state') \Rightarrow bool$$
Correct Step Predicates
$$CorrectSteps : ((state \Rightarrow state) \times state \times nat) \Rightarrow bool$$
$$CorrectSteps' : ((state' \Rightarrow state') \times state' \times nat) \Rightarrow bool$$

Figure 4.2: Signatures for System Comparison

we compare an original and a translated system they will always start with states that are in such a tuple.

2. Two state transition functions. One from each system.

3. A predicate stating correspondence of original and translated system states (*state correspondence predicate*). It takes a state from the original and from the transformed system and returns a boolean value. This predicate is generic. It puts all requirements upon state correspondence that we regard as necessary to say that two states are related to each other. A common instantiation would be to guarantee that certain outputs that have occurred and are encoded in the state are equivalent in the related states, e.g. the label functions of both states in relation have to denote the same output value.

4. Predicates stating whether several consecutive steps of state transitions may be treated as a single step. They take the following arguments: a state transition function, the first state in a consecutive step sequence, and the number of steps to be treated as a single step. With this treatment, we can allow that several steps within the original systems correspond to a number of steps in the translated system. It is possible to put restrictions on the treatment of consecutive steps as single steps via these predicates. For instance several outputs may occur within a consecutive sequence of steps and we do not want to treat this as a single step.

The formalization of the corresponding initial states H_0 as a set and the state correctness C as a predicate is done for convenience reasons.

The correctness criteria used to relate original and transformed systems to each other in this thesis are always an instance of the simulation based correctness criterion shown in Figure 4.3: the *Generic Correctness Criterion*. The criterion takes two state transition functions, the set of pairs of initial states, the *state correspondence predicate*, and the two predicates (one for each system) that indicate whether a sequence of steps may be treated as a single step as input. The predicate ensures behavioral equivalence via the following items (cp. Figure 4.4):

GenericCorrectnessCriterion($next, next', H_0, C, CorrectSteps, CorrectSteps$)

initial requirements
∃ H.
∃ NEXT NEXT'.

classical (bi)simulation conditions
$\forall\ s_0\ s_0'.\ (s_0, s_0') \in H_0 \longrightarrow$ H$(s_0, s_0') \wedge$
$\forall\ s\ s'.$ H$(s,s') \longrightarrow$ H (NEXT(s), NEXT'$(s')) \wedge$

further conditions
$\forall\ s\ s'.$ H$(s,s') \longrightarrow C(s, s') \wedge$
$\forall\ s\ .\ \exists\ i.$ apply_n $next\ s\ i =$ NEXT $s \wedge CorrectSteps\ next\ s\ i \wedge$
$\forall\ s'\ .\ \exists\ i.$ apply_n $next'\ s'\ i =$ NEXT' $s' \wedge CorrectSteps'\ next'\ s'\ i$

Figure 4.3: Definition of the *Generic Correctness Criterion*

1. The initial requirements say that there has to be a simulation relation H (which has type *state* × *state'*). We also require the existence of two state transition functions NEXT and NEXT' (types *state* ⇒ *state* and *state'* ⇒ *state'*).

2. The classical (bi)simulation conditions require that each pair of initial states has to be in the simulation relation H. Furthermore, for each pair of states in H the succeeding states have to be in H again. The succeeding states are calculated using two state transition functions NEXT and NEXT'.

3. Further requirements ensure properties on the choice of the simulation relation H: Each pair of states in the simulation relation must fulfill the *state correspondence criterion* C; thus, H has to be at least as strong as C. Apart from the most basic requirements on state correspondence ensured by C the simulation relation H can contain additional requirements.

   Each step of the state transition functions NEXT and NEXT' has to denote the same result as a finite number of consecutive applications of the original state transition functions of the two systems *next* and *next'* (cp. Section 3.3 for the definition of apply_n). Furthermore, each step of the NEXT and NEXT' functions have to fulfill the requirements on treating sequences of steps as a single step ensured by the predicates *CorrectSteps* and *CorrectSteps'*.

Relation to Weak Bisimulation

The introduced correctness criterion is a derivative of weak bisimulation. It features the ability to put special requirements on both state correspondence and steps. Common to all notions of simulation is that the initial states have to be in the simulation relation

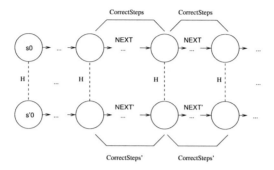

Figure 4.4: Two Traces Compared with the *Generic Correctness Criterion*

and succeeding states of states in the simulation relation have to be in it again. This is captured by the first two paragraphs of our *Generic Correctness Criterion*. In weak bisimulation, a finite sequence of steps may be treated as a single step. However, there is one restriction: only one label other than τ – which corresponds to one output written to some device – may occur during such a sequence. This is treated in our last paragraph of the *Generic Correctness Criterion*. In this subsection, we present a proof that assuming the fact that our state definitions are rich enough to define a simulation relation that determines a possible number of steps that have to be taken in order to arrive at states that are in the simulation relation again, the *Generic Correctness Criterion* with step correctness predicates instantiated in an appropriate way is implied by weak bisimulation for deterministic state transition systems with label memory. Thereby, we examine the main characteristics of the *Generic Correctness Criterion*.

Consider the condition that allows H to be called a weak bisimulation relation for deterministic labeled deterministic transition systems with label memory from Section 3.2:

1. For every state s_1 and natural numbers i such that $s_1 = next^i(s)$, $next^i(s)$ contains at most one non-silent transition,

   a) there exists a state s_1' and natural number j such that $s_1' = next'^j(s')$, $next'^j(s')$ contains at most one non-silent transition,

   b) $H(s_1, s_1')$ holds,

   c) $prevlabel(s_1) = prevlabel'(s_1')$ holds.

2. For every state s_1' and natural numbers j such that $s_1' = next'^j(s')$, $next'^j(s')$ contains at most one non-silent transition,

   a) there exists a state s_1 and natural number i such that $s_1 = next^i(s)$, $next^i(s)$ contains at most one non-silent transition,

   b) $H(s_1, s_1')$ holds,

   c) $prevlabel(s_1) = prevlabel'(s_1')$ holds.

These conditions can be rewritten in a more formal way. We get the following formula stating weak bisimulation of labeled transition systems with label memory:

- $\forall s \; s'.$
  $H(s, s')$
  $\longrightarrow$
  $\forall \; s_1 \; i. \; s_1 = next^i(s) \wedge next^i(s)$ contains at most one non-silent transition
  $\longrightarrow$
  $\exists \; s_1' \; j \; .$
  $\qquad s_1' = next'^j(s'), \; next'^j(s')$ contains at most one non-silent transition $\wedge$
  $\qquad H(s_1, s_1') \; \wedge$
  $\qquad prevlabel(s_1) = prevlabel'(s_1')$
  $\qquad \qquad \wedge$
  $\forall \; s_1' \; j. \; s_1' = next'^j(s') \wedge next'^j(s')$ contains at most one non-silent transition
  $\longrightarrow$
  $\exists \; s_1 \; i \; .$
  $\qquad s_1 = next^i(s), \; next^i(s)$ contains at most one non-silent transition $\wedge$
  $\qquad H(s_1, s_1') \; \wedge$
  $\qquad prevlabel(s_1) = prevlabel'(s_1')$

This can be equivalently rewritten:

- $\forall s \; s'.$
  $H(s, s')$
  $\longrightarrow$
  $\forall \; s_1 \; i \; s_1' \; j.$
  $\quad s_1 = next^i(s) \wedge next^i(s)$ contains at most one non-silent transition
  $\quad \longrightarrow$
  $\quad \exists \; s_1' \; j \; .$
  $\qquad s_1' = next'^j(s'), \; next'^j(s')$ contains at most one non-silent transition $\wedge$
  $\qquad H(s_1, s_1') \; \wedge$
  $\qquad prevlabel(s_1) = prevlabel'(s_1')$
  $\qquad \qquad \wedge$
  $\quad s_1' = next'^j(s') \wedge next'^j(s')$ contains at most one non-silent transition
  $\quad \longrightarrow$
  $\quad \exists \; s_1 \; i \; .$
  $\qquad s_1 = next^i(s), \; next^i(s)$ contains at most one non-silent transition $\wedge$
  $\qquad H(s_1, s_1') \; \wedge$
  $\qquad prevlabel(s_1) = prevlabel'(s_1')$

The following formula is implied:

- $\forall s \; s'.$
  $H(s, s')$
  $\longrightarrow$
  $\exists \; s_1 \; i \; s_1' \; j.$

$$s_1 = next^i(s) \land next^i(s) \text{ contains at most one non-silent transition}$$

$$\longrightarrow$$

$$\exists\ s_1'\ j\ .$$

$$s_1' = next'^j(s'),\ next'^j(s') \text{ contains at most one non-silent transition} \land$$
$$H(s_1, s_1') \land$$
$$prevlabel(s_1) = prevlabel'(s_1')$$

$$\land$$

$$s_1' = next'^j(s') \land next'^j(s') \text{ contains at most one non-silent transition}$$

$$\longrightarrow$$

$$\exists\ s_1\ i\ .$$

$$s_1 = next^i(s),\ next^i(s) \text{ contains at most one non-silent transition} \land$$
$$H(s_1, s_1') \land$$
$$prevlabel(s_1) = prevlabel'(s_1')$$

There is at least one i and j that lets the preconditions of the implications come true (1 will always do). This allows us to equivalently rewrite the formula:

- $\forall s\ s'.$

$$H(s, s')$$

$$\longrightarrow$$

$$\exists\ s_1\ i\ s_1'\ j.$$

$$s_1 = next^i(s) \land next^i(s) \text{ contains at most one non-silent transition}$$

$$\land$$

$$\exists\ s_1'\ j\ .$$

$$s_1' = next'^j(s'),\ next'^j(s') \text{ contains at most one non-silent transition} \land$$
$$H(s_1, s_1') \land$$
$$prevlabel(s_1) = prevlabel'(s_1')$$

$$\land$$

$$s_1' = next'^j(s') \land next'^j(s') \text{ contains at most one non-silent transition}$$

$$\land$$

$$\exists\ s_1\ i\ .$$

$$s_1 = next^i(s),\ next^i(s) \text{ contains at most one non-silent transition} \land$$
$$H(s_1, s_1') \land$$
$$prevlabel(s_1) = prevlabel'(s_1')$$

This implies the following formula:

- $\forall s\ s'.$

$$H(s, s')$$

$$\longrightarrow$$

$$\exists\ s_1\ i\ s_1'\ j.$$

$$s_1 = next^i(s) \land next^i(s) \text{ contains at most one non-silent transition}$$

$$\land$$

$$\exists\ s_1'\ j\ .$$

$$s_1' = next'^j(s'),\ next'^j(s') \text{ contains at most one non-silent transition} \land$$

$$H(s_1, s_1') \wedge$$
$$prevlabel(s_1) = prevlabel'(s_1')$$

The resulting formula can be simplified and written like this:

- $\forall s\ s'.$
    $H(s, s')$
    $\longrightarrow$
    $\exists s_1\ s_1'\ i\ j.$
        $s_1 = next^i(s) \wedge$
        $next^i(s)$ contains at most one non-silent transition $\wedge$
        $s_1' = next'^j(s') \wedge$
        $next'^j(s')$ contains at most one non-silent transition $\wedge$
        $H(s_1, s_1') \wedge$
        $prevlabel(s_1) = prevlabel'(s_1')$

This can be rewritten equivalently:

- $\forall s\ s'.$
    $H(s, s')$
    $\longrightarrow$
    $\exists i\ j.$
        $H(next^i(s), next'^j(s')) \wedge$
        $next^i(s)$ contains at most one non-silent transition $\wedge$
        $next'^j(s')$ contains at most one non-silent transition $\wedge$
        $prevlabel(next^i(s)) = prevlabel'(next'^j(s'))$

By pulling the existential quantifiers to the front we have the following condition derived via an equivalence transformation:

- $\forall s\ s'.\exists i\ j.$
    $H(s, s')$
    $\longrightarrow$
    $H(next^i(s), next'^j(s')) \wedge$
    $next^i(s)$ contains at most one non-silent transition $\wedge$
    $next'^j(s')$ contains at most one non-silent transition $\wedge$
    $prevlabel(next^i(s)) = prevlabel'(next'^j(s'))$

Assuming that s and s' determine the number of steps that have to be taken in the next transition for a given simulation relation. We can rewrite this by introducing the $NEXT$ and $NEXT'$ functions:

- $\exists NEXT\ NEXT'.$
    $\forall s\ s'.\exists i\ j.$
        $H(s, s')$
        $\longrightarrow$

$$H(NEXT(s), NEXT'(s')) \land$$
$$NEXT(s) = next^i(s) \land$$
$next^i(s)$ contains at most one non-silent transition $\land$
$$NEXT'(s') = next'^j(s') \land$$
$next'^j(s')$ contains at most one non-silent transition $\land$
$$prevlabel(NEXT(s)) = prevlabel'(NEXT'(s'))$$

This implies the following formula:

- $\exists NEXT\ NEXT'.$

  $\forall s\ s'.$

  $H(s, s')$

  $\longrightarrow$

  $H(NEXT(s), NEXT'(s')) \land$

  $\forall s\ \exists i.\ H(s, s') \longrightarrow$

  $\quad NEXT(s) = next^i(s) \land$

  $\quad next^i(s)$ contains at most one non-silent transition $\land$

  $\forall s\ \exists j.\ H(s, s') \longrightarrow$

  $\quad NEXT'(s') = next'^j(s') \land$

  $\quad next'^j(s')$ contains at most one non-silent transition $\land$

  $\quad prevlabel(NEXT(s)) = prevlabel'(NEXT'(s'))$

This can be rewritten in the way shown below, since we can set $NEXT(s) = next^0(s)$ and $NEXT'(s') = next'^0(s')$ for states s if there is no s' such that $H(s, s')$ holds and for states s' if there is no s such that $H(s, s')$ holds respectively.

- $\exists NEXT\ NEXT'.$

  $\forall s\ s'.$

  $H(s, s')$

  $\longrightarrow$

  $H(NEXT(s), NEXT'(s')) \land$

  $\forall s\ \exists i.$

  $\quad NEXT(s) = next^i(s) \land$

  $\quad next^i(s)$ contains at most one non-silent transition $\land$

  $\forall s'\ \exists j.$

  $\quad NEXT'(s') = next'^j(s') \land$

  $\quad next'^j(s')$ contains at most one non-silent transition $\land$

  $\quad prevlabel(NEXT(s)) = prevlabel'(NEXT'(s'))$

The following changes are introduced to derive our *Generic Correctness Criterion*:

1. The fact that a transition step must contain at most one non-silent transition is generalized to the step correctness predicates.

2. In our *Generic Correctness Criterion*, we are able to put further restrictions on the simulation relation via the state correspondence predicate. These are a generalized form of the condition $prevlabel(NEXT(s)) = prevlabel'(NEXT'(s'))$.

GCC1:1($next,next',H_0,C$)
   $\exists$ H.

$$\forall\ s_0\ s_0'.\ (s_0, s_0') \in H_0 \longrightarrow \mathsf{H}(s_0, s_0')\ \wedge$$
$$\forall\ s\ s'.\ \mathsf{H}(s,s') \longrightarrow \mathsf{H}\ (next(s),\ next'(s'))\ \wedge$$
$$\forall\ s\ s'\ .\ \mathsf{H}(s,s') \longrightarrow C(s,s')$$

Figure 4.5: Definition of the *Generic 1:1 Correctness Criterion*

Moreover, we take the condition for initial states from the definition of weak bisimulation and use it in our *Generic Correctness Criterion*.

Discussion of the *Generic Correctness Criterion*

Our *Generic Correctness Criterion* is generic in three ways:

1. It is generic with respect to the classes of systems used. We may instantiate the type used for *state* and *state'* freely. Hence, any two classes of systems that can be formalized as deterministic state transition systems may be put in relation using one instance of our criterion.

2. It is generic for use with different systems of a class. Any two systems for fixed types of states may be put in relation. This item is a further concretization of the feature mentioned in the first item.

3. It is generic with respect to the used notion of correctness. By instantiating C, *CorrectSteps*, and *CorrectSteps'* appropriately different notions of translation correctness may be realized.

Note the *CorrectSteps*, and *CorrectSteps'* predicates are only needed if we treat several steps as one using the NEXT and NEXT' functions.

4.1.2 Derived Correctness Criteria

In our implemented certifying translations we do not use the *Generic Correctness Criterion* from Figure 4.3 directly, but rather use derived criteria.

    If we do not merge steps – i.e. each step in the original system corresponds to a single step in the transformed system – we can use the *Generic 1:1 Correctness Criterion* shown in Figure 4.5. Its behavior for relating two system traces is shown in Figure 4.6. It is a simplification of the *Generic Correctness Criterion*. Since we do only regard single steps, we do not need the functions NEXT and NEXT' encapsulating several steps. The step correctness predicates become obsolete since the correctness requirements of the behavior of a single step may be captured using solely the C state correspondence criterion. This *Generic 1:1 Correctness Criterion* corresponds to bisimulation of systems.

    Another version of the *Generic Correctness Criterion* – the *Generic 1:n Correctness Criterion* – is presented in Figure 4.7. An example application for one trace is shown in Figure 4.8. As the 1:n suggests, it relates one step in the original system to a finite

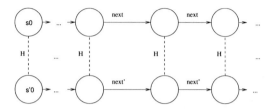

Figure 4.6: Two Traces Compared with the *Generic 1:1 Correctness Criterion*

GCC1:n(*next*,*next'*,H_0,*C*,*CorrectSteps'*)
   ∃ H.
   ∃ NEXT'.
      ∀ s_0 s_0'. $(s_0, s_0') \in H_0 \longrightarrow$ H$(s_0, s_0') \wedge$
      ∀ s s'. H$(s,s') \longrightarrow$ H $(next(s),$ NEXT'$(s')) \wedge$
      ∀ s s' . H$(s,s') \longrightarrow C(s,s') \wedge$
  ∀ s' . ∃ i. apply_n *next'* s' i = NEXT' $s' \wedge$ *CorrectSteps'* *next'* s' i

Figure 4.7: Definition of the *Generic 1:n Correctness Criterion*

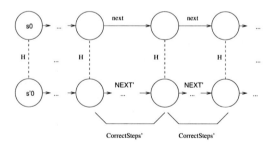

Figure 4.8: Two Traces Compared with the *Generic 1:n Correctness Criterion*

number of steps in the translated system. We do only need the NEXT' function from the *Generic Correctness Criterion* treating several steps of the translated system as a single step. The correctness of this treatment is ensured using the *CorrectSteps'* predicate.

The *Generic 1:n Correctness Criterion* corresponds to the special case of weak bisimulation where one step in the original system may correspond to several steps in the translated system. Note that unlike the *Generic Correctness Criterion* and the *Generic 1:1 Correctness Criterion* the *Generic 1:n Correctness Criterion* is asymmetric by definition even if the systems are defined on the same type of states.

Apart from the two presented instances of the *Generic Correctness Criterion* other instances may be constructed without problems. Nevertheless, in the scope of this thesis we only need to deal with the two correctness criteria presented in this section.

4.1.3 Applying the *Generic Correctness Criteria* to Verification Scenarios

To use the *Generic Correctness Criteria* within a verification task involving system translations, we need to find out if the presented framework is applicable, i.e. we have to deal with deterministic systems, a certain number of execution steps performed in one system has to correspond to a certain number of steps in the translated system. Furthermore, we need to specify:

- the classes of systems in consideration,

- a notion of state correspondence,

- notions of step correctness (if applicable),

- what are initial states and which initial state in one system corresponds to one in the translated system.

The remainder of this chapter presents some principles to perform these tasks.

Furthermore, we need to establish a proof generation mechanism if we are working on certifying translations or prove the translation algorithm correct if we are working with certified translations.

4.2 Embedding System Descriptions into the Framework – Shallow and Deep Embedding

This section is especially aimed at formalization issues of system descriptions for a theorem prover. Thus, it helps to bridge the gap between our *Generic Correctness Criteria* family and its applications.

Central to our system descriptions are the notions of states and state transition function. Most systems, however, are represented using some kind of textual language. For instance a program is usually represented using a programming language. This section describes two general ways to bridge the gap between system descriptions comprising state transition functions and textual program representations: *deep embedding* and *shallow embedding*.

- A *deep embedding* formalizes a programming language's syntax within the language of the theorem prover. An interpretation function is defined upon the syntactical elements. Datatypes in the programming language are often reformalized in the theorem prover language.

- A *shallow embedding* does not need a syntax formalization. It defines semantic entities such as state transition functions directly using the theorem prover's syntax.

The most common way to represent systems given in a textual language is to do a deep embedding of this textual language into the theorem prover. This comprises the following steps:

1. Define a type to represent the language's syntax: the *language syntax definition*. Most common choices are inductive types.

2. Define a type to represent states, e.g. some kind of tuple.

3. Define functions that interpret concrete syntactical structures. A function taking a system's concrete syntactical representation, and a concrete state, returning another state is used as a state transition function.

Note that these steps have to be done only once and for all systems to be represented by a concrete kind of textual representation – most commonly a programming language. To go coherent with the system definition from Figure 4.1 a deep embedding further requires formalizing the concrete initial states and the concrete syntactical representation for each system in the theorem prover. If our translations are based on the transformation of some textual representation, these two items are created by a usually relatively simple transformation out of the provided non-theorem prover syntax representation of a system.

While a state transition function that is generic for a complete language requires the system's syntax as an argument, the state transition function for a concrete system is created by currying this generic state transition function to the given concrete system's syntax. For this reason, we end up with a state transition taking and returning nothing but single states.

Since a shallow embedding does not formalize a system's syntax in the theorem prover, there is no generic state transition function for a language. Each system's state transition function is directly encoded using the theorem prover's syntax. The definition of a system's state is not affected by the choice of deep or shallow embedding in our applications.

Discussion

There is usually a close link between the syntax representation of a concrete system in the theorem prover and in the non-theorem prover world. For example a program represented as source code and the theorem prover representation of it tend to look very similar in a deep embedding. The transformation from some kind of system representation into a shallow embedding is often less clear. Directly encoded state transition functions and their relation to their non-theorem prover world equivalents can be hard to understand. Thus, to make people confident in ones verification work, a deep embedding is often preferable.

A deep embedding has also the feature that it is possible to reason about syntactical structures such as inductive term definitions by induction. Nevertheless, this is especially valuable for algorithm verification since algorithm verification has to verify properties about possible unknown syntactical structures and their transformed counterparts. In certifying translations, we always have concrete instances of system representations. For this reason there is no need to use such general techniques in this thesis. Another advantage of a deep embedding is the fact that a small generic state transition function instantiated with some human readable textual representation of a system is usually easier to debug than a large generated state transition function without syntactical elements that are human readable.

Some work has been done comparing deep and shallow embedding in theorem provers. Wildmoser and Nipkow [WN04] present a comparison between deep and shallow embedding in the Isabelle/HOL environment. They tend to prefer deep embedding over shallow embedding. This, however, is probably due to the fact that they are mostly dealing with algorithm verification. Thus, structural induction over syntactical elements is often needed in their work.

As a concluding remark we suggest that whenever there is a clear syntax definition of a language in the non-theorem prover world and it is possible to port it to a theorem prover we should do so and do a deep embedding.

4.3 Working with the *Generic Correctness Criteria* Family

In this section we present basic notions and techniques that ease the use of our correctness criteria introduced in Section 4.1 in verification scenarios. We discuss general semantic issues that have not been addressed yet. Furthermore, we reason about how to combine correctness criteria.

4.3.1 Partial Orders of Correctness Criteria, State Correspondence and Simulation Relations

When checking whether we accept a translation run as correct, it is sometimes easier to check that the original and translated system fulfill a correctness criterion other than the criteria of our *Generic Correctness Criteria* family. Such a criterion has to imply one of the criteria from the *Generic Correctness Criteria* family intended in the first place.

In this subsection, we discuss relations between predicates used as correctness criteria for relating systems with each other. These predicates are based – among other conditions – on state correspondence predicates that indicate whether two states from an original and a translated system correspond to each other (cp. Section 4.1.1). For this reason, we discuss the relation between state correspondence predicates and simulation

We call a criterion CC more strict or logical equivalent than CC'
(denoted $CC \trianglelefteq CC'$) iff:

> for each two systems $s1$ and $s2$
> > whenever $CC(s1,s2)$ holds then $CC'(s1,s2)$ holds as well.

Figure 4.9: Definition: Strictness of Criteria Relating Systems

relations derived from them. We establish a partial order of predicates and criteria that help conducting our proofs.

Relating Correctness Criteria

This subsection compares correctness criteria for fixed classes of systems that do not necessarily have to be part of the *Generic Correctness Criteria* family.

At an early point of the development of many certifying translation (including compiler transformations), we choose a criterion from our *Generic Correctness Criteria* family, the classes of systems considered, and define the instantiation of state correspondence and step correctness predicates (cp. Section 4.1.3). Thus, all parameters except for the actual systems are fixed once a transformation is implemented that shall generate certificates for stating its correct behavior. It can be regarded as a binary predicate $CC(s1,s2)$ stating whether one system $s2$ is a correct translation of another $s1$.

Usually several formalizations of correctness criteria are possible for the same kinds of systems. For this reason, notions to relate different criteria with the same signatures are desirable.

1. When we are talking about two criteria being *syntactical equal* we mean, that they are formalized in syntactical the same way.

2. We call two criteria *logical equivalent*, if we allow them to be syntactical different but require them to be equivalent in a logical sense. This means that for two system descriptions, two logical equivalent criteria will denote the same boolean value. The notions of logical equivalence and syntactical equality used here corresponds to definitions in standard textbooks on mathematical logic (cp. e.g. [EFT96]).

Sometimes, it can be a tedious task to prove that two criteria are indeed just two different formalizations of the same thing (i.e. they are equivalent). Some criteria may be stricter than others. A definition of strictness is given in Figure 4.9. Correctness criteria for given classes of systems are either incomparable, logical equivalent or one of them is more strict than the other. Since the strictness relation ($\trianglelefteq$) – unlike the criteria it relates – is reflexive, antisymmetric, and transitive, we can construct a partial order of system correctness criteria using the strictness relation. With $CC_t(p1,p2) = True$ being the least strict criterion (top element) and $CC_b(p1,p2) = False$ being the most strict (bottom element) we can even construct a lattice of correctness criteria. Note, once we have established such a lattice and proved that the strictness relation between criteria holds it can be used to make our proofs easier.

In practice a notion of correctness may be easy to formulate using instances of our *Generic Correctness Criteria* family since only the instantiation of the state correspondence and step correctness predicates is required. Nevertheless, for practical proving a more strict criterion may turn out to be the better choice. We may want to put stronger requirements on step correctness and state correspondence. These requirements may make proofs easier. If we have these two different correctness criteria and proved the strictness relation between the criteria using the established strictness ordering, we can be sure that once we have conducted the correctness proof in the stricter criterion it will also hold in the other.

Using stricter criteria usually does not preserve completeness. Two systems may be regarded as a false translation of each other in the stricter criterion, even if they are regarded as a correct translation by the original less strict criterion.

When regarding a concrete class of transformations, we construct an additional lattice containing all the correctness criteria where we would intuitively accept the definition as correct or semantics preserving. This additional lattice of valid criteria is best constructed containing an instance of our *Generic Correctness Criteria* family with an instantiation that contains only the most necessary semantic restrictions as the top element. Hence, we can select every criterion in the lattice to conduct a proof attempt that the correctness criterion is indeed fulfilled by two systems. Sometimes, different formalizations of a non-formal correctness criteria may be adequate. Their logical equivalence may be difficult to prove. Moreover, we may be able to find a criterion that is more strict than the different formalizations of our desired correctness criterion, but still general enough to serve as a correctness criterion. If we can prove the more strict relation between this criterion and our criteria established in the first place, we might want to regard it as an adequate formalization of a refined notion of correctness and put it on top of a new lattice to work with.

In general, we can only construct a lattice based on logical equivalence and implication. With syntactical equality – which is always decidable and usually much easier than logical equivalence – we can not construct a lattice of correctness criteria although there is a more strict ordering on its elements, too. Nevertheless, there is no such thing as a top or bottom element since the criteria CC_t and CC_b from above may be represented syntactically in many ways.

Simulation Relation and State Correspondence

Other partial orders may be defined for simulation relations. The set inclusion is used as the underlying order relation. Similarly partial orders may be defined upon state correspondence criteria for given types of states. State correspondence criteria and simulation relations from the same classes of states are comparable via this order.

The partial orders on simulation relations and state correspondence criteria have an immense practical value. We use in all our proofs a simulation relation that is constructed by demanding all items required by a state correspondence criterion. This is strengthened until we arrive at a simulation relation that is suitable for our proofs.

In our verification scenarios, state correspondence is usually independent of concrete systems while an adequate simulation relation is constructed for every pair of original and translated system. We can even define a lattice of state correspondence criteria: The empty set is the bottom element, the set containing all possible pairs of states is the top element.

4.3.2 Handling Inputs and Non-Determinism

We have already discussed that outputs may be encoded as labels in labeled transition systems. We further put outputs occurring during a system run in consideration in Sections 1.1 and 4.1. As suggested with the definition of labeled transition systems with label memory (Definition 8) we propose the solution to encode occurred outputs into the states, e.g. keep a list of so far accumulated output.

To formalize systems reacting to input we also need a formalization of inputs. In the scope of this thesis, input might for example occur due to user interaction with a program or sensors delivering data to a system. It may occur during any time of the execution of a system.

Input occurring during system execution brings up some non-deterministic elements into our framework. Nevertheless, in our framework we are able to handle input to systems. We suggest two possible formalizations:

- It may be formalized as streams: A stream of inputs is encoded in a system state. During a state transition the first element of the stream is consumed and deployed as currently occurring input.

- It may be formalized as a function returning an input value to a given index. The index is increased during the execution of the system.

The verification of system translations for all possible inputs requires to consider all possible pairs of initial states of original and translated system with corresponding – usually equal – input streams or functions.

The non-determinism provided by inputs is from a semantic point of view fundamentally different to non-determinism due to ambiguous programming language elements (cp. non-deterministic evaluation of expressions in the C programming language [KR88]). Our framework is able to handle inputs in an appropriate way. We are able to handle non-deterministic programming language elements as well, but only via indirections. One could for example artificially introduce an input on which the handling of the non-deterministic programming language depends. Nevertheless, the standard way of handling non-deterministic programming language elements would be to use inference rules for state transitions instead of state transition functions (cp. e.g. [NN92]).

4.3.3 Combining Correctness Criteria

So far we have presented correctness criteria for verifying single translations correct – single, not only in the sense of distinct translation runs, but also in the sense that there

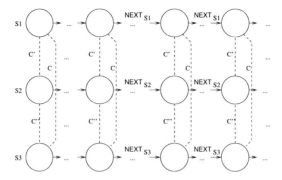

Figure 4.10: Composing and Decomposing Generic Correctness Criteria

is only one translation conducted per system. In this subsection, we investigate what happens if the translation is part of a consecutive chain of translations. For practical verification problems, we are often interested in correctness of such a chain of translations as a whole. Furthermore, one of our primary goals in this thesis is to point out a way to engineer trusted systems. This might even involve the combination of different verification techniques or the splitting of a verification task into different sub-tasks. For example one might want to split a single translation transforming a system into another system into different sub translations – an approach common to compilers. Each of those sub translations might produce an intermediate system. If each of these intermediate systems have a distinct semantics, it should be possible to formalize distinct correctness criteria for each sub translation. To achieve a correctness result for the complete transformation we have to find a way to combine the correctness criteria for the sub translations into an overall correctness criterion.

The criteria from our *Generic Correctness Criteria* family are based on simulation. Simulation based criteria may be combined into a more comprehensive simulation based criterion.

If one does make only restricted use of the step correctness predicates (step correctness predicates of intermediate representations are not considered) two criteria from our *Generic Correctness Criteria* family may be combined (or decomposed) in the way graphically depicted in Figure 4.10. Suppose, that a class of systems $S1$ is given. These systems are transformed into systems of the class $S2$. Systems of the class $S2$ are themselves transformed to systems of a class $S3$. $S1$ is related to $S2$ and $S2$ to $S3$ by an instance of our *Generic Correctness Criteria* family. These correctness criteria use state correspondence criteria C' (between systems of $S1$ and $S2$) and C'' (between systems of $S2$ and $S3$) which are given as a predicate defining a relation. Furthermore, they use step correctness predicates $CorrectSteps_{S1}$, $CorrectSteps_{S2}$ and $CorrectSteps_{S3}$. State transition functions of concrete systems of the classes $S1$, $S2$, and $S3$ are denoted: $next_{S1}, next_{S2}$, and $next_{S3}$. They are used for the definitions of the state transition functions for performing "merged steps": $NEXT_{S1}$, $NEXT_{S2}$, and $NEXT_{S3}$.

The new *Generic Correctness Criterion* relating systems of classes $S1$ and $S3$ is constructed in the following way:

- We construct a new state correspondence criterion C between $S1$ and $S3$:

$$C(a, c) = \exists t.\ C'(a, t) \wedge C''(t, c)$$

- The overall *Generic Correctness Criterion* is instantiated:

  GenericCorrectnessCriterion
  $$(next_{S1}, next'_{S3}, H_0, C, CorrectSteps_{S1}, CorrectSteps_{S3})$$

  using an appropriate relation of initial states H_0 and the state transition functions

If we prove a correctness criterion based on C' and C'', we can be sure that the new correctness criterion based on C also holds.

Proofs on combining simulation relation like the process sketched above can be found in e.g. [Gla01]. The sketched principle may be applied recursively (to achieve transitivity). Hence, it can be used to combine simulation based correctness proofs and criteria of an arbitrary number of sub translations into a single proof and criterion.

The sketched technique omits the step correctness predicates of possible intermediate representations. This is sufficient if one is only interested in step correctness predicates to ensure the same observable behavior of source and target program during a step.

If the correctness criteria do make other use of the step correctness predicates, combining them is in general less easy. It deserves a specialized treatment for each distinct pair of classes of systems that are considered. Nevertheless, since the restrictions specified via the step correctness predicates usually stay the same during each sub translation, it is in most practical relevant cases not a difficult task. The following technique of combining two step correctness predicates $CorrectSteps_{S1}$ and $CorrectSteps_{S2}$ for systems of classes $S1$ and $S2$ with state transition functions $next_{S1}$ and $next_{S2}$ may be used and introduced as a further constraint into a correctness criterion if necessary:

- $CorrectSteps_{S1S2}\ (next_{S1}\ o\ next_{S2})\ s_{S1}\ i = CorrectSteps_{S1}\ next_{S1}\ s_{S1}\ i\ \wedge$
  $\forall s_{S2}\ C''(s_{S1}, s_{S2})\ \longrightarrow\ CorrectSteps_{S2}\ next_{S2}\ s_{S2}\ i$

When proving a concrete instantiation of this criterion correct, one proves the items on the right-hand side first to derive the left hand side.

4.4 Our Correctness Criteria and their Relation to Other Formalisms

In this section we discuss properties of our *Generic Correctness Criteria* family and their relation to other possible notions of correct translation. We give an overview of the representation and methodologies to reason about trace based semantics in theorem provers.

4.4.1 Final Value Semantics

A classical approach to program transformation correctness is to compare the final values that are computed by the original and the transformed program for equality. For instance when looking at functions, the return values might be regarded (cp. Section 1.1 for a brief motivation on this problem). This is especially suitable for verifying functions that always terminate. Many classical textbooks on programming language semantics (e.g. Nielson and Nielson [NN92] introducing denotational, operational, and axiomatic program verification in a "final value" way) as well as Hoare style [Hoa69] program verification are based on this kind of semantics.

Compared to our *generic correctness criteria* family such a final value semantics corresponds to comparing the last states – or in some cases the last outputs – of terminating system runs with each other. In our framework, this can be achieved by using step correctness predicates that require the encapsulation of an entire finite system run by ensuring that a step reaches a final state at its end.

For this reason final value semantics may be regarded as a special case of trace based semantics.

The main disadvantage of the final value semantics is that non-terminating systems have to be regarded as either always correct or always incorrect translations of each other. Furthermore, even for terminating systems the run-time behavior is usually not taken into account.

4.4.2 Explicit Trace Representations in Transition Systems

In our system definitions, we have an implicit trace representation via initial states and a state transition function. The definitions of a transition system and a Kripke structure in Section 3.2 have a slightly more explicit representation of traces: they comprise a transition relation defined on states.

Such a transition relation may as well be created for our transition systems. A given *deterministic state transition system* with a set of initial states S_0 and a state transition function *next* may be represented as a transition system (S, S_0, R) featuring a set of encountered states S, the set of initial states, a transition relation R. The set S is inductively defined as:

- $S_0 \subseteq S$

- $s \in S \longrightarrow (next\ (s)) \in S$

The transition relation R is defined similarly:

- $s_0 \in S_0 \longrightarrow (s_0, next\ (s_0)) \in R$

- $(s, s_1) \in R \longrightarrow (s_1, next\ (s_1)) \in R$

Instead of regarding single steps we may use a state transition function that treats several steps as one (cp. definition of R^+ in Section 3.2). This is used to define a transition relation for our more general instances of the *Generic Correctness Criteria* family.

Note, that transition relations in general transition systems may contain transitions that do not belong to a system run, since they are never reached. Thus, comparing transition relations for equality is not the same as comparing system execution traces for equality.

Representing Traces as Functions

An even more explicit way to encode traces of deterministic system executions into an even more explicit representation is to use a function that maps a number i to the ith encountered state like in the following definition for a given initial state s_0 ($next^i$ (s_0) denotes the application of i times $next$ to the value s_0):

$$state \ (i) = next^i \ (s_0)$$

A similar function may be defined if one is only interested in outputs (given by the label function $nextlabel$ as defined for deterministic labeled state transition systems):

$$output \ (i) = nextlabel(next^i \ (s_0))$$

If one is only interested in outputs other than τ the following definition of $output'$ is appropriate:

$$\begin{aligned} &nextoutputstate \ (s) = \\ &\quad \text{if } nextlabel(next \ (s)) \neq \tau \text{ then} \\ &\quad\quad next \ (s) \text{ else } nextoutputstate(next \ (s)) \\ &output' \ (i) = \text{if } nextlabel \ (s_0) \neq \tau \text{ then} \\ &\quad\quad nextlabel(nextoutputstate^i \ (s_0)) \text{ else } nextlabel(nextoutputstate^{i+1} \ (s_0)) \end{aligned}$$

It makes use of the function $nextoutputstate$ and returns the ith output occurring in a system run with 0 being the first output.

Based on these functions, other set based trace representations may be derived. The sketched way to represent output traces as functions has the advantage that traces may be compared by using equality of functions.

4.4.3 Coalgebraic Trace Representations

Coalgebraic types are used for infinite datatypes as algebraic types are used for finite datatypes. They can be seen as an explicit way to represent traces, too. Values of coalgebraic types consist of destructors.

The coalgebraic view allows observing and defining operations on coalgebraic values using their outermost destructors like the algebraic view allows to observe the outermost constructor of a value of an algebraic type (e.g. in definitions of primitive recursive functions in functional programming languages). No primitive recursive function definition is possible on coalgebraic datatypes since they do not have to be finite structures. For this reason operations defined in a primitive recursive style do not need to terminate on a coalgebraic datatype.

Since we are dealing with deterministic systems in this thesis, the only coalgebraic type we are interested in are infinite streams. Other words used for stating a coalgebraic interpretation of list like structures comprise lazy lists and streams. A trace may be represented by a (co)datatype using standard list constructors. These are, however, interpreted in a coalgebraic way: as destructors. Thus, the following definition may be used to represent streams:

$$\begin{aligned} \text{statelist} = \\ \text{NIL} \mid \\ \text{LCONS state statelist} \end{aligned}$$

Coalgebraic datatypes are not constructed starting with some kind of basic constructor (e.g. NIL for lists without any element). They rather assume that a list that may even consist of an infinite consecutive application of LCONS is given.

Traces representing a program run are defined in a non-constructive(!) way by saying that the initial state is the first element, and each succeeding element is defined as the application of the state transition function to the direct predecessor. This is shown in the following trace where s_0 is the initial state, next is the state transition function and the innermost "..." may be infinitely long.

$$\text{trace} = \text{LCONS} \ (\ s_0 \ (\text{LCONS} \ (\text{next} \ s_0) \ (... \ \text{LCONS} \ s_i \ (\text{LCONS} \ (\text{next} \ s_i) \ ... \ ) \ ... \ ))$$

We refer to Jacobs' and Rutten's 1997 tutorial [JR97] for a comprehensive introduction to coalgebras and their usage in semantics of systems.

In recent times coalgebraic trace representations have gained some interest from the compiler verification community. See e.g. Leroy's work on coinductive big-step semantics [Ler06a] and some investigations I have been involved in [GB06, GLB06, BGL05].

In principle proving the equivalence of traces in a coalgebraic way and the equivalence proofs of traces in a transition system way are very similar as long as we base the notion of equivalence on bisimulation. Thus, correctness proofs based on bisimulation may be conducted in a very similar fashion for both formalisms. The coalgebraic way compares foremost states in traces and relates traces in a bisimulation relation to each other. The initial traces have to be in such a relation. Moreover, for each two traces in such a relation the remaining traces resulting from taking the first states away from such a trace have to be in the bisimulation relation again. This is very similar to bisimulation on transition systems where for two states in the bisimulation relation the succeeding states (which define the remaining traces) have to be in the bisimulation relation again. The similarity in usage is remarkable due to different foundations of both formalisms.

Using Coalgebraic Traces in Theorem Provers

The Coq theorem prover provides the keywords *Coinductive* and *Cofixpoint* for defining coinductive datatypes and functions working on them. Leroy's work [Ler06a] is based on these features. Isabelle/HOL does not have a native concept to reason about coinductive datatypes. Nevertheless, Paulson provides a formalization for coalgebraic traces in his Lazy List package [Pau00]. This is used in the work by Glesner, Blech, and Leitner [GB06, GLB06, BGL05]. Like in our system definition, such a Lazy List is defined via an initial state and a state transition function.

4.4.4 Explicit vs. Implicit Trace Representation

Apart from our *Generic Correctness Criterion* which does not feature an explicit value representing a system's behavior as a trace we have discussed translation relations, functions mapping indices to corresponding output or states, and coalgebraic structures as explicit ways to represent program behavior in traces. Explicit ways of representing program traces as values feature the ability to relate them via equality.

When proving the correctness of translations on deterministic state transition systems – e.g. equality of two traces of outputs – the proofs always break down to checking the correspondence of pairs of initial states and the correspondence of steps, either with or without explicit trace representations. This is even true for algorithm verification working on deterministic state transition system. Furthermore, this is true independent of the formalism used for trace representation. No matter if we use coalgebraic, function or set based traces in verification, we always have to break these structures down to their defining elements which are initial states and state transition functions. Hence, for the task of verifying translation runs there is no need for an explicit trace representation nor do we strictly need our non-explicit formalism.

If one wants to reason on a meta level about correctness proofs – e.g. if one wants to combine them – an explicit trace representation may be useful. This is especially true if one wants to use formalisms that are designed for a more general class of systems, i.e. non-deterministic state transition systems that do not necessarily come with a notion of a state transition function but may have notions of correctness based on traces.

However, the author of this thesis believes that the non-explicit ways of representing a system's semantics as a state transition system and base the notion of correctness on some kind of simulation is the most widely accepted notion of translation correctness both in the compiler verification and the model checking community. To his knowledge, the advantage of not having to construct an explicit trace representation from a state transition system's defining elements – which may be a sophisticated procurement we have to trust – outwages the advantage of using the mathematical equality between explicit structures. Since our code generation addresses the compiler verification community and the system abstractions case study addresses the model checking community a simulation based notion of correctness like the *Generic Correctness Criterion* seems to be the best choice to base our notion of translation correctness upon.

Corresponding Initial States (alternative 1)

$\forall$ i i' t. CC (...,((i , 0) , (i' , t , 0)),...)

: (... $\times$ ((val $\times$ nat)$\times$ (val $\times$ val $\times$ nat)) $\times$ ...)

Corresponding Initial States (alternative 2)

$\forall$ i t. CC (...,((i , 0) , (i , t , 0)),...)

Figure 4.11: Initial State Correspondence

4.5 Discussion: Formalizing the Framework in a Theorem Prover

This section aims to bridge the gap between our framework as described in this chapter and the following more application oriented chapters.

We have formalized the definitions concerning our basic framework from this chapter in the theorem provers Isabelle/HOL and Coq. Most of them are formalized very close to the mathematical definitions. This is also true for most items of the systems as described in Figure 4.1 and their relation as described in Figure 4.2 in Section 4.1. However, there are two exceptions to this: the handling of the initial states and input streams.

Handling the Initial States in a Theorem Prover

In our definitions in Section 4.1, we have sets of initial states in the definition of a single system. We have sets of pairs of initial states for relating two systems. When using higher-order theorem provers, we found it to be more convenient to formalize the set of initial states as a single, but underspecified state. The set of pairs of corresponding initial states is formalized as a single pair of underspecified states, respectively. The underspecification is achieved using variables inside the state definition. These have to be universally quantified over the term they appear in.

To exemplify this, we consider the running example from Figure 1.1 in Section 1.1 comprising code generation for a very small program. We did not give a type for states in this example so far. A very simple state choice for the intermediate language uses a tuple consisting of two components: the value of the variable i and the line of code we are currently executing. In the corresponding machine code a tuple serving as a state representation may comprise three components: the values of the two registers r1 and r2 and the program counter. Two different examples showing ways of formalizing single pairs of underspecified initial states are given in Figure 4.11. A single pair in this theorem prover formalization represents a set of pairs of initial states in a mathematical notation. They are used in the context of serving as a parameter to a correctness criterion CC. In the first alternative we demand that we start with actual line of code 0 in the intermediate program and program counter 0 in the machine code. In contrast to that the values of the variable in the intermediate language – given by the variable i – and the registers – given by the variables i', and t – are not specified directly. They are specified by universally quantified variables on a top level taking the places of concrete values. In the given example the variable and the registers may have any value. And when using this definition in a proof we have to consider all possible values for i, i', and t. All value combinations have to be examined. The second alternative uses universally quantified variables, too. However, in this version we demand that the values of the variable in the intermediate language and register r1 have to be the same (denoted by variable i) no matter which value they represent.

The presented technique is aimed at formalizing correspondences between states – we can represent an infinite number of corresponding initial states in a very compact form. We have applied it in compiler code generation and system abstraction scenarios.

Handling Input as Volatile Variable

Instead of using streams of inputs one may formalize the input occurring during a state transition as a special kind of variable. This variable is part of a state. Its value is assumed to change non-deterministically during every execution step. Such *volatile variables* may be regarded as current values of implicitly universally quantified input streams. When comparing two systems via a correctness criterion one may use the same volatile variable in both system descriptions. Thus stating that both systems react to the same input.

Volatile variables are easy to achieve within Isabelle/HOL and Coq. Although they do not fit directly into the definition of our *Generic Correctness Criteria* they can be used for proving subgoals appearing in the proof of our original criterion. We recommend this solution and use it in our case studies because it frees us from dealing with streams and their formalizations for use as variables' values.

This approach for handling inputs is common to various works in formal verification and specification especially when using higher-order theorem provers. It should be noted that most model checkers would not be able to deal with such volatile variables since they have to work on explicitly constructed traces.

5 Certifying Code Generation

In this chapter we present our certifying code generation phase. We regard code generation from an intermediate language into MIPS [PH98] assembler code.

A major focus of this chapter is on creating and checking the certificates for code generation. We present techniques to speed up the checking process – which is the bottleneck of certifying compilation.

Our certifying code generation is part of a compiler using a standard architecture. The architecture is shown in Figure 5.1 and comprises several phases: A program written in a higher imperative programming language (a C subset) is parsed into an abstract syntax tree and transformed into an intermediate language. Some optimizations are performed using this intermediate representation. The last phase in our compiler is code generation. In this phase we generate MIPS assembler code from the intermediate language representation, we do register allocation, jump target resolution and some optimizations as well.

Correctness results from different compiler phases can be combined into a complete correctness guarantee for a compiler or a compilation run, if compatible notions of correctness are used throughout all phases [1]. Correctness results may even be combined if different techniques are used for guaranteeing correctness of compilation runs such as a combination of certified compiler phases with certifying compiler phases.

The used intermediate language is quite close to the source language. Therefore we regard the optimization (depending on the optimizations performed!) and the code generation phase as the most challenging compiler phases to verify. Thus, code generation is a good case study for evaluating the feasibility of our certifying translations methodology for compilers in general.

In Section 5.1 we describe the used intermediate language. The MIPS code is described in Section 5.2. We present the code generation algorithm in Section 5.3. The principle approach to verify a code generation run is shown in Section 5.4. The implementation of our certifying code generation is described in Section 5.5. Finally, we present approaches to improve the certifying code generation phase based on distinct checker predicates. These guarantee properties of artifacts used in the proof process by checking them very fast. The principle methodology and a first example is presented in Section 5.6. Section 5.7 presents a larger checker predicate.

---

[1]The topic of how to combine correctness proofs for different compiler phases has been extensively discussed in the Verifix project (cp. e.g. [DHVG02] (Section 4) on this).

source language →〔 parsing 〕 AST →〔 transformation 〕 IL →〔 optimization 〕 IL →〔 code generation 〕 target language

Figure 5.1: Our Compiler Architecture

operand ::=
      CONST val | VAR var | ARCONST var val | ARVAR var var

expression ::=
      OPERAND operand |
      PLUS operand operand | MINUS operand operand | MULT operand operand |
      LT operand operand | LE operand operand

statement ::=
      ASSIGN_V var expression | ASSIGN_AC var val expression | ASSIGN_AV var var expression |
      BRANCH expression loc | GOTO loc |
      CALLn var procid (var list) | RET var |
      PRINT var | EXIT

procedure ::=
      PROC pid (var set) (var list) (statement list)

program ::=
      PROG pid (var set) (procedure set)

Figure 5.2: Intermediate Language Syntax

5.1 Syntax and Semantics of an Intermediate Language

Semantics of our intermediate language is defined on top of the syntactical elements of the language in a small step operational way. It is defined via a state transition function.

The syntax of our intermediate language is depicted in Figure 5.2 using the EBNF (Extended Backus-Naur Form). Our intermediate language is quite close to a higher imperative programming language and comprises statements made up from assignments, branches, output operations, and procedure calls. Our syntax has definitions for expressions and operands which are combined to form statements which themselves are used to form procedures and programs. We have arrays and primitive variables which may be local – accessible only in the context of a procedure – or global – accessible in an entire program.

Operands are defined using values val and variable var types. They comprise constants, read accesses to primitive variables (referenced via var) as well as arrays with constant (referenced via var and val for array name and index) or variable indices referenced via two vars for array name and index. Operands are used for defining expressions.

ilstate =
$$(\text{val list}) \times \text{pid} \times (\text{var} \Rightarrow \text{val}) \times ((\text{pid} \times \text{loc} \times \text{var} \times (\text{var} \Rightarrow \text{val})) \text{ list}) \times \text{loc}$$

Figure 5.3: Intermediate Language State

Addition, subtraction, multiplication, and two comparison operations *less than* and *less or equal than* are expressions. Expressions are used for defining statements. Statements comprise assignments to primitive and array variables with constant and variable indices. Furthermore, they consist of conditional (target location has type loc to index program locations) and unconditional branches, procedure calls and return statements. Finally, there is a print statement for writing a variable's value to an output device and an exit statement for immediate program termination. Procedures comprise an identifier pid, a set of local variables, a list of arguments, and a list of their statements. Statements can be picked from a list of statements via a value of type loc which may be regarded as a natural number denoting a position in the list of statements. A program definition consists of the identifier of the main procedure, a set of global variables as well as a set of procedures.

States in our intermediate language are tuples (cp. Figure 5.3). They comprise

1. a list of accumulated output val list,

2. an identifier of the current procedure pid,

3. a function mapping global primitive and array variables to values (var ⇒ val).

4. In addition there is a stack for handling recursive procedure calls (formalized as a list: (pid × loc × var × (var ⇒ val)) list). Once a procedure is called by another procedure the calling procedure's data is put on the stack. Such a stack element comprises an identifier of the procedure from which the call has occurred pid, a return location loc – a kind of program counter –, the variable name a return value will be assigned to once the called procedure returns var, and a mapping from local variables to values of the called procedure (var ⇒ val).

5. Furthermore, a state comprises the actual program counter for the current procedure loc.

Variables from the variable type var, used in mappings from variables to values and in the definition of sets of local and global variables are encoded as tuples: The first component of the tuple denotes the actual variable name. The second an index. Thus, each element of an array is handled as a single element in such variable sets. Primitive variables have the index 0. When accessing arrays in our semantics definitions we explicitly write the tuple consisting of the variable name and the index value. Primitive variables access is written for convenience reasons just by giving the primitive variable's name. This can be seen as an abbreviation for a tuple consisting of the variable's name and the index 0. The notion $v \in V$ with v being a variable name and V being a set of variables is an abbreviation for $\exists i.(v, i) \in V$.

evaloperand L G locvals globvals (CONST c) = c

$$\text{evaloperand L G locvals globvals (VAR v)} = \begin{cases} v \in L & \text{then locvals v} \\ v \in G & \text{then globvals v} \end{cases}$$

$$\text{evaloperand L G locvals globvals (ARCONST (v, ci))} = \begin{cases} v \in L & \text{then locvals (v,ci)} \\ v \in G & \text{then globvals (v,ci)} \end{cases}$$

$$\text{evaloperand L G locvals globvals (ARVAR (v, vi))} = \begin{cases} v \in L \wedge vi \in L & \text{then locvals (v,locvals vi)} \\ v \in L \wedge vi \in G & \text{then locvals (v,globvals vi)} \\ v \in G \wedge vi \in L & \text{then globvals (v,locvals vi)} \\ v \in G \wedge vi \in G & \text{then globvals (v,globvals vi)} \end{cases}$$

Figure 5.4: Operand Evaluation

The intermediate language statement evaluation function for defining the small step operational semantics of our intermediate language is shown in Figure 5.6. The transition function makes use of auxiliary functions for evaluating operands and expressions as defined in Figure 5.4 and Figure 5.5. Operands are evaluated by a function requiring a set of local variables, a set of global variables, mappings from local and global variables to values and the actual syntactical operand as inputs. Depending on the fact whether a variable used in an operand is global or local, the value is picked from the appropriate mapping.

Similar to operands, expressions are evaluated by a function requiring sets of local and global variables, mappings for local and global variables, and an expression as inputs. In the definition we make explicit use of the constant 1 representing a boolean value true. Statement evaluation is done by taking a program definition, sets for local and global variables, and the actual state. The statement evaluation function returns the succeeding state. Notice that the set of local variables will change during consecutive applications of the statement evaluation function if a procedure call or return statement is evoked. Similar to operand evaluation, statement evaluation handles the updating of the variable to value mapping by making case distinctions whether a variable is local or global. The conditional branch statement evaluates an expression. Depending on this evaluation the program counter is either set to the jump destination or just increased by one. For the unconditional branch it is just set to the jump destination.

The call statement makes use of a function assignargvals. It takes a program definition, a procedure identifier, a lists of variables serving as arguments as well as variable value mappings for current local and global variables. A new local memory is returned. Values – resolved from the variables that are passed as arguments – are assigned to the variables whose names occur in the called procedure definition. When returning from a procedure, the value of the local variable returned is assigned to the variable name stored on the stack: either one of the callers local variables or a global variable.

The print statement appends the value of a variable to the list of accumulated outputs. These outputs have occurred so far during the program execution. The exit statement

evalexpression L G locvals globvals (OPERAND o1) = evaloperand L G locvals globvars o1

evalexpression L G locvals globvals (PLUS o1 o2) =
    evaloperand L G locvals globvals o1 + evaloperand L G locvals globvals o2

evalexpression L G locvals globvals (MINUS o1 o2) =
    evaloperand L G locvals globvals o1 - evaloperand L G locvals globvals o2

evalexpression L G locvals globvals (MULT o1 o2) =
    evaloperand L G locvals globvals o1 * evaloperand L G locvals globvals o2

evalexpression L G locvals globvals (LT o1 o2) =
    if (evaloperand L G locvals globvals o1 < evaloperand L G locvals globvals o2)   then 1
                                                                                        else 0

evalexpression L G locvals globvals (LE o1 o2) =
    if (evaloperand L G locvals globvals o1 ≤ evaloperand L G locvals globvals o2)   then 1
                                                                                        else 0

Figure 5.5: Expression Evaluation

appends a special termination token to this list.

The exit statement appends a special termination token to the list of outputs. The program counter is not changed. Thus, the succeeding instruction to an exit statement will always be the exit statement itself. The complete state transition function for the intermediate language is depicted in Figure 5.7. It takes a program definition and a state and returns the succeeding state. Auxiliary functions for looking up the set of local variables from a given procedure identifier and a program (getLocals), for looking up the set of global variables from a program (getGlobals) as well as the look-up of a statement from a procedure identifier, a program counter and a program (getStatement) are used.

Discussion of the Intermediate Language

In the semantics definition at hand we did not entirely specify the effect of every possible state transition. The following list contains items that are intentionally left open in the semantics definition and ways we handled them in our implementation:

1. Array index out of bounds access: may either lead to an error state (a special token appended to the output list) or in case of read accesses return an arbitrary value, in case of write accesses may have no effect at all. Depending on the array formalization it may be an even easier solution to treat arrays in the intermediate language like they where potentially infinitely long (cp. Appendix A.1 for a Coq implementation of this solution).

2. Jumps to a non existing statement/out of the procedure code: will lead to an

evalstatement P L G (outp,pid,gvs,(rpid,raddr,rvar,lvs)::stack,pc) (ASSIGN_V v e) =
  if(v ∈ L)   then (outp,pid,gvs,(rpid,raddr,rvar,lvs(v:=evalexpression L G lvs gvs e))::stack,pc+1)
  if(v ∈ G)   then (outp,pid,gvs(v:=evalexpression L G lvs gvs e),(rpid,raddr,rvar,lvs)::stack,pc+1)

evalstatement P L G (outp,pid,gvs,(rpid,raddr,rvar,lvs)::stack,pc) (ASSIGN_AC ci e) =
  if(v ∈ L)   then (outp,pid,gvs,(rpid,raddr,rvar,lvs((v,ci):=evalexpression L G lvs gvs e))::stack,pc+1)
  if(v ∈ G)   then (outp,pid,gvs((v,ci):=evalexpression L G lvs gvs e),(rpid,raddr,rvar,lvs)::stack,pc+1)

evalstatement P L G (outp,pid,gvs,(rpid,raddr,rvar,lvs)::stack,pc) (ASSIGN_AV vi e) =
  if(v ∈ L ∧   then
    vi ∈ L)   (outp,pid,gvs,(rpid,raddr,rvar,lvs((v,lvs vi):=evalexpression L G lvs gvs e))::stack,pc+1)
  if(v ∈ L ∧   then
    vi ∈ G)   (outp,pid,gvs,(rpid,raddr,rvar,lvs((v,gvs vi):=evalexpression L G lvs gvs e))::stack,pc+1)
  if(v ∈ G ∧   then
    vi ∈ L)   (outp,pid,gvs((v,lvs vi):=evalexpression L G lvs gvs e),(rpid,raddr,rvar,lvs)::stack,pc+1)
  if(v ∈ G ∧   then
    vi ∈ G)   (outp,pid,gvs((v,gvs vi):=evalexpression L G lvs gvs e),(rpid,raddr,rvar,lvs)::stack,pc+1)

evalstatement P L G (outp,pid,gvs,(rpid,raddr,rvar,lvs)::stack,pc) (BRANCH e lab) =
  if(evalexpression L G lvs gvs e = 1)   then (outp,pid,gvs,(rpid,raddr,rvar,lvs)::stack,lab)
                        else (outp,pid,gvs,(rpid,raddr,rvar,lvs)::stack,pc + 1)

evalstatement P L G (outp,pid,gvs,(rpid,raddr,rvar,lvs)::stack,pc) (GOTO lab) =
        (outp,pid,gvs,(rpid,raddr,rvar,lvs)::stack,lab)

evalstatement P L G (outp,pid,gvs,(rpid,raddr,rvar,lvs)::stack,pc) (CALLn rv pid',argvars) =
        (outp,pid',gvs,(pid,pc+1,rv,assignargvs P pid argvars lvs gvs)::(rpid,raddr,rvar,lvs)::stack,0)

evalstatement P L G (outp,pid,gvs,(rpid1,raddr1,rvar1,lvs1)::(rpid2,raddr2,rvar2,lvs2)::stack,pc)
        (RET var) =
  if(rvar1 ∈ L)   then (rpid1,outp,gvs,(rpid2,raddr2,rvar2,lvs2(rvar1:=lvs1 var))::stack,raddr1)
  if(rvar1 ∈ G)   then (rpid1,outp,gvs(rvar1:=lvs1 var),(rpid2,raddr2,rvar2,lvs2)::stack,raddr1)

evalstatement P L G (outp,pid,gvs,(raddr,rvar,lvs)::stack,pc) (PRINT v) =
  if(v ∈ L)   then ((lvs v)::outp,pid,gvs,(rpid,raddr,rvar,lvs)::stack,pc)
  if(v ∈ G)   then ((gvs v)::outp,pid,gvs,(rpid,raddr,rvar,lvs)::stack,pc)

evalstatement P L G (outp,pid,gvs,(rpid,raddr,rvar,lvs)::stack,pc) (EXIT) =
        (termination::outp,pid,gvs,(rpid,raddr,rvar,lvs)::stack,pc)

Figure 5.6: Intermediate Language Semantics

ilnext P (outp,pid,gvals,stack,pc) =
        evalstatement P (getLocals pid P) (getGlobals P) (outp,pid,gvals,stack,pc) (getStatement pid pc P)

Figure 5.7: Intermediate Language State Transition Function

error state (error token will be appended to the output list) or the execution of an implicit exit statement (cp. Appendix A.1 for a Coq implementation of the latter solution).

3. No return or exit statement at the end of a procedure definition: have the effect that no state marked as procedure return statement or final state is reached with the last statement. Thus, if the last statement is no branch or jump we will reach a non-existing statement in the next step and item 2 will be encountered.

The presented language is feasible as an intermediate language for compilers. One may use it for compiling many source languages to some kind of target code. The source language, however, may not contain arbitrary pointers. Moreover, arbitrary gotos that cross procedure boundaries are not possible. Further arithmetic operations can be easily included. In fact in some of our implementations we use a much larger set of arithmetic operations. Since the main focus of this thesis is on presenting the methodology and demonstrating its general feasibility we have omitted these additional operations for clarity reasons.

The language can easily be extended with reference semantics and a more complicated type system in the syntax and semantics definition. However, using a non-trivial reference semantics in equivalence proofs requires many assumptions during the proof process that have to be guaranteed on source code level. Thus, we have omitted them in the presented definition. Moreover, if we use realistic reference handling with a non-trivial type system, a type safety proof of the intermediate language is highly preferable. Such a type safety proof is already a large bunch of work that goes beyond the scope of this thesis. See e.g. Nipkow's and von Oheimb's work [NO98] for a formal type safety proof of a subset of Java carried out in Isabelle/HOL.

A very simple reference semantics allowing only a single primitive type to be referenced, may be realized in the following way within our language:

- Tag one distinct array serving as a kind of memory for values.

- Ordinary variables when used as an index to this array are references and may be treated in any way normal references are treated. Using this treatment we are able to use standard arithmetic operations for reference arithmetics.

- Accessing an array element via such a variable is an access via a reference.

Moreover, it should be noted that we do not have a mechanism for dynamic memory allocation. The reasons for this are similar to the reasons why we do not have integrated non-trivial reference semantics. It should be noted, that our chosen intermediate language definition guarantees constant heap size and constant size of stack frames.

Procedure calls are formalized using a call by value semantics. We allow only the passing of values referenced by primitive variables and array elements. Whole arrays may not be passed.

The intermediate language at hand was chosen to demonstrate the general feasibility of the certifying translations approach for code generation. It should, however, be only slightly more complicated to port these results to a more complex intermediate language, e.g. static single assignment form as used in many modern compilers (see e.g. the work by Blech, Glesner et al. [BGLM05, BG04] for static single assignment semantics formalized in Isabelle/HOL).

The defined language does not make a restriction on the used integer arithmetic. We found that a concrete arithmetic formalization can be exchanged with another relatively easy. For this reason, we are able to use different arithmetics for different processors the compiler generates code for. Typical integer arithmetics are 32 or 64 bit signed and unsigned integers. Overflow handling is typically done by taking the value of an unsigned integer to be stored modulo the largest number plus one and storing the result [2].

Instead of making the case distinction whether a variable is local or global in Figure 5.4 we provide in our implemented semantics different syntactic constructs for accessing local or global variables. Furthermore, we encode a special termination flag into the state definition instead of using a distinct termination output token. This flag is also useful for indicating certain states of program execution such as a procedure call that has just occurred. A Coq formalization of the intermediate language is given in Appendix A.1.

The formalization of the syntax definition is done in Isabelle using the *datatype* construct (cp. Section 3.3). In Coq we use the *Inductive* construct for an inductively defined type (cp. Section 3.4). The state transition functions in Isabelle are formalized using the *primrec* construct for primitive recursive definitions. Although there is no recursion in the state transition functions, the use of *primrec* eases the case distinction on the statements. In Coq we use a simple *Definition* for this purpose.

5.2 Syntax and Semantics of MIPS code

In this section we describe our formalization of syntax and semantics of the MIPS [PH98] code.

Figure 5.8 shows the definition of the MIPS syntax. Most instructions work with registers reg and constants const. Instructions for basic arithmetic operations are provided. The shift left instruction SHL is a special case of multiplication and has no direct correspondence in the intermediate language. Moreover, there is the family of *set less than* and *set less or equal than* instructions. They are used for conditional statements. Especially common are combinations with the conditional branch instruction. The SYSCALL statement is used to provide system functionality such as printing a register value to an output device. MIPS programs are lists of instructions.

States in our MIPS formalization are defined as shown in Figure 5.9. They consist of a list of outputs (val list) that have occurred so far, a mapping from registers to values (reg $\Rightarrow$ val), a mapping from memory addresses to values (val $\Rightarrow$ val), and a program counter loc.

Like for the intermediate language, the MIPS semantics is defined with the help of a function for instruction evaluation (cp. Figure 5.10). Addition and subtraction are

---

[2]See e.g. the work by Glesner and Blech [GB03] on integer constant folding. Featuring a schema how to formalize different integer arithmetics within Isabelle/HOL

```
datatype instruction ::=
    ADD reg reg reg | ADDI reg reg const | SUB reg reg reg | MLT reg reg | SHL reg const
    SLT reg reg reg | SLTI reg reg const | SLE reg reg reg | SLEI reg reg const |
    STORE reg const reg | LOAD reg const reg |
    BGTZ reg loc | J loc |
    SYSCALL const


datatype MIPSprogram ::= instruction list
```

Figure 5.8: MIPS Syntax

```
MIPSstate =
    (val list) × (reg ⇒ val) × (val ⇒ val) × loc
```

Figure 5.9: MIPS State Definition

defined on registers. The add immediate function ADDI adds a constant to a register. Since the MIPS architecture does not have an explicit move statement ADDI can be also used for moves. The MIPS machine has several special purpose registers. lo and hi are used for storing the upper and lower part of a multiplication. This is due to the fact that the size of a multiplication result can be twice as large as its operands in bits. Another special purpose register is 0. It has a constant value of zero. The shift left instruction shifts the contents of a register a given number of bits to the left. Thus, within the range length of the register, it is equivalent to a multiplication by two to the power of bits to be shifted. The *set less than* instruction compares the values of two registers and sets a one or a zero in a third register based on the result of the comparison. Different versions of this instruction exist: *set less than or equal* and *set less than immediate, set less than or equal immediate*, respectively. The latter ones take constants as one argument instead of a register. The branch instruction decides on whether a branch is taken or not by the value of a register. The jump instruction performs an unconditional jump. Finally, the system call SYSCALL is used for various purposes. Based on the value of a certain register in our formalization we use it for writing a register's value to an output device and for program termination.

Program termination is encoded similar to the intermediate language: a termination token is added to the list of outputs, the program counter and the rest of the state are not changed.

Based on the instruction evaluation function a state transition function tlnext is defined in Figure 5.11. The tlnextn function executes n consecutive instructions at a time.

Discussion of the MIPS Language

Many different versions of the MIPS processor have evolved since its introduction in 1985. The MIPS processor is designed in a RISC (Reduced Instruction Set Computer) way. The instruction sets of different types of MIPS processors differ in several ways. Our introduced formalization is a generic standard sub set common to all MIPS proces-

evalinstruction (outp,regs,mem,pc) (ADD r1 r2 r3) = (outp,regs(r1:= (regs r2) + (regs r3)),mems,pc+1)

evalinstruction (outp,regs,mem,pc) (ADDI r1 r2 c) = (outp,regs(r1:= (regs r2) + c),mems,pc+1)

evalinstruction (outp,regs,mem,pc) (SUB r1 r2 r3) = (outp,regs(r1:= (regs r2) - (regs r3)),mems,pc+1)

evalinstruction (outp,regs,mem,pc) (MLT r1 r2) = (outp,regs((lo,hi):= (regs r1) * (regs r2)),mems,pc+1)

evalinstruction (outp,regs,mem,pc) (SHL r c) = (outp,regs(r:= (regs r) * 2^c),mems,pc+1)

evalinstruction (outp,regs,mems,pc) (SLT r1 r2 r3) =
        if(regs r2 < regs r3)   then (outp,regs(r1:=1),mems,pc + 1)
                             else (outp,regs(r1:=0),mems,pc + 1)

evalinstruction (outp,regs,mems,pc) (SLTI r1 r2 c) =
        if(regs r2 < regs c)   then (outp,regs(r1:=1),mems,pc + 1)
                          else (outp,regs(r1:=0),mems,pc + 1)

evalinstruction (outp,regs,mems,pc) (SLE r1 r2 r3) =
        if(regs r2 ≤ regs r3)   then (outp,regs(r1:=1),mems,pc + 1)
                             else (outp,regs(r1:=0),mems,pc + 1)

evalinstruction (outp,regs,mems,pc) (SLEI r1 r2 c) =
        if(regs r2 ≤ c)   then (outp,regs(r1:=1),mems,pc + 1)
                       else (outp,regs(r1:=0),mems,pc + 1)

evalinstruction (outp,regs,mem,pc) (STORE r1 offset r2) =
        (outp,regs,mems(offset + (regs r2):= (regs r1)),pc + 1)

evalinstruction (outp,regs,mem,pc) (LOAD r1 offset r2) =
        (outp,regs(r1 := mems (offset + (regs r2))),mems,pc + 1)

evalinstruction (outp, regs, mems, pc) (BGTZ r1 lab) = $\left\{ \begin{array}{ll} \text{if}(0 < \text{regs r1}) & \text{then (outp,regs,mems,lab)} \\ & \text{else (outp,regs,mems,pc + 1)} \end{array} \right.$

evalinstruction (outp,regs,mem,pc) (J lab) = (outp,regs,mems,lab)

evalinstruction (outp, regs, mems, pc) (SYSCALL c) = $\left\{ \begin{array}{ll} c = 1 & \text{then ((regs a1)::outp,regs,mems,lab)} \\ c = 10 & \text{then (termination::outp,regs,mems,pc)} \end{array} \right.$

Figure 5.10: MIPS Semantics

tlnext P (outp,regs,mems,pc) =
        evalinstruction (outp,regs,mems,pc) (getInstruction pc P)

tlnextn P state 0 = state
tlnextn P state n =
        tlnextn P (tlnext P state) (n-1)

Figure 5.11: MIPS State Transition Functions

sors. It is sufficient for serving as a target language for higher imperative programming languages. In our implementations, however, we have introduced additional macros that stand for one or several consecutive MIPS instructions. We have done this mostly for easing up the development process of our certifying compilers and the verification process. Most of them encapsulate several instructions, others are special cases of the instructions presented.

We did not regard any pipeline issues so far. Integer width can vary dependent on the MIPS processor used. Early MIPS machines have 32 bit wide registers. Since the introduction of the R4000 machines 64 bit wide registers do also exist. In our defined semantics we do not make restrictions on the integer width but allow it to be set according to the needs of the compiler user.

Note, that in our semantics locations of instructions are indexed in a way that each instruction corresponds to one cell in the memory where the code is stored. Depending on the actual machine other storage schema might be appropriate. We would likewise increment the program counter by e.g. 4 if one instruction corresponds to a 32 bit integer.

Similar to the intermediate language semantics, we do not mention possible restrictions on memory addresses or registers in our MIPS semantics. Accesses of not existing memory locations and registers are intentionally underspecified. Several solutions are possible to resolve this underspecification: Such accesses may either lead to error states. A second solution is that read accesses result in an arbitrary value and write accesses have no effect. Another solution used in the Coq implementation in Appendix A.2 is to assume an unlimited memory for writing and reading values. Program counters indexing locations that contain no executable instruction are handled in a way that an exit statement is executed.

The MIPS processor was chosen because of its simple architecture, its wide area of usage, and the availability of a simulator: SPIM [Jam]. Programs of the introduced subset of the MIPS language can be run within this simulator (the macros mentioned above have to be unfolded).

Like in the intermediate language the formalization of the syntax definition is done in Isabelle using the *datatype* construct and in Coq using the *Inductive* construct. The state transition functions are formalized using the *primrec* construct in Isabelle and the *Definition* construct in Coq. For the tlnextn function we use *Fixpoint* construct in Coq due to the functions recursive definition on the argument n. A Coq formalization of the MIPS language can be found in Appendix A.2.

5.3 The Code Generation Algorithm

Our code generation algorithm compiles procedures independently of each other. It comprises three passes over the sequential program representation.

In the first pass of our code generator register allocation is performed. It is determined for every program point whether a variable's values shall be stored in a register or memory.

We have implemented various register allocation algorithms and found out that they have in general little effect on our correctness proofs. As a result of this, it is possible to use sophisticated register allocation strategies and simple proof schemes to prove them correct.

Based on the information provided by the register allocation we allocate memory locations next. This does not require an additional pass over the program representation. We allocate memory locations for the non-register mapped variables. One result of register and memory allocation is a mapping from intermediate language variables – and sometimes program points – to registers and memory addresses (*variable mapping*). This mapping is not only used during the compilation process but is also vital for conducting our correctness proofs.

In the next pass the intermediate language program is processed sequentially and for each statement one or more MIPS instructions are generated. Thus, we have a 1:n relation between intermediate language statements and MIPS instructions. This generation is done via simple standard compiler textbook algorithms. Hence, some small optimizations are applied to each instruction code sequence representing an intermediate language statement. A byproduct of this pass is a relation of intermediate language and MIPS code program points that correspond to each other: the *program counter relation*.

In a last pass through the MIPS program jump targets are resolved with the help of this *program counter relation*. This relation is also very helpful for generating and the conduction of the correctness proof.

The whole compiler is implemented using the ML programming language. We did investigate several different implementations of the code generation phase. None has exceeded a few thousand lines of code. It took no longer than one person-week to realize a single implementation for someone with a background in compiler construction.

5.4 Correct Code Generation

In this section we present our way of guaranteeing correct code generation using our certifying system translation methodology.

We describe our overall notion of correctness for code generation in Subsection 5.4.1. It is based on our *Generic Correctness Criteria* family. We briefly describe how we generate and check generated proof scripts in Subsection 5.4.2. A general technique for performance evaluation of proving strategies is described in Subsection 5.4.3. The technique uses the O-notation to represent the worst case performance of proof scripts. It is based on counting the number of rewriting steps applied during the proving process. The presented performance evaluation technique is used for the analysis of different parts of our proof scripts which are described in detail in Subsections 5.4.4, 5.4.5, 5.4.6, and 5.4.7. Furthermore, typical proof steps are presented together with examples. We discuss how to structure the conduction and generation of proofs in these subsections.

1. $H = createsimulation$ CI

2. $correct$ H

3. $H(s0_{IL}, s0_{MIPS})$

4. $\forall s_{IL}\ s_{MIPS}\ s'_{IL}\ s'_{MIPS}.$
   $s'_{IL} = ilnext\ P_{IL}\ s_{IL} \wedge s'_{MIPS} = tlnextn\ P_{MIPS}\ s_{MIPS}\ (steplength\ s'_{MIPS}\ CI)$
   $H(s_{IL}, s_{MIPS}) \longrightarrow H(s'_{IL}, s'_{MIPS})$

Figure 5.12: Code Generation Correctness Criterion

5.4.1 Adapting the *Generic Correctness Criterion*

Based on the *Generic 1:n Correctness Criterion* from Figure 4.7 we define the *Code Generation Correctness Criterion* as shown in Figure 5.12. It allows one step in the intermediate language to correspond with one or more steps in the MIPS assembler code. In the first line we say that the simulation relation H is created from information that has been computed during the compilation process: *CI (compilation information)*. These informations are rather a hint on how to create the simulation relation. Thus, the first line is not a condition we have to verify. The compilation information comprises the *variable mapping* and the *program counter relation*. The second line states that the simulation relation is indeed correct. This means, it preserves state correspondence and thus implies correctness of the transformation on state comparison level (cp. Chapter 4). In our cases this means that the values written to an output device are the same for both states in the simulation relation. This is ensured by the predicate **correct** which takes the simulation relation as argument. The third line states that initial states have to be in the simulation relation (cp. the remarks in Section 4.5 on the encoding of this). The fourth line encapsulates the simulation step: If two states are in the relation, the succeeding states have to be in the relation, too. There is always one step in the intermediate language. Thus, we chose *ilnext* P_{IL} as state transition function. There can be several steps on the MIPS side. The existentially quantified function NEXT' encapsulating several target language steps in the *Generic 1:n Correctness Criterion* is realized in the figure at hand via the *tlnextn* P_{MIPS} function. The number of steps taken in the MIPS code is determined by the *program counter relation*.

We do not explicitly make use of the step correctness predicate from Figure 4.7. This may be used to put constraints on consecutive steps that are treated as a single step. Putting constraints on the simulation relation using the state correspondence predicate from our framework is sufficient to guarantee our desired semantical property: Equality of output streams. Nevertheless, there is one correctness constraint we are interested in that cannot explicitly be formulated as a constraint on the simulation relation. It is the guarantee of the fact that at most one output value is written during consecutive steps in the MIPS code piece that correspond to a single intermediate language statement. This is implicitly guaranteed by the fact that we always regard a single step in the intermediate language – where only one element may be written to an output device –, the fact that the simulation relation requires the same output sequences before and after the steps ensured by the *correct* predicate, and the fact that there is no MIPS instruction that can undo outputs that have already occurred during a previous instruction.

Derivation of the Code Generation Correctness Criterion

In this paragraph we show that the Code Generation Correctness Criterion is more specialized than *Generic 1:n Correctness Criterion*. This means that it is an instantiation of it. We show this by proving that the Code Generation Correctness Criterion is implied by the *Generic 1:n Correctness Criterion*.

To prove this, we start with the definition of the *Generic 1:n Correctness Criterion* and strengthen the conditions. We instantiate it with the appropriate state transition functions of intermediate language and the MIPS code as the first two arguments. Since we only look at correctness of single procedures, our code generation correctness criterion does only care about the parts of the programs P and P' serving as arguments to the state transition function that belong to this procedure. This procedure is determined from the initial states. Further arguments are initial states, our notion of step correspondence ensuring equal output values in states (done by the predicate *output_equiv*), and our step correctness predicate in the MIPS language. The latter always returns true as discussed above.

GCC1:n($next \leftarrow ilnext\ P, next' \leftarrow tlnext\ P'$,
   $H_0 \leftarrow \{(s0_{IL}, s0_{MIPS})\}$,
   $C \leftarrow output\_equiv$,
   $CorrectSteps' \leftarrow \lambda\ f\ s'\ i.true$)
$\exists$ H.
$\exists$ NEXT'.
   $\forall\ s_0\ s'_0.\ (s_0, s'_0) \in H_0 \longrightarrow H(s_0, s'_0)\ \wedge$
   $\forall\ s\ s'\ .\ H(s,s') \longrightarrow C(s, s')\ \wedge$
   $\forall\ s\ s'.\ H(s,s') \longrightarrow H\ (next(s),\ NEXT'(s'))\ \wedge$
$\forall\ s'\ .\ \exists\ i.$ apply_n $next'\ s'\ i =$ NEXT' $s' \wedge CorrectSteps'$ next' $s'\ i$

Doing so results in the following criteria:

$\exists$ H.
$\exists$ NEXT'.
   $\forall\ s_0\ s'_0.\ (s_0, s'_0) \in \{(s0_{IL}, s0_{MIPS})\} \longrightarrow H(s_0, s'_0)\ \wedge$
   $\forall\ s\ s'\ .\ H(s,s') \longrightarrow output\_equiv(s, s')\ \wedge$
   $\forall\ s\ s'.\ H(s,s') \longrightarrow H\ (ilnext\ P\ (s),\ NEXT'(s'))\ \wedge$
$\forall\ s'\ .\ \exists\ i.$ apply_n $(tlnext\ P')\ s'\ i =$ NEXT' $s' \wedge ((\lambda\ f\ s'\ i.true)\ (tlnext\ P')\ s'\ i$

We can rewrite this equivalently by simplifying the condition for the initial states and evaluating the λ-expression:

70

∃ H.
∃ NEXT'.
$\quad$ H($s0_{IL}, s0_{MIPS}$) ∧
$\quad$ ∀ s s' . H(s,s') $\longrightarrow$ $output\_equiv(s, s')$ ∧
$\quad$ ∀ s s'. H(s,s') $\longrightarrow$ H ($ilnext$ P (s), NEXT'(s')) ∧
∀ s' . ∃ i. apply_n ($tlnext$ P') s' i = NEXT' s'

This can be rewritten equivalently by pulling the existential quantification of the NEXT' function more to the end:

∃ H.
$\quad$ H($s0_{IL}, s0_{MIPS}$) ∧
$\quad$ ∀ s s' . H(s,s') $\longrightarrow$ $output\_equiv(s, s')$ ∧
∃ NEXT'.
$\quad$ ∀ s s'. H(s,s') $\longrightarrow$ H ($ilnext$ P (s), NEXT'(s')) ∧
$\quad$ ∀ s' . ∃ i. apply_n ($tlnext$ P') s' i = NEXT' s'

We can group the different elements such that they correspond to the different items from our Code Generation Correctness Criterion:

1. ∃ H.

2. ∀ s s' . H(s,s') $\longrightarrow$ $output\_equiv(s, s')$ ∧

3. H($s0_{IL}, s0_{MIPS}$) ∧

4. ∃ NEXT'.
$\quad$ ∀ s s'. H(s,s') $\longrightarrow$ H ($ilnext$ P (s), NEXT'(s')) ∧
$\quad$ ∀ s' . ∃ i. apply_n ($tlnext$ P') s' i = NEXT' s'

The next transformation step is an implication. In the context of this proof this means that the formula above is implied by the following formula. We instantiate the existentially quantified NEXT' variable such that:

NEXT' s' = *tlnextn P' s' (steplength s' CI)*

Thus, the existentially quantified i is instantiated with:

steplength s' CI

CI represents the compiler provided information which is fixed for each compilation run.

1. $\exists$ H.

2. $\forall\ s\ s'$. H$(s,s') \longrightarrow$ *output_equiv*$(s, s') \wedge$

3. H$(s0_{IL}, s0_{MIPS}) \wedge$

4. $\forall\ s\ s'$. H$(s,s') \longrightarrow$ H ($ilnext\ P\ (s)$, $tlnextn\ P'\ (s')\ (steplength\ s'\ Cl)) \wedge$
   $\forall\ s'$. apply_n ($tlnext\ P'$) s' ($steplength\ s'\ Cl$) $=$ $tlnextn\ P'\ s'$ ($steplength\ s'\ Cl$)

The last step is another strengthening of the formula: The existentially quantified H is instantiated as shown in the first item of our Code Generation Correctness Criterion. The second item is rewritten using the definition of **createsimulation** and *output_equiv*. The last line of the last item in the previous formula can be statically evaluated to true. Thus, we arrive at the Code Generation Correctness Criterion:

1. H $=$ *createsimulation Cl*

2. *correct H*

3. H ($s0_{IL}, s0_{MIPS}$)

4. $\forall s_{IL}\ s_{MIPS}\ s'_{IL}\ s'_{MIPS}$.
   $s'_{IL} = ilnext\ P\ s_{IL} \wedge s'_{MIPS} = tlnextn\ P'\ s_{MIPS}$ ($steplength\ s'_{MIPS}\ Cl$)
   H($s_{IL}, s_{MIPS}) \longrightarrow$ H(s'_{IL}, s'_{MIPS})

The theorem prover formalization of the Code Generation Correctness Criterion and its actual instantiation is written for each code generation run into a separate theorem prover file. A Coq formalization for the compilation of a procedure is shown in Appendix B.

5.4.2 Proof Sketch on Proving Code Generation Runs Correct

Since code generation is done for each procedure independently we verify each compilation run of a procedure independently, too. To prove a code generation run correct we have to show that each intermediate language procedure and its compiled MIPS counterpart fulfill the *Code Generation Correctness Criterion* instantiated and presented in Section 5.4.1.

First we establish a simulation relation for the concrete code generation run based on information provided by the compiler. We prove that it indeed implies correctness, i.e. it ensures the same output traces (cp. first two items of the code generation correctness criterion). We have a generic simulation relation which is instantiated with the information provided by the compiler. Since we have proved that this generic simulation relation always leads to a correct concrete simulation relation this proof is rather trivial when conducted for a certain code generation run.

Next we prove that the initial states of both procedures are in the simulation relation. Using the encoding for initial states as suggested in Section 4.5 this turns out to be an easy task.

For showing that for each two states in the simulation relation the succeeding states are in the relation again, we make a case distinction on possible locations in the intermediate language code (program counter). An intermediate language state being in a simulation relation with some MIPS state requires that it must point to some intermediate language statement. In addition, the MIPS program counter has to point to a corresponding MIPS program point and the *program counter relation* has to indicate the exact number of corresponding MIPS instructions to the intermediate language instruction. We make a case distinction on all possible intermediate language program points. Hence we split intermediate language and MIPS code into corresponding slices which have to semantically correspond to each other. For each corresponding pair of slices we prove in the theorem prover a separate lemma that they compute equivalent values, store them at equivalent locations, reach equivalent program points, call equivalent procedures with equivalent parameters, return equivalent values or produce equivalent outputs. Of course a typical MIPS program may compute a lot of intermediate values that do not appear in the intermediate language. We handle this by requiring only values of variables appearing in the intermediate language procedure and the appropriate memory locations to correspond to each other.

To prove such a single step correct we require a number of prerequisites. Various properties concerning the mapping from variables to memory have to be ensured in a *first phase*. Crucial to our proofs is the fact that the mapping between variables and memory is injective: If we change a variable and a corresponding memory cell no other variable's memory cell is affected.

The lemmata realizing the case distinction on the intermediate languages program points are established in a *second phase*. We call such a lemma a *step lemma*. Finally, it is all put together in a *third phase* proving the *Code Generation Correctness Criterion* (cp. Figure 5.12). We call the phase where the properties that are invariant to a code generation run like the implication of one criterion by another the *phase zero* within this terminology.

This case distinction on program points of the given procedures is the key to proving the equivalence of intermediate language code and MIPS code. It should be noted that proving such a step correct is not a direct execution of certain instructions in certain states since the variables', registers', and memory values in such states are not fixed. It is the deduction of an abstract successor state from another abstract state with the rules defining the semantics as introduced in Section 5.1 and Section 5.2. Hence this procurement lifts the dynamic nature of trace based semantics to a static view enhancing the possibility to reason about possibly infinite state systems in a theorem prover.

5.4.3 Analyzing Proving Effort

Throughout the next subsections we use the O-notation to estimate the time it takes to conduct a certain proof script. We count the number of basic rewriting steps a theorem prover has to perform for a certain task, e.g. whenever some function is applied to evaluate a datastructure or some formulas are derived from other formulas.

In our evaluation, V is the size of the set of variables to be considered. Each array element occurs as a single element within these sets (cp. Section 5.1). P is the size of the involved procedure, i.e. the number of intermediate statements occurring in it.

Thus, if we say that a proof script performs within $O(f(V, P))$ time we mean that there exists constants i and j such that the number of rewriting steps performed by the script is less than or equal $i + j \cdot f(V, P)$ for all possible sizes of sets of variables V and procedure sizes P.

Although our proving strategies depend on the number of involved MIPS memory locations and the size of the MIPS code, these do not directly appear in our O-notation terms since they are proportional to the number of elements in the set of variables and the size of the intermediate language procedure.

Limitations of our Analysis

In Isabelle 2005 most rewriting steps require some form of higher-order unification. The time spent for unification is by far the most time consuming part in Isabelle 2005. In Coq 8.1, however, many rewriting steps in datastructures may be applied without doing unification, but can be done in a more native way directly on the underlying datatypes. Therefore our given O-notation estimations are less valuable for proof scripts processed by Coq 8.1. Moreover, unification times may be different for different formula to be matched with each other. Especially when dealing with very long formula this is a factor having a larger effect on our proving times. Nevertheless, we believe that our O-notation estimations give a good first classification of how good proof scripts do perform in practice.

Since certificate checking is the bottleneck in certifying code generation our O-notation estimation is especially beneficial for analyzing possible problems especially with potential extensions of the involved languages before one actually implements them.

5.4.4 Setting up the Proof: Establishing the Simulation Relation

Before conducting the actual proof we have to establish a simulation relation. We do this by instantiating a generic simulation relation proved to ensure correctness of the compilation run with information provided by the compiler.

The only condition from a correctness point of view on a simulation relation used for proving a code generation run is that it has to ensure the following fact: accumulated outputs in the intermediate language and in the MIPS code are the same in corresponding states.

Using the facts about implication of different correctness criteria – especially the orders on correctness criteria and their counterparts on simulation relations as discussed in

Chapter 4 (especially Section 4.3.1) we can strengthen the generic simulation relation by adding further conditions without loosing its ability to prove correctness of a transformation. To prove a code generation run correct using the *Code Generation Correctness Criterion* we strengthen our simulation relation with the following properties that shall be ensured for states being in the simulation relation:

- We require that variables in the interpretation of the intermediate language have the same values as the memory cells or registers they are mapped to in the execution of the MIPS code.

- We require that program points in both states correspond to each other.

- When encountering procedure calls we require that certain calling conventions are fulfilled: Parameters are passed at distinct specified locations in registers and memory. The old program pointer has to be saved at a distinct location as well.

- When returning from a procedure returning conventions have to be preserved: The return value has to be written to the memory location of the variable it is assigned to. This memory location has been saved on the stack. The old program pointer has to be restored.

- Depending on the used machine some areas of memory may not be written to. This can also be ensured in the simulation relation.

Thus, we only need to instantiate a generic simulation relation with sets of variables under consideration, the *variable mapping*, the *program counter relation*, and some distinct specified locations for special values to get a simulation relation for a concrete code generation correctness proof.

Discussion

Note, that the locations for passing parameters and storing program counters can be anywhere within the memory or register set. It has to be ensured, however, that the program pointer is stored and restored from the same location and parameters are stored and fetched from the same locations. Furthermore, the locations may not interfere with other locations used for storing other variables. For different target systems these locations may vary and may be subject to e.g. operating system policies.

Since we do look at the compilation of distinct procedures and not of entire programs we do not need to relate a procedure call stack in the intermediate language with a corresponding stack area in the MIPS memory within the simulation relation. We rather assume that this has been done correctly before the procedure in consideration has been called and assume that every procedure that is called does this correctly. For each compiled procedure we verify that these calling and returning conventions are fulfilled. The simulation relation has, however, to ensure that other stack frames are not accessed other than for calls and returns.

An array a is correctly aligned iff

for all valid indices i:
the address of $a[i]$ is the address of $a[0] + (integer width) * i$

Figure 5.13: Array Alignment Property

5.4.5 Proving the Prerequisites

After we have established the simulation relation we begin with the first phase of the proof. In the *first phase* of the correctness proof for a code generation run we prove properties about information provided by the compiler during the compilation process. These properties are formulated as lemmata in our theorem provers and are used in later phases of the correctness proof.

Several properties of the *variable mapping* have to be proved:

- The *variable mapping* has to be injective. This means that two different variables' corresponding memory cells are different.

- The array alignment has to be correct. For each array involving dynamic accesses the property described in Figure 5.13 has to hold. Typical values for *integer width* are 4 or 8 depending whether we use 32 bit or 64 bit integers.

- Local variables have addresses in memory relative to a stack pointer. To make deduction of the stack size easier we require them to be aligned without wasting stack space, i.e. each memory cell on the stack belongs to a variable.

- Unless we assume unlimited memory in a verification scenario, memory size is limited, so we have to prove that we do not have more variables in the system than available memory space. Moreover, we must not allocate memory dedicated to the stack or used for program code for global memory.

- Some registers and memory areas are reserved for intermediate values occurring during the MIPS computations. For this reason no variable must be mapped to them.

The proof of injectivity of the *variable mapping* between variables and memory locations is done in an *inductive* way. We use the following scheme:

- We prove that a mapping with one variable and memory/register location is injective.

- With adding additional variables we prove that the mapping comprising the additional *variable to new memory location* is still injective.

To do this in a simple way we use a memory counter. All prior variable's memory locations are below this memory counter. Hence, if we assign a new memory location and it is equal or above this counter, the resulting mapping will be injective again.

In terms of rewriting steps the time it takes to complete this injectivity proof solely depends on the number of variables the *variable mapping* maps to memory or register locations. Since each addition of a new variable can be done in $O(1)$ time denoting a constant number of rewriting steps the complete proof takes $O(V)$ time. To make the reuse of our injectivity proofs easier we create different *variable mappings* for global and local variables. These can be combined into a larger complete *variable mapping* for a complete program with very little effort.

The proof of correct array alignment can be done in $O(V^2)$ time. For each array we have to prove that the alignment is correct. This is done by looking the definition – a relatively small arithmetic term realizing the array alignment similar to the one displayed in Figure 5.13 – of the mapping for an array up from the function realizing the *variable mapping*. Since this function grows linear with the size of the variables the proof for one array can be done in $O(V)$ time.

The remaining properties about the *variable mapping* can be done together with its inductive definition. We basically have to prove that a variable's memory location is below or above a certain address. Requiring for each property at most one fact to be proved in $O(1)$. Since we only have a constant number of facts for each variable these proofs can be done in $O(V)$.

The complete proof for *variable mapping* properties can be done in $O(V^2)$.

Discussion of the *First Phase*

Since we have different *variable mappings* for each procedure and one for global variables we have different proofs as well. This splitting helps to make the approach scalable for larger programs. To do so means that the potentially quadratic behavior of each correctness proof of a single procedure is less problematic.

The injectivity proof for the *variable mapping* can only be done in the sketched manner if the locations the variables are mapped to do not change within a procedure for local variables (relative to a stack pointer) or in a program for global variables. While this is a realistic assumption for variables mapped to memory locations, variables mapped to registers may change during the execution of a procedure. We handle this by adding an additional parameter to the *variable mapping* denoting the current program counter. Of course the injectivity proof gets more complicated with the number of program points we have to distinguish.

The injectivity proof for local variables is done relative to a stack pointer and is not much different from the one used for global variables.

Regarding elements of arrays as distinct variables which are contained in the sets of global and local variables respectively does not change the complexity issues addressed in this section. However, we experienced that it eases formulation of correctness theorems and the deduction of correctness proofs.

Note, that we can do the proof of correct array alignment together with the injectivity proof during the inductive definition of a set of variables.

The amount of time used to prove correct array alignment is usually much lower than $O(V^2)$ would suggest. The $O(V^2)$ occurs only in rather pathological cases. When counting array elements as distinct variables there has to be a very large number of arrays each consisting of very few elements to come close to the $O(V^2)$ time behavior. With an efficient encoding of the *variable mapping* the time for the proof for the correct array alignment is usually neglectible.

5.4.6 Proving the Steps Correct

Having conducted the proofs from the *first phase* we encounter our *second phase*: We prove symbolic execution steps correct. These are formalized within step lemmata. To prove a step correct we have to prove that for two states that are in the simulation relation and having corresponding program points the succeeding states are in the simulation relation again. Since we know the involved program points we can determine which intermediate language statement is involved in the step and base the choice of the proof principle upon it.

Typically we have different kinds of step lemmata correctness proofs for assignments with arithmetic operations, branches and special statements like procedure calls or returns and syscalls.

In this subsection we present such typical steps. Instead of giving a general principle how to prove a class of step lemmata correct we present easily generalizable examples on how to handle a class of steps.

As mentioned in Section 1.2 an important characteristics of certifying compilation is that we can guarantee correctness, i.e. if our proof scripts are accepted by the theorem prover we can be sure that the compilation task has been carried out correctly. Thus, correctness is encoded and guaranteed by the languages' semantics, the correctness criterion and the trusted computing base, comprising the theorem prover. It is not an issue of the proof script.

On the other hand we can not guarantee completeness of our certifying compilation infrastructure, i.e. a generated proof script might fail, even if the compilation task has been done correctly. This procurement results in less complicated proofs than in algorithm verification, which guarantee completeness. In the case of the proving principles for step lemmata, this means that we have no guarantee that the presented proof principles will always lead to a successful proof script generation. Nevertheless, we think that our examples convince the reader that the presented technique is sufficiently complete for practical relevant usage.

Please also note that while for a given compiler a completeness proof should be at least in theory possible it is impossible for an unknown compiler. Complementary to this, it is possible to construct some usable certificates for distinct runs of unknown compilers.

Assignments

An example for an assignment including an arithmetic operation is shown in Figure 5.14. A variable x is assigned the value of y + 1. In the MIPS code the value of y is stored at memory address 1004 (offset 1004 + value of register 0, which is always 0) it is loaded into a register a10. The value of a10 is increased by one and stored at memory address 1000.

We assume that the two code pieces are at position 100 in the intermediate language code and start at 400 in the MIPS code. Furthermore, x and y are both global variables. To prove the step correct, we must be able to conclude that whenever the two states before the step are in the simulation relation (shown in the figure) the states after the step must be in the relation, too. In the intermediate language the only change happening during the state transition is a change of the value of x and the incrementation of the program counter. In the MIPS language the register a10 is altered two times. The value of this register is then assigned to a memory location. The program counter is incremented by three. The resulting MIPS state can be simplified as shown in the figure to make the conduction of the proofs easier.

We do not know the context in which the step occurs. Hence, we only know what the simulation relation ensures for the states before encountering the step. Most importantly that comprises that variables' values and the memory and register set have values corresponding to each other as specified by the *variable mapping*.

The correctness proof of our assignment step breaks down to check the following items – the items demanded by our simulation relation:

- We do not know which outputs have occurred so far, but can conclude: Since the states before the step are in the simulation relation, ILoutp and MIPSoutp have to be the same. Hence, since no output occurs during the steps, the outputs are still the same after the step.

- Variables in the intermediate language and corresponding memory and register locations have the same values before the step. The only variable's value altered is x it gets the value of y + 1. On the MIPS machine the register a10 is altered for use with an intermediate value which has no direct correspondence within the intermediate language. Moreover, the memory cell 1000 gets the value of the memory cell 1004 plus the constant 1 assigned. If we can derive from the *variable mapping* that x corresponds to memory cell 1000 and y corresponds to memory cell 1004 we can conclude that x and memory cell 1000 will have the same values after the step.

  We usually have many variables in a program that are not altered during a step. To prove that the values of their corresponding memory cells and registers do not change during the step as well, we use the properties proved during the *first phase*. They ensure that the *variable mapping* is injective, thus no other variable than x has the corresponding memory cell 1000. Moreover, the fact that some registers (including a10) are left free for intermediate results is guaranteed.

- We have to ensure that the resulting program counters are in the intermediate language again. This is done via a look-up in the compiler provided *program counter relation*.

In general we need for the verification of an assignment as presented above $O(P+V)$ time. We need $O(P)$ time for a single look-up of an actual statement or instruction belonging to the intermediate and MIPS code from a procedure definition since statements and

Intermediate Language Code

    ASSIGN_V 'x' (PLUS (VAR 'y') (CONST 1))

MIPS Code

      LOAD a10 1004 0

      ADDI a10 a10 1

      STORE a10 1000 0

Intermediate Language's and MIPS States before the Step

    (ILoutp,pid,gvars,stack,100)

    (MIPSoutp,regs,mem,400)

Intermediate Language's and MIPS States after the Step

    (ILoutp,pid,gvars(x:= (gvars y) + 1),stack,101)

    (MIPSoutp,regs(a10 := mem 1004,a10 := a10 + 1),

           mem(1000 := (regs(a10 := mem 1004,a10 := a10 + 1)) a10),403) =

    (MIPSoutp,regs(a10 := (mem 1004 + 1)),mem(1000 := (mem 1004) + 1),403)

Figure 5.14: An Assignment to a Variable

instructions are stored in lists. For an assignment, we require a roughly constant number of look-ups to the procedure definitions – depending on the number of MIPS instructions that correspond to an intermediate language statement. Furthermore, we need to make one look-up to the program counter relation, which is a list. Hence it can be done in $O(P)$ as well. We need to make a constant number of look-ups to know whether a variable corresponds to a memory cell or register. Since the *variable mapping* grows linear with the number of variables, a look-up takes $O(V)$ time.

A more complex example for two code pieces doing an assignment to an array element is shown in Figure 5.15. An array a is assigned at position i the value of a[i] + x. While i corresponds to memory cell 1008, the array a starts at memory cell 2000 and x corresponds to memory cell 1000. To access an array element in the machine code the value used for the index is multiplied by four (the shift left) and added to the array's base address (offset 2000). While the principle properties stated in the first example still hold, the check that the array element altered and the corresponding memory cell have the same values is more complicated since we do not know which array element is affected – it depends on the unknown value of the index i.

However, the index i has a corresponding memory cell and this memory cell is used for the computation of the address from which the element's corresponding value is fetched in the MIPS machine. We can conclude that no matter which array element is changed, its corresponding memory cell is altered in the same way. This can be concluded directly for all valid indices with the help of the array alignment property of the *variable mapping* from the first phase (cp. Figure 5.13).

One problem occurs in this example: We can only prove the array alignment correct for the *variable mapping* for valid indices. What happens if no array element at all – an out of bounds access – is referenced? As discussed in Section 5.1 this is intentionally left open in the intermediate language definition: we can handle it in the intermediate language semantics with e.g. a termination of the program. On the MIPS machine we can not capture out of bounds accesses directly. An unrestricted variable used as an index may have any value since it is in general undecidable which values a variable will be assigned to during a program run. An access might result in a memory access to a cell belonging to another variable.

To apply the properties proved on correct alignment in the *first phase* we have to either ensure that no out of bounds access occurs or deal with them in another way. This may be done in the following ways:

1. We can provide a fact proved on source code level that no invalid index will ever be used, accordingly no out of bounds access will ever occur. We can conclude from this that only valid indices will be used in the MIPS machine as well. If a proof for this fact is provided in the theorem prover language, we do not have to rely on a tool other than our theorem prover.

2. We can use the *set less than* instruction family to make a test whether a register's value is in a certain bound before making an access to fetch an array element on the MIPS machine. If this test does not succeed, we must encounter an error state (implemented via a termination syscall on the MIPS machine) in both intermediate and MIPS language.

3. We can define that an out of bounds access in the intermediate language denotes an error state and adopt our correctness criterion in a way that any state on the MIPS side corresponds to an intermediate language's error state. Thus, no application of alignment properties is needed.

We have implemented and tested all solutions. While the second one generates more code overhead, it is always applicable and we do not have to trust a tool doing source code verification as in the first one. The third solution is easy to implement, it can be fitted into the *Generic Correctness Criterion* easily by defining the properties put on the simulation relation appropriately. However, some users might not like a certifying compiler that does not guarantee the absence of array out of bounds accesses.

Once we have ensured valid array accesses, we can apply the array alignment property and the proof succeeds.

Branches

Apart from assignments we have to handle branches. Typical example code pieces for a branch are shown in Figure 5.16. These code pieces might realize a loop. In the intermediate language we compare a variable x to the constant 500. If this comparison yields true the branch is taken and the program counter is set to 40. Otherwise it is increased by one resulting in 103 in our example. In the MIPS code we load the corresponding value of x stored at memory address 1000 into register a10. We perform a *set less than immediate* operation on a10 with the constant 500 as second parameter. The register a10 contains a 1 if the value of a10 was indeed below 500. Otherwise it is set to 0. If the register was set to 1, we perform the branch, thus end up with a program

Intermediate Language Code

ASSIGN_AV 'a' 'i' (PLUS (ARVAR 'a' 'i') (VAR 'x')) |

MIPS Code

```
        LOAD a10 1008 0
        SHL a10 2
        LOAD r11 2000 a10
        LOAD r12 1000 0
        ADD r12 r12 r11
        STORE r12 2000 a10
```

Intermediate Language's and MIPS States before the Step

    (ILoutp,pid,gvars,stack,101)

    (MIPSoutp,regs,mem,403)

Intermediate Language's and MIPS States after the Step

    (ILoutp,pid,gvars((a,gvars i):= gvars(a,gvars i) + gvars x),stack,102)

    (MIPSoutp,regs(a10 := (mem 1008) * 4,r11 := mem(2000 + regs a10),

        r12 := mem 1000 + mem(2000 + regs a10)),

        mem(2000 + ((mem 1008) * 4) := mem (2000 + (mem 1008) * 4) + mem 1000),409)

Figure 5.15: Array Assignment

counter of 100. Otherwise the program counter is just increased by the number of MIPS instructions executed.

To prove this step correct we have to do a case distinction whether x < 500 is true or not. For both cases we can conclude that the branch is either taken in both the intermediate language and the MIPS code or not. This conclusion is done using the fact that x and memory cell 1000 must have the same values since the intermediate language and MIPS states steps are in the simulation relation before the step. What remains is to prove that no matter if the branch is taken or not the program counters of intermediate language and MIPS are in the *program counter relation* again. In our case the program counter 40 in the intermediate language and 100 in the MIPS code as well as 102 in the intermediate language and 412 in the MIPS code have to correspond to each other.

Like in the assignment case, the verification of such a step takes $O(P + V)$ time since we have to look up statements and instructions ($O(P)$) as well as variable memory correspondence ($O(V)$).

Procedure Invocation

Figure 5.17 shows intermediate language call and return instructions and sketches corresponding MIPS code. Like in other steps, we start with two states being in the simulation relation, invoke the call and have to prove that the states afterwards are in the simulation relation again. In this case we want the called procedure 42 to start at address 42000. This procedure expects to fetch its first argument: the value of the variable x originally stored at memory address 1000 out of a register a0. Hence, an appropriate

Intermediate Language Code

    BRANCH (LT (VAR 'x') (CONST 500)) 40

MIPS Code

    LOAD a10 1000 0

    SLTI a10 a10 500

    BGTZ a10 100

Intermediate Language's and MIPS States before the Step

    (ILoutp,pid,gvars,stack,102)

    (MIPSoutp,regs,mem,409)

Intermediate Language's and MIPS States after the Step

    (ILoutp,pid,gvars,stack,if (gvars x < 500) then 40 else 103)

    (MIPSoutp,regs(a10 := if (mem 1000) < 500 then 1 else 0), if (mem 1000) < 500 then 100 else 412)

Figure 5.16: A Conditional Branch

load operation is carried out. In addition to that the return program counter is saved as very first element on the stack and the address the return value is written to as the second element. Since the stackpointer sp is increased by 40, this leaves space for eight local variables. When a return from a procedure is invoked, the return value is written to the memory address that was given by the caller and the old stack pointer and program counter are restored.

The steps involving a procedure call or a return statement start within a concrete procedure and end outside of it. Since we regard every procedure independently, we do not trace what is happening outside the procedure at hand. We rather require that the step fulfills the calling conventions manifestated in the simulation relation. From the theorem proving point of view this is a very simple static check of some properties on states. To guarantee correct code generation we show on a meta level the following: If within a program only procedures are called that are correct according to the criteria discussed within this section and called and calling procedures use the same correct calling conventions the whole program is compiled correctly.

System Calls

Figure 5.18 shows an example for a step in which an output occurs. In the intermediate language the value of variable x is printed out. As a result of this it is added to the accumulated output list of the state. Likewise we load the value of the corresponding memory cell 1000 into a register a1 and output its content via the appropriate system call in the MIPS code. Using the correspondence between x and memory cell 1000 we can easily conclude that the output lists in intermediate language and MIPS code are extended by the same values. Using the fact that no variable is mapped to a1 – thus no variable's mapped value is overwritten – and that the resulting program counters are in the *program counter relation* we can conclude that the states after the step are still in the simulation relation.

Intermediate Language Code
    CALLn 'x' 42 'y'
MIPS Code
    LOAD a0 1000 0
    ADDI sp sp 40
    'save return program counter at sp'
    'save return values memory address (1004) at sp + 4'
    J 42000

Intermediate Language Code
    RET 'n'
MIPS Code
    'save value of n at address stored at sp + 4'
    'restore program counter at sp and decrease sp by 40'

Figure 5.17: A Procedure Call and a Return

Intermediate Language Code
    PRINT 'x'
MIPS Code
    LOAD a1 1000 0
    SYSCALL 10
Intermediate Language's and MIPS States before the Step
    (ILoutp,pid,gvars,stack,104)
    (MIPSoutp,regs,mem,414)
Intermediate Language's and MIPS States after the Step
    ((gvars x) :: ILoutp,pid,gvars,stack,105)
    ((mem 1000) :: MIPSoutp,regs(a1 := mem 1000),mem,416)

Figure 5.18: An Output Occurring

Like the other steps, the verification of an output step takes $O(P + V)$ time since we have to look up statements and instructions ($O(P)$) as well as variable memory correspondence ($O(V)$).

Using Program Optimizations to Make Proofs Easier

Optimizations carried out during the compilation process can be among the hardest things to prove correct in certifying or certified compilers. However, some local optimization can not only be used to produce faster code, but speed the proof up and help to keep the proof scripts simple!

Figure 5.19 shows an example how both – proof and code – benefit from a local optimization. An intermediate language statement assigns the value of *1 + 2* to a variable x. Our naive code generation algorithm generates code for loading the two

Intermediate Language Code
```
ASSIGN_V 'x' (PLUS (CONST 1) (CONST 2))
```
Naive MIPS Code
```
ADDI a8 0 1
ADDI a9 0 2
ADD a10 a8 a9
STORE a10 1000 0
```
Optimized MIPS Code
```
ADDI a10 0 3
STORE a10 1000 0
```

Figure 5.19: Optimizing MIPS Code

constants into registers, do an addition on these registers and storing the result into memory. We can, however, do a constant folding and store the value of *3* directly into memory. Doing so has several advantages:

- It makes the code faster since fewer instructions have to be executed.

- It makes the determination of the abstract successor states in the theorem prover faster for the same reason.

- The proof scripts get easier since we do not have to show that the registers a8 and a9 are reserved for temporary intermediate values.

Typical optimizations beneficial to both proofs and code are the folding of local constants and some peep hole optimizations.

Discussion of the *Second Phase*

We have presented a number of step lemma verification principles that are typical for programs. All step lemmata we have examined in real programs can be handled by the principles introduced. All examined step lemmata can be verified in $O(P+V)$ time. We believe that all step lemmata from code pieces from our code generation algorithm can be handled in $O(P+V)$. We do, however, have no proof for this.

The $O(P+V)$ time complexity for a step lemma may be reduced by using more efficient data structures. So far we assumed an encoding of the *variable mapping*, the *program counter relation* and the procedure code – as defined in the IL and MIPS syntax – as lists or list like structures. If we use search trees instead, we end up with $O(log\ P + log\ V)$. Nevertheless, in practice search trees are sometimes tedious to handle in a theorem prover.

Instead of passing the memory address the return value of a called procedure shall be written to on the stack most compilers would pass it in a register. They would insert right after the call has happened in the source code a piece of code that stores the returned value into its appropriate memory cell. This technique, however, makes verification of code generation runs more hard since a single intermediate instruction (the call) is split into two corresponding code pieces: call and fetch of return value. Between the call and the fetch of the return value from a procedure possibly infinite instructions may be executed. In order to apply our technique to standard compilers, we can deal with this problem by indicating that the value fetch part of the call belongs to the intermediate instruction right after the procedure call. The simulation relation and call convention would have to be modified appropriately.

Since the actual calling conventions can vary for different machines, we use in our implementations special instructions to denote a procedure call and return in the MIPS code. During the process of linking different procedures to a complete program these special instructions are replaced with the MIPS code representing the actual calling conventions.

5.4.7 Putting it All Together

In the *third phase* we prove that the *Code Generation Correctness Criterion* from Figure 5.12 is fulfilled.

We prove the correspondence of the initial states first. This is done by checking that the simulation relation holds for the initial states and is usually a relatively simple proof.

Furthermore, we prove that two states in the simulation relation are in the simulation relation again after a step is performed. As sketched in Section 5.4.2 we make a case distinction on the intermediate language program counter – denoting a statement – and derive the corresponding code piece from the MIPS program. For each such intermediate language program point we apply the fact that the symbolic execution step that can be performed from it and on the corresponding MIPS code is correct as proved in the *second phase*.

The checking of the initial states takes $O(V + P)$ time in a standard encoding, since we may have look-ups to the *variable mapping* and have to check that the program counters are in the *program counter relation*. The check of the *Code Generation Correctness Criterion* takes $O(P)$ time. We have to apply for each intermediate language statement one fact about the symbolic execution step that can be performed on it.

5.5 Generating and Handling of the Certificates

In this section we describe our implementation realizing a certificate generator for certifying code generation. Furthermore, we describe how to represent the certificates and intermediate language and MIPS code for checking by a theorem prover. Parts of this section have been published in 2008 [BG08a].

A refined version of the certifying translation approach (cp. Figure 1.4) to our code generation phase is shown in Figure 5.20. Like in the original scenario source code is transformed into a piece of target code. Thereby the compiler provided information info is emitted which is used by a *certificate generator* to build the proof script. The theorem prover processes the proof script and states whether the proof succeeds. Not shown in the figure are the provided formalized notion of correctness including the semantics it is based on. Preproved lemmata are added to the proving process as well. Furthermore, for

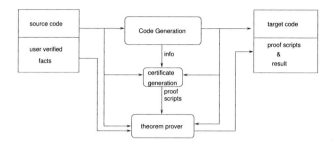

Figure 5.20: Overview of Our Certifying Code Generation

clarity reasons, the mechanisms that are used to generate the program representations are not shown.

As pointed out in Section 5.3 the compiler provided information *info* comprises sets of variables used in the intermediate language, the *variable mapping*, and the *program counter relation* which are generated and emitted during the code generation.

Section 5.4.6 suggests the use of user provided facts in the context of array index bounds properties proved on source code level to be added into the verification process. These are also shown in the figure. As with proof carrying code one might imagine scenarios in which it is advantageous to keep the proof script so that other people using the program can be convinced that they have indeed a correctly compiled procedure with respect to a piece of source code.

It should be noted that when performing complicated optimizations in a compiler phase, it is very helpful to emit optimization relevant information such as analysis results among the other *info* items. The compiler needs only very small modifications in order to emit such information. This is because the information is computed anyway (e.g. as a base to carry out an optimization). The certificate generator – responsible for the actual generation of the proof scripts – can be realized by an independent program.

5.5.1 Program Representation Generation

Before generating the proof scripts and the theorem stating code generation run correctness, we generate representations of intermediate language and MIPS code. In addition, we generate representations of the variable sets, and formalizations of the *program counter relation*, and *variable mapping* to be used by the theorem prover. The program representations in intermediate language and MIPS code are the only parts in a certified compiler implementation that have to be trusted. For this reason it is important to make this part as simple as possible. While we do not have a standard textual representation for the intermediate language, it is also important that the MIPS code formalization looks like MIPS assembler code to help people to agree that this is indeed a very small gap in the verification chain.

The generation mechanisms for the program representations are implemented in ML in a very simple, standard way. They write each statement or instruction one after another into a theorem prover file.

5.5.2 Certificate Generation Algorithm

Based on the information provided through *info* and the actual intermediate language and MIPS program code the certificate generator generates the proof scripts.

Generating the Prerequisites

The simulation relation is established using the sets of variables and the *variable mapping* as described in Section 5.4.4. Next the certificate generator generates proof scripts to state and prove the properties of the *variable mapping*. The mapping is constructed inductively as stated in Section 5.4.5 using the sets of variables and the *variable mapping* as emitted by the compiler.

Generating the Proofs of the *Second Phase*

The proof scripts for the *second phase* make use of all the information the compiler omits plus the intermediate language and MIPS program code. For each step we make a case distinction on the syntactical structure of the intermediate language statement to be handled. We have different raw proof script template covering the different cases. Such a template has some blanks in it. The certificate generator fills them up with information from the corresponding MIPS code and from the compiler provided information.

Figure 5.21 shows a proof script template and conditions under which we can apply it. It is used for an array assignment. It consists of an intermediate language statement it has to be mapped against, an optional MIPS code piece, a priority, and the actual proof script template that is completed to serve as the generated prove script by filling up names of variables, facts, and case distinctions.

In the figure an array element is assigned the value of another array element plus something else. Something else is presumably a constant since rules have priorities and more complicated cases have more distinct patterns they are matched against and higher priorities. *MemMap* is a function – which is constant to the whole program. In contrast to that, *varvals* and *mem* are variables. Different elements can be distinguished in the proof code:

- The evaluation of terms like in the first two lines.

- The split of a proof goal into sub goals (third line).

- The assertion and proving of some more basic facts (next five lines).

- The rewriting of a term by something equivalent (last line of the first sub-goal).

- The *qed* denotes a sub-goal that can be trivially finished. Usually some kind of equation needs to be proved in the last step.

IL:
  ASSIGN_AV (a,b,PLUS(ARVAR (c,d),e))
MIPS:
  -

Priority: 10
ProofCode:
evaluate succeeding IL state representation
evaluate succeeding MIPS state representation
split_goal_into_subgoals:
1. memorycorrespondence:
  assert (varvals (v, i) = mem (MemMap (v, i))) for all valid v and i
    prove that a is a valid array
    prove that c is a valid array
    prove or use that b is a valid index
    prove or use that d is a valid index
  use injectivity + assertion to rewrite variable accesses with
        memory accesses in variable store representation
  qed
2. programcounter correspondence:
  look up whether program counters correspond to each other
  qed

Figure 5.21: Proof Script Template for an Array Assignment

The parts in this proof template that need to be instantiated are the first four lines in
the assertion of the first sub-goal. The corresponding variable names have to be put
into locations. Furthermore, if we use user provided facts that prove whether a memory
location is a valid index or not some adaptation to the proof script needs to be made. We
have implemented a mechanism to reference and manage such facts in the proof script
generation. If we do not use user provided facts, we need to make a case distinction on
the range of the index. Thus, we need to make some adaptation to the proof script, too.
This is done by referencing the index variable's name again.

When handling conditional branches we have to make a case distinction on the value,
on which the taking of the branch depends. To do this case distinction we have to insert
the variable's name and corresponding memory location explicitly at some point in the
proof script. A template for a branch is shown in Figure 5.22.

A more comprehensive list of proof script templates from one of our Coq implementations can be found in Appendix C. The templates shown here are given in pseudo proof
code which omits the more trivial steps. A typical generated proof for a step consists of
roughly about 100 applications of Coq tactics.

Note that many proof script templates for similar tasks tend to look very similar and
relatively few adaptation by the certificate generator is required for each instantiation.
Due to these facts we are able to encode the proof script templates in the ML implementation of our certificate generator in a very compact form which outperforms even the
pseudo code representation in terms of lines of code: We encapsulate common sequences

```
IL:
  BRANCH (VAR a,target)
MIPS:
  -

Priority: 10
ProofCode:
```
evaluate succeeding IL state representation
evaluate succeeding MIPS state representation
split_goal_into_subgoals:
1. memorycorrespondence:
*   qed*
2. programcounter correspondence:
*   assert (varvals a = mem (MemMap a))*
*   prove that a is a valid variable*
*   prove that assertion holds*
*   rewrite proof goal with assertion*
*   case a = 1:*
*   look up whether program counters correspond to each other*
*   else:*
*   look up whether program counters correspond to each other*
*   qed*

Figure 5.22: Proof Script Template for a Branch Statement

of tactic application in templates themselves. As a result of this we end up with an encoding scheme for proof templates that can encode one template in 1 to a few lines of ML code.

Completing the Certificate Generation

The generation of the scripts for the *third phase* only needs information on the sets of variables, the *variable mapping* and the *program counter relation*. The sets of variables and the *variable mapping* are only needed to prove the correspondence of the initial states.

The generation of the proof script proving the steps correct is by far the most complicated process. The proposed methodology has the advantage that it can be refined during the development process. We can start with a generic proof script for a step that may be able to prove some steps correct. We go on refining this script depending on the statements, expressions, and operators occurring in the intermediate language. We can go further on with the refinement by looking at the compiler provided information and the MIPS code.

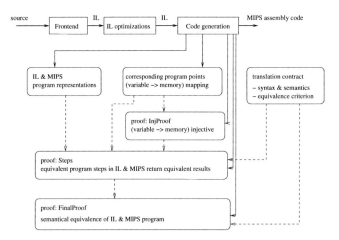

Figure 5.23: The Compiler and the Generated Theory Files with Dependencies

5.5.3 Preparing for the Theorem Prover

While the basic principles of proving a code generation run correct are presented in Section 5.3, in this section we describe the actual deployment of generated scripts and the invocation of the theorem provers. We have implemented two versions of the certificate generator for use with two different theorem provers:

- The Isabelle/HOL version generates proof scripts by creating different files for different phases and data. Intermediate language and MIPS code, the *variable mapping*, and the *program counter relation* are each stored within separate files as shown in Figure 5.23. These data files contain no proof scripts or lemmata. Properties proved during the proof phases are stored in a *InjProof* file (*first phase*), a *Steps* file(*second phase*), and a *FinalProof* file (*third phase*). The properties proved are described as lemmata followed by a proof script using Isabelle's *apply tactic* style (cp. Section 3.3). To process the generated proof scripts within Isabelle/HOL we need to use formalizations of syntax and semantics of the involved languages as well as a correctness criterion (subsumed as translation contract in the Figure). In addition to that we provide preproved lemmata to make some often reoccurring transformations easier.

- The Coq version's principal architecture is very similar to the Isabelle's. The file structure is the same. In Coq, however, we need less preproved lemmata since computations – which might have been avoided in Isabelle using a lemma – are generally conducted faster on their own.

91

5.6 Using Checker Predicates to Optimize the Proof Process

In this section we describe the use of checker predicates to further speed up the proof process. Most of the contents of this and the following section have highly benefited from discussions and work done together with Benjamin Grégoire.

Checker predicates are used for increasing the speed of distinct sub tasks of certificate checking and can be used instead of traditional tactic application based proof scripts thereby simplifying the proof script generation. The general idea behind the techniques described in this section is the fact that functions formalized in an executable way in Coq may be evaluated very fast. Other steps involving unification or rewriting of terms are considerably slower. Thus, we want to keep as much executable as possible. Instead of verifying a fact directly with respect to some declarative correctness notion we formalize in an executable way ("implement") a predicate in Coq that computes whether the fact holds. To be applicable within our proof process the predicate has to be proved correct with respect to the original declarative correctness notion. From a logical perspective this means that it either implies or is equivalent to the original notion of correctness. This correctness proof is done once and forall. Accordingly we can now use the executable predicate instead of the declarative correctness notion in a normal proof script.

5.6.1 The Nature of Checker Predicates

During our proofs it is often necessary to show that some pieces of data $c_1, ..., c_n$ – e.g. build from constructors of an inductive datatype – fulfill some property D. This means that our theorem prover has to prove a subgoal that looks like:

$$D(c_1, ..., c_n) = \text{true}$$

D is usually a generic property that needs to be fulfilled by a large class of programs. It is formalized in a declarative way that is relatively easy to understand for humans – it may even be part of the correctness criterion. The $c_1, ..., c_n$ are different for each compilation run. One way to prove this lemma correct is to generate and run a script consisting of some tactic applications. The faster way is to use checker predicates.

In our case we may formalize a checker predicate E in an executable way that checks whether the property formalized by D holds. Its correctness is guaranteed by proving the following lemma once and for all:

$$\forall x_1, ..., x_n . E(x_1, ..., x_n) = \text{true} \longrightarrow D(x_1, ..., x_n) = \text{true}$$

This correctness lemma can be applied via a classical implication rule each time a subgoal as sketched above appears within a proof. It will transform the sketched subgoal into another subgoal:

$$E(c_1, ..., c_n) = \text{true}$$

```
check_inj' MemMap l max =
    match l with
    | nil => true
    | cons x l =>
    let im := MemMap x in
            if (is_greater im max) then check_inj' MemMap l im
            else false
    end.

check_inj MemMap l =
    match l with
    | nil => true
    | cons x l => check_inj' MemMap l (MemMap x)
    end.
```

Figure 5.24: Injectivity Checker

We can now use the executable formalized checker predicate instead of the declarative correctness notion in our proof script to solve this subgoal.

5.6.2 A Fast Injectivity Proof

One example of using checker predicates is in the injectivity proof. Figure 5.24 shows two functions – close to a theorem prover formalization – used for a fast computation of the injectivity of a *variable mapping*. Both take a function realizing the *variable mapping* and a list of variables as inputs. The first function takes an additional max argument as input. It checks whether all variables in the list of memory addresses are sufficiently larger than the address(es) the previous element is mapped to. The address(es) of the previous element is kept in the max argument. The second function is initially called and sets the value of max to the address(es) of the first variable in the list. To use this function in our proofs we have proved that whenever a variable mapping fulfills this check_inj predicate with respect to a list of variables, it is indeed injective with respect to the list and our original formalization of injectivity. Thus, we can rewrite a proof goal containing the original injectivity specification with a proof goal that contains the checker definition. This is usually solved much faster.

Discussion

In principle the algorithm realized by the check_inj predicate is not much different from the one described in Section 5.4.5. However, by using checker predicates we do not explicitly prove facts for each new variable which is very time consuming in theorem provers, but use a function implicitly computing and using them instead.

The max may be implemented as a single value or an address range. Static addresses or addresses with respect to an offset register are possible. The is_greater has to be implemented appropriately. It can also be used to relate registers and memory addresses to each other.

We have implemented the injectivity checker predicate and proved it correct in Coq in 2008 [BG08b].

5.7 A Checker Predicate for Semantical Equivalence

We can use checker predicates to speed up the checking of the correctness of our simulation steps from the *second phase*. Such checker predicates are presented in this section. To formalize them we prepare an important prerequisite: semantics of our languages that allow the encoding of abstract, underspecified states as constant terms. We develop such a checker semantics for our intermediate language and MIPS code. We prove that instead of using step lemmata based on our semantics defined in the first part of this chapter we can use our checker semantics definitions used within checker predicates instead. Hence, we prove the correctness of the checker semantics with respect to the semantics presented in the first part of this chapter. Based on this we prove our checker predicates correct. Changes in the languages syntax definitions are not needed to use our checker semantics and checker predicates.

In the context of this section we refer to our semantics defined in the first part of this chapter as the non-checker or original semantics.

The idea behind the approach presented in this section is that state, value, memory, or program counter representations that do not contain any variables of the theorem prover's logic may be processed much faster by the theorem prover than those containing some variable or underspecified parts. The proof objects containing only constant values can be used directly in computations, whereas those containing variable parts need the application of unification and rewriting steps on the theorem prover's tactics level. Thus, the handling of proofs using non-checker semantics breaks down to the handling of proof goals containing many declarative, non-executable parts whereas the handling of proofs using the checker semantics has many executable proof goals in the proving process (cp. Section 5.6).

In the original semantics of intermediate and MIPS language presented in Sections 5.1 and 5.2 we use underspecified or variable parts in states to reason about execution steps that may occur at certain program points. In the checker semantics presented in this section we use abstract state definitions made up from special datatypes formalizing constant terms instead of variables to represent underspecified values! From these terms we compute an abstract successor state which is itself a constant term. Hence, our checker semantics is abstract in the sense that a constant term may be used to represent a set of states.

We define checker predicates that compare states using constant term representation thereby ensuring the correctness of a step. For this reason, the computation of an abstract successor state and state comparison can be conducted very fast. No unification or inference rule style reasoning is required for the tasks done by our checker predicates presented in this section.

This section comprises a description of the checker semantics for the intermediate language and the MIPS code in Subsections 5.7.1 and 5.7.2. Furthermore, we describe how to prove steps correct with our checker semantics in Subsection 5.7.3. We introduce our step correctness checker predicates defined on the checker semantics in Subsection 5.7.4. We explain what correctness of our checker semantics and correctness of the step correctness checker predicate means and finally we sketch how to prove our checker predicates correct in Subsection 5.7.5.

5.7.1 Our Checker Intermediate Language Semantics

The first step to establish a checker semantics for the intermediate language is to find an adequate state representation. To represent potentially underspecified states as constant terms we need abstract values to define abstract *variable mappings* and abstract memory. These are subsumed as abstract stores in this section.

Figure 5.25 shows the definitions of abstract values, an abstract store for variables' values, and an abstract representation of locations. Abstract values may be build from constants and standard arithmetic operations. Moreover, we need a constant term representation for variable read accesses. These are encoded via an abstract read constructor comprising the variable name and an abstract store for variables' values. Different constructors exist for accessing primitive variables, arrays with constant and dynamic indices. The abstract store definition for storing variables' values consists of an initial constructor INIT representing a store containing completely unspecified values and write constructors writing abstract values to this store. For this reason, two stores that are made up only from the INIT constructor are from a semantical point of view incomparable since they both contain completely unspecified values! Different write constructors exist for primitive variables and arrays with constant and dynamic indices. Finally, there is a representation for abstract locations. Locations may be known or unknown. Unknown locations are the result of a conditional branch. In this case the branch target depends on an abstract value: the result of the branch condition.

Read access to our abstract variables' values store is shown in Figure 5.26. The function read is defined for accesses to primitive variables and arrays with constant and dynamic index. The read function is overloaded for use with both primitive and array variables. In the case of read accesses to arrays with dynamic index the representation of the index may be converted to a constant representation by looking up the abstract value of the index variable.

Write access to an abstract store is straight forward as defined in Figure 5.27 and makes use of the abstract store constructors. An important feature of abstract stores and values is that a term representing an abstract value or a store may be simplified. For this reason, apart from the read and write functions we have defined simplification functions that apply some simplifications on terms representing abstract stores and values. Figure 5.28 shows a small excerpt of these rules to exemplify their nature. All simplifications based on these rules may be computed directly without the need for unification and are thus very fast. The first simplification rule states that whenever a variable's value is read from an abstract store where it was written to immediately before it may be returned

absval::=
        ABSCONST val | ABSPLUS absval absval | ABSMINUS absval absval | ABSMULT absval absval |
        ABSLT absval absval | ABSLE absval absval |
        VARGET var absvarstore | ACGET var absval absvarstore |
        AVGET var var absvarstore

absvarstore ::=
        INIT | VARUPD var absval absvarstore | ACUPD var absval absval absvarstore |
        AVUPD var var absval absvarstore

absloc ::=
        LOCKNOWN loc | LOCUNKNOWN absval loc loc

Figure 5.25: Abstract Representations of IL Values and Abstract Store

directly. The next two simplification rules state that no primitive variable's value may be altered by write accesses to arrays. For this reason array write accesses may be discarded from an abstract store if one is only interested in a primitive variable's value. The next two lines formalize similar optimizations for array read accesses. The last example rule corresponds to constant folding in abstract states. It can be done without any unification, too. Many other algebraic and read access simplification laws are integrated into the simplification functions. Simplification is used to keep the terms resulting from the conduction of execution steps small. They speed up further computation and more importantly make terms comparable since they also provide some form of normalization. Some simplification rules are very close to analysis and transformations known from compiler optimization. To use a simplification rule it has to be proved that the result is always semantical equivalent to the original term. This again is done once and for all.

In addition to abstract values, stores and program counters we need abstract lists. These are used to represent lists of potentially unknown length. They are defined in Figure 5.29. Like ordinary lists, they comprise constructors for empty lists NIL and concatenation CONS of an element e to an existing (abstract) list. In addition there is a constructor representing an undefined list UNDEFINED.

Abstract intermediate language states in Figure 5.30 are defined analogous to standard intermediate language states. Instead of lists we use abstract lists for representing accumulated output and the stack. Elements of the accumulated output are abstract values. Local and global variables' values are hold in abstract stores. The current program counter is encoded as an abstract type (abstract location) to deal with unknown program counters. Note that the return location of a procedure stored in a stackframe on the stack is always known. Hence we do not need an abstract location here.

Figure 5.31 shows operand evaluation for abstract intermediate language states. Compared to the non-checker semantics we evaluate a constant operand to an abstract constant value in the first line. Furthermore, we exchange the way read accesses are done by replacing them with the appropriate read function and abstract store. Abstract ex-

Read Access: Primitive Variables
    read (INIT) v = VARGET v INIT
    read (VARUPD v1 aval store) v =
            if v = v1 then aval else (read store v)
    read (ACUPD v1 indval aval store) v = (read store v)
    read (AVUPD v1 iv aval store) v = (read store v)

Read Access: Arrays with Constant Index
    read (INIT) (v,c) = ACGET v c INIT
    read (VARUPD v1 aval store) (v,c) = (read store (v,c))
    read (ACUPD v1 indval aval store) (v,c) =
            if (v,c)=(v1,indval) then aval else (read store (v,c))
    read (AVUPD v1 iv aval store) (v,c) =
            if (v,c) = (v1,read store iv) then aval else (read store (v,c))

Read Access: Arrays with Variable Index
    read (INIT) (v,i) = AVGET v i INIT
    read (VARUPD v1 aval store) (v,i) = (read store (v,read (VARUPD v1 aval store) i))
    read (ACUPD v1 indval aval store) (v,i) =
            if (v,read store i)=(v1,indval) then aval else (read store (v,(read store i)))
    read (AVUPD v1 iv aval store) (v,i) =
            if (v,read store i) = (v1,read store iv) then aval else (read store (v,read store i))

Figure 5.26: Read Access to an Abstract Store

    write store v aval = (VARUPD v aval store)
    write store (v,c) aval = (ACUPD v c store)
    write store (v,i) aval = (AVUPD v i aval store)

Figure 5.27: Write Access to an Abstract Store

pression evaluation is done as defined in Figure 5.32. Each operator occurring in the expression is replaced by its corresponding abstract value representative. Simplification may be used to actually compute the value of an expression. However, simplification of the resulting abstract value is not always necessary. If we compare the abstract value resulting from an expression evaluation to a similar unoptimized term computed in a corresponding MIPS code piece it can be advantageous to keep both terms in their unoptimized representation for ease of comparison.

Figure 5.33 shows our abstract statement evaluation functions. Reads and writes to abstract stores are implemented. We use the function assignabsargvs to assign initial values passed as parameters upon calling a function to local variables.

The evaluation of a statement always assumes a known program counter. It is undefined for unknown program counters. Contrary to that it may deliver a program counter of unknown value. One might believe that this could be a problem when considering

VARGET v (VARUPD v aval store) = aval
VARGET v (ACUPD v1 indval aval store) = VARGET v store
VARGET v (AVUPD v1 iv aval store) = VARGET v store
...
ACGET v c (VARUPD v1 aval store) = ACGET v c store
ACGET v c (ACUPD v c aval store) = aval
...
ABSPLUS (ABSCONST a) (ABSCONST b) = ABSCONST (a+b)
...

Figure 5.28: Some Simplification Rules

alist ::=

NIL *alternatively represented by '[]' |*

CONS e alist *alternatively written with infix operator '::' |*

UNDEFINED

Figure 5.29: Abstract Lists

absilstate =
    (absval alist) × pid × absvarstore × ((pid × loc × var × absvarstore) alist) × absloc

Figure 5.30: Abstract IL States

evaloperand L G locvals globvals (CONST c) = (ABSCONST c)

$$\text{evaloperand L G locvals globvals (VAR v)} = \begin{cases} v \in L & \text{then read locvals v} \\ v \in G & \text{then read globvals v} \end{cases}$$

$$\text{evaloperand L G locvals globvals (ARCONST (v,ci))} = \begin{cases} v \in L & \text{then read locvals (v,ci)} \\ v \in G & \text{then read globvals (v,ci)} \end{cases}$$

$$\text{evaloperand L G locvals globvals (ARVAR (v,vi))} = \begin{cases} v \in L \wedge vi \in L & \text{then} \\ & \text{read locvals (v,locvals vi)} \\ v \in L \wedge vi \in G & \text{then} \\ & \text{read locvals (v,globvals vi)} \\ v \in G \wedge vi \in L & \text{then} \\ & \text{read globvals (v,locvals vi)} \\ v \in G \wedge vi \in G & \text{then} \\ & \text{read globvals (v,globvals vi)} \end{cases}$$

Figure 5.31: Abstract Operand Evaluation in IL

evalexpression L G locvals globvals (OPERAND o1) = evaloperand L G locvals globvars o1

evalexpression L G locvals globvals (PLUS o1 o2) =
     ABSPLUS (evaloperand L G locvals globvals o1) (evaloperand L G locvals globvals o2)

evalexpression L G locvals globvals (MINUS o1 o2) =
     ABSMINUS (evaloperand L G locvals globvals o1) (evaloperand L G locvals globvals o2)

evalexpression L G locvals globvals (MULT o1 o2) =
     ABSMULT (evaloperand L G locvals globvals o1) (evaloperand L G locvals globvals o2)

evalexpression L G locvals globvals (LT o1 o2) =
     ABSLT (evaloperand L G locvals globvals o1) (evaloperand L G locvals globvals o2)

evalexpression L G locvals globvals (LE o1 o2) =
     ABSLE (evaloperand L G locvals globvals o1) (evaloperand L G locvals globvals o2)

Figure 5.32: Abstract Expression Evaluation

the following scenario: We regard a sequence of consecutive state transition function applications and have an unknown program counter in between this sequence. Thus, we would have to consider both branches. This is not possible within a sequence of state transition function applications. In practice, however, branches will only occur at the end of a sequence of steps in consideration and we are thus able to handle them. Remember that if a branch occurs at the end of some sequence of statements we can regard the different jump targets independently. For this reason each of them has a known program counter.

We would run into the same problem in the non-abstract semantics, however, the fact that we would have to consider both branches would not have been stated by an explicit constructor but rather by the inability of the theorem prover to determine a concrete value for the branching state's program counter.

The state transition function in Figure 5.34 is defined using the abstract statement evaluation function. In the concrete theorem prover implementation we do make use of the option datatype as result type for the state transition function. We have to do so because we can not syntactically restrict the function definition to states with only known program counters. We return NONE in the case – that should not occur in our verification scenarios that no abstract successor state can be computed.

5.7.2 Our Checker MIPS Semantics

The definition of the checker MIPS semantics has the same design goals as the definition of the checker intermediate language semantics. One unifying goal is to keep abstract value, store, and location representations comparable with their counterparts from the

evalstatement P L G (outp,pid,gvs,(rpid,raddr,rvar,lvs)::stack,LOCKNOWN pc) (ASSIGN_V v e) =
if(v ∈ L)   then (outp,pid,gvs,(rpid,raddr,rvar,write lvs v (evalexpression L G lvs gvs e))::stack,
             LOCKNOWN pc+1)
if(v ∈ G)   then (outp,pid,(write gvs v (evalexpression L G lvs gvs e)),(rpid,raddr,rvar,lvs)::stack,
             LOCKNOWN pc+1)

evalstatement P L G (outp,pid,gvs,(rpid,raddr,rvar,lvs)::stack, LOCKNOWN pc)
             (ASSIGN_AC v ci e) =
if(v ∈ L)   then (outp,pid,gvs,(rpid,raddr,rvar,write lvs (v,ci) (evalexpression L G lvs gvs e))::stack,
             LOCKNOWN pc+1)
if(v ∈ G)   then (outp,pid,write gvs (v,ci) (evalexpression L G lvs gvs e),(rpid,raddr,rvar,lvs)::stack,
             LOCKNOWN pc+1)

evalstatement P L G (outp,pid,gvs,(rpid,raddr,rvar,lvs)::stack,LOCKNOWN pc)
             (ASSIGN_AV v vi e) =
if(v ∈ L ∧   then
   vi ∈ L)   (outp,pid,gvs,(rpid,raddr,rvar,write lvs (v,read lvs vi) (evalexpression L G lvs gvs e))::stack,
             LOCKNOWN pc+1)
if(v ∈ L ∧   then
   vi ∈ G)   (outp,pid,gvs,(rpid,raddr,rvar,write lvs (v,read gvs vi) (evalexpression L G lvs gvs e))::stack,
             LOCKNOWN pc+1)
if(v ∈ G ∧   then
   vi ∈ L)   (outp,pid,write gvs (v,read lvs vi) (evalexpression L G lvs gvs e),(rpid,raddr,rvar,lvs)::stack,
             LOCKNOWN pc+1)
if(v ∈ G ∧   then
   vi ∈ G)   (outp,pid,write gvs (v,read gvs vi) (evalexpression L G lvs gvs e),(rpid,raddr,rvar,lvs)::stack,
             LOCKNOWN pc+1)

evalstatement P L G (outp,pid,gvs,(rpid,raddr,rvar,lvs)::stack, LOCKNOWN pc)
             (BRANCH e lab) =
      (outp,pid,gvs,(rpid,raddr,rvar,lvs)::stack,
             LOCUNKNOWN (evalexpression L G lvs gvs e) (pc +1) lab)

evalstatement P L G (outp,pid,gvs,(rpid,raddr,rvar,lvs)::stack,LOCKNOWN pc) (GOTO lab) =
             (outp,pid,gvs,(rpid,raddr,rvar,lvs)::stack,LOCKNOWN lab)

evalstatement P L G (outp,pid,gvs,(rpid,raddr,rvar,lvs)::stack,LOCKNOWN pc) (CALLn rv pid',argvars) =
             (outp,pid',gvs,(pid,pc+1,rv,assignabsargvs P pid argvars lvs gvs)::(rpid,raddr,rvar,lvs)::stack,
             LOCKNOWN 0)

evalstatement P L G (outp,pid,gvs,(rpid1,raddr1,rvar1,lvs1)::(rpid2,raddr2,rvar2,lvs2)::stack,
             LOCKNOWN pc) (RET var) =
if(rvar1 ∈ L)   then (rpid1,outp,gvs,(rpid2,raddr2,rvar2,write lvs2 rvar1 (read lvs1 var)))::stack,raddr1)
if(rvar1 ∈ G)   then (rpid1,outp,write gvs rvar1 (read lvs1 var)),(rpid2,raddr2,rvar2,lvs2)::stack,raddr1)

evalstatement P L G (outp,pid,gvs,(raddr,rvar,lvs)::stack,LOCKNOWN pc) (PRINT v) =
if(v ∈ L)   then ((read lvs v)::outp,pid,gvs,(rpid,raddr,rvar,lvs)::stack,LOCKNOWN pc)
if(v ∈ G)   then ((read gvs v)::outp,pid,gvs,(rpid,raddr,rvar,lvs)::stack,LOCKNOWN pc)

evalstatement P L G (outp,pid,gvs,(rpid,raddr,rvar,lvs)::stack,LOCKNOWN pc) (EXIT) =
             (termination::outp,pid,gvs,(rpid,raddr,rvar,lvs)::stack,LOCKNOWN pc)

Figure 5.33: Abstract Statement Evaluation

```
ilnext P (outp,pid,gvals,stack,LOCKNOWN pc) =
      SOME (evalstatement
              P
              (getLocals pid P)
              (getGlobals P)
              (outp,pid,gvals,stack,LOCKNOWN pc)
              (getStatement pid pc P))

ilnext P (outp,pid,gvals,stack,LOCKUNKNOWN exp pc' pc") =
      NONE
```

Figure 5.34: Abstract IL State Transition Function

```
absval ::=
      ABSCONST val | ABSPLUS absval absval | ABSMINUS absval absval | ABSMULT absval absval |
      ABSLT absval absval | ABSLE absval absval |
      REGGET reg absregstore | MEMGET absval absmemstore

absregstore ::=
      INIT | REGUPD reg absval absregstore


absmemstore ::=
      INIT | MEMUPD absval absval absmemstore


absloc ::=
      LOCKNOWN loc | LOCUNKNOWN absval loc loc
```

Figure 5.35: Abstract Representations of MIPS Values, Register, and Memory Store

other language.

Figure 5.35 shows the abstract representations of MIPS values, register store, memory store, and program counter selection depending on an abstract value. Its definition is very similar to the corresponding definitions in the intermediate language. Note that we have two abstract stores: register set and memory. Hence, there are two read access constructors REGGET and MEMGET in the abstract value definition. Read and write access function to an abstract register set and memory are given in Figure 5.36. They are analogous defined to the read and write functions for the intermediate language. Registers can not be addressed indirectly. Accordingly we can define a standard look up function on them. Note, however, that when updating a memory cell the address can not always be resolved. In this case an abstract unevaluated term is returned. Abstract states for MIPS are defined as shown in Figure 5.37. Like in the abstract intermediate language state definition, an abstract list (cp. Figure 5.29) of accumulated output is defined for abstract values. Abstract stores for register set and memory are contained

Read Access to Registers
    read (INIT) r = REGGET r INIT
    read (REGUPD reg aval store) r =
        if reg = r then aval else (read store r)

Read Access to Memory
    read (INIT) r = MEMGET r INIT
    read (MEMUPD addr aval store) a =
        case addr = a of
          true : aval
          ?   : MEMGET a (MEMUPD addr aval store)
          false : read store a

Write Access to Registers
    write store r aval = REGUPD r aval store

Write Access to Memory
    write store addr aval = MEMUPD addr aval store

Figure 5.36: Read and Write Access to an Abstract Store for MIPS

MIPSstate =
    (absval alist) × absregstore × absmemstore × absloc

Figure 5.37: Abstract MIPS State Definition

in the abstract MIPS state, too. The program counter is formalized using an abstract location term. The instruction evaluation function for the checker semantics of MIPS is shown in Figure 5.38. Like in the intermediate language, program counters have to be known to perform an instruction evaluation step. Arithmetic operations are evaluated to their abstract value representation and simplifications may be performed on them. Based on the evalinstruction function we define in Figure 5.39 a state transition function that is capable of evaluating several consecutive instructions if the program counters in between are known. Like in the intermediate language it is realized using an option datatype.

5.7.3 Verifying Steps using the Checker Semantics

In this subsection we examine the general principles how checker predicates using our checker semantics definition of intermediate language and MIPS code work by looking at an example.

Consider the Figure 5.40. It shows the same syntactical array assignment as in Figure 5.14 for our concrete semantics. Both states in intermediate language and MIPS code have unspecified initial variables' values, memory, and register set. This INIT value corresponds to an universally quantified store in the original semantics. The succeeding states consist of terms indicating the computations done during the step transition. Our

evalinstruction (outp,regs,mem,LOCKNOWN pc) (ADD r1 r2 r3) =
    (outp,write regs r1 (ABSPLUS (read regs r2) (read regs r3)),mems,LOCKNOWN pc + 1)

evalinstruction (outp,regs,mem,LOCKNOWN pc) (ADDI r1 r2 c) =
    (outp,write regs r1 (ABSPLUS (read regs r2) (ABSCONST c)),mems,LOCKNOWN pc + 1)

evalinstruction (outp,regs,mem,LOCKNOWN pc) (SUB r1 r2 r3) =
    (outp,write regs r1 (ABSMINUS (read regs r2) (read regs r3)),mems,LOCKNOWN pc + 1)

evalinstruction (outp,regs,mem,LOCKNOWN pc) (MLT r1 r2) =
    (outp,write regs (lo,hi) (ABSMULT (read regs r1) (read regs r2)),mems,LOCKNOWN pc + 1)

evalinstruction (outp,regs,mem,LOCKNOWN pc) (SHL r c) =
    (outp,write regs r (ABSMULT (read regs r) (ABSCONST 2^c)),mems,
        LOCKNOWN pc + 1)

evalinstruction (outp,regs,mems,LOCKNOWN pc) (SLT r1 r2 r3) =
    (outp,write regs r1 (ABSLT (read regs r2) (read regs r3)),mems,LOCKNOWN pc + 1)

evalinstruction (outp,regs,mems,LOCKNOWN pc) (SLTI r1 r2 c) =
    (outp,write regs r1 (ABSLT (read regs r2) (ABSCONST c)),mems,LOCKNOWN pc + 1)

evalinstruction (outp,regs,mems,LOCKNOWN pc) (SET r1 r2 r3) =
    (outp,write regs r1 (ABSLE (read regs r2) (read regs r3)),mems,LOCKNOWN pc + 1)

evalinstruction (outp,regs,mems,LOCKNOWN pc) (SLEI r1 r2 c) =
    (outp,write regs r1 (ABSLE (read regs r2) (ABSCONST c)),mems,LOCKNOWN pc + 1)

evalinstruction (outp,regs,mem,LOCKNOWN pc) (STORE r1 offset r2) =
    (outp,regs,write mems (ABSPLUS (ABSCONST offset) (read regs r2)) (read regs r1),
        LOCKNOWN pc + 1)

evalinstruction (outp,regs,mem,LOCKNOWN pc) (LOAD r1 offset r2) =
    (outp,write regs r1 (read mems (ABSPLUS (ABSCONST offset) (read regs r1)),mems,
        LOCKNOWN pc + 1)

evalinstruction (outp,regs,mems,LOCKNOWN pc) (BGTZ r1 lab) =
    (outp,regs,mems,PCUNKNOWN (read regs r1) pc lab)

evalinstruction (outp,regs,mem,LOCKNOWN pc) (J lab) = (outp,regs,mems,LOCKNOWN lab)

evalinstruction (outp,regs,mems,LOCKNOWN pc) (SYSCALL c) =
  if(c = 1)   then ((read regs a1)::outp,regs,mems,LOCKNOWN pc)
  if(c = 10)   then (termination::outp,regs,mems,LOCKNOWN pc)

Figure 5.38: Abstract MIPS Instruction Evaluation

```
tlnext P (outp,regs,mems,LOCKNOWN pc) =
        SOME (evalinstruction (outp,regs,mems,LOCKNOWN pc) (getInstruction pc P))
tlnext P (outp,regs,mems,LOCUNKNOWN exp pc pc') =
        NONE


tlnextn P state 0 = state
tlnextn P NONE n = NONE
tlnextn P (SOME state') n =
        tlnextn P (tlnext P state') (n-1)
```

Figure 5.39: Abstract MIPS State Transition Functions

Intermediate Language Code
    ASSIGN_V 'x' (PLUS (VAR 'y') (CONST 1))
MIPS Code
    LOAD a10 1004 0
    ADDI a10 a10 1
    STORE a10 1000 0
Intermediate Language's and MIPS States before the Step
    (ILoutp,pid,INIT,stack,100)
    (MIPSoutp,INIT,INIT,400)
Intermediate Language's and MIPS States after the Step
    (ILoutp,pid,
        VARUPD x (ABSPLUS (VARGET y INIT) (ABSCONST 1)) INIT,stack,LOCKNOWN 101)
    (MIPSoutp, ...,
        MEMUPD (ABSCONST 1000) (ABSPLUS (MEMGET (ABSCONST 1004) INIT)
        (ABSCONST 1)) INIT, LOCKNOWN 403)

Figure 5.40: An Assignment to a Variable Using the Checker Semantics

checker predicates compare these terms from both intermediate and MIPS code. They
are syntactically very similar: Both consist of an assignment to some kind of store. The
value assigned is represented in both cases as a term consisting of an ABSPLUS constructor with comparable arguments. The checker predicate is defined on such terms. All it
has to derive is the look-up that the variable 'x' corresponds to the memory location
ABSCONST 1000 and 'y' corresponds to ABSCONST 1004. The checker predicate can
do the whole checking process without the need for a unification at any point. Moreover,
the checker predicate may need to rewrite the terms serving as its arguments but it never
needs to rewrite any proof goals within the theorem prover logic.

5.7.4 A Checker Predicate Implementation for Fast Step Correctness Checking

We use checker predicates that ensure the correctness of single steps for the *second phase* of our proving methodology. Such a checker predicate proves that if one state in the intermediate language corresponds to one state in the MIPS language the succeeding states will correspond to each other. In our checker semantics the two states that correspond to each other before the step will always be represented in the same way except for the program counters. This is due to the fact that all other parts of these states are unknown and are always represented by the same constants. The original program counters are only needed to fetch the appropriate statement and instructions. For these reasons when looking at a single step we do not need the states before the step as parameters to our checker predicate.

Hence, our checker predicates that prove a step correct take the intermediate and MIPS program code as parameters. Furthermore two program counters for intermediate and MIPS code, and finally the number of steps taken in the MIPS code is passed to the checker predicates. They return a boolean value stating whether the succeeding states correspond to each other or not.

So far we implemented several different checker predicates for checking simulation steps which differ in completeness and execution speed. Our description in the following subsections focuses on the most comprehensive checker predicate for which we managed to establish a correctness proof.

A Complete Step Checker Predicate

We have implemented a checker predicate that is general enough to check arbitrary steps. Moreover, it is based on a function that does not only indicate whether a step lemma from the second phase is correct but in case it cannot prove a step correct it returns a list of conditions that have to be proved to regard the step as correct. This can be combined with user provided facts from the source code: The user may provide the facts that could not be proved by the checker. The study of this checker predicate is very interesting because it can be seen as the fastest way to conduct a correctness proof for the *second phase*. For this reason the time measured for this checker provides some kind of practical lower bound for what the reduction of the time a correctness proof for the *second phase* takes may achieve. Of course if one is content with the correctness criterion as it is formalized within this checker predicate one may even use it to conduct the correctness proofs of our *second phase* for language elements that have not yet been included in the checker's correctness proof.

We did prove that the checker predicate works correctly on a large subset of our introduced languages with respect to the original correctness criterion. This subset comprises primitive and array variables, arithmetic expressions, and branches. The checker predicate that works only on this language subset is called checker (cp. Figure 5.41).

Furthermore, we did implement several other special purpose checker predicates which manage special cases of the complete step checker predicate. These checker predicates

```
checker_step (MemMap,Vars,PCRel,P_IL,P_MIPS,pc_IL,pc_MIPS) =
    let ais := mk_il_rawstate pc_IL in
    let ats := mk_tl_rawstate pc_MIPS in
    match AS.ilnext P_IL ais with
       | Some (aoutp,pid,agvs,(rpid,raddr,rvar,alvs)::stack,apc) =>
       match TAS.tlnextn P_MIPS ats n with
          | Some (tlaoutp,aregs,amem,tlapc) =>
             compmem MemMap Vars agvs alvs amem aregs ++
             comppc MemMap Vars PCRel apc tlapc ++
             compoutp MemMap Vars aoutp tloutp
          | None => Cfalse :: nil
       end
       | None => Cfalse::nil
    end.

checker(MemMap,Vars,PCRel,P_IL,P_MIPS,pc_IL,pc_MIPS) ≡
    checker_step(MemMap,Vars,PCRel,P_IL,P_MIPS,pc_IL,pc_MIPS) = []
```

Figure 5.41: The checker Checker Predicate

are aimed at proving some special steps correct. Thus speeding up the proving process.

Special purpose checker predicates may be derived from the complete checker predicate by abandoning term optimizations and other cases which are difficult to be proved correct once and for all. Once we have shown their correctness they can be used within our generated proof scripts.

The Step Checker Predicate checker

The following describes the implementation of our step correctness checker predicate checker shown in Figure 5.41. It uses a helper function checker_step. This helper function computes a list of conditions that need to be true in order to regard a symbolic execution step as correct.

First underspecified initial states are generated using the functions mk_il_rawstate and mk_tl_rawstate. Using them the succeeding abstract state representations are computed. These are compared using the functions compmem, comppc, and compoutp. The function compmem compares abstract store representations for global and local variables, registers and memory. Comparing program counters is done by comppc. Output lists are handled by compoutp. These functions are defined inductively on the term structure of the terms representing abstract stores and program counters as sketched in Section 5.7.3. compoutput only regards the last value in the list –if any is computed. Thereby a list of conditions that these functions cannot prove on their own is generated (concatenated by ++). Usually this list is empty. checker only checks whether the list is empty or not. If an error occurs a constant Cfalse representing the boolean value *false* is added to the list of conditions that need to be verified.

5.7.5 Checker Predicate Correctness

In this subsection we describe what correctness of the checker semantics with respect to original semantics means and motivate and sketch the corresponding correctness proofs. Furthermore, we describe what correctness of our checker predicates for the *second phase* means, sketch a correctness proof, and review how they are applied within our generated proof scripts.

The correctness proofs sketched in this section are based on the checker predicate for a subset of our intermediate language comprising primitive and array variables, arithmetic expressions, and branches: checker. Thus procedure call and return statements are not part of the correctness proofs. We only have to regard a single stack frame comprising one set of local variables.

Proving the Checker Semantics Correct

In order to prove a checker predicate working with our checker semantics correct, we first have to prove that the checker semantics is correct.

To do this in the intermediate language we need a function (Figure 5.44) that interprets abstract intermediate states and returns a concrete representation: interp_ilstate. It takes variables representing non-abstract, but undefined initial global gvals and local variable stores lvals and successively modifies these stores according to the terms the abstract stores are made of. Furthermore, a variable representing a non-abstract, undefined list of accumulated output output serves as third argument. The last argument is the abstract intermediate language state. The function interp_ilstate makes use of functions for interpreting abstract global and local variable stores (interp_gstore,interp_lstore) as well as abstract program counters (interp_pc) and output (interp_output). Excerpts of these helper functions are shown in Figure 5.42. They are defined mutually recursive on the term structure of the abstract state using another helper function interpreting abstract values (interp_val) shown in Figure 5.43.

The state interpretation function for the MIPS language interp_tlstate is defined analogously. It takes variables representing non abstract, but undefined memory and register stores and a variable representing abstract, undefined so far accumulated output as arguments. Moreover, the abstract MIPS state is an argument. Instead of heaving to deal with global and local variable stores it is defined on memory and register stores.

The correctness of the abstract intermediate language semantics is formulated via the lemma shown in Figure 5.45. Assuming that an abstract state ast has a concrete representation s we have to derive that the succeeding abstract state ast' is interpreted in a concrete state representation equal to the succeeding concrete state s'. CS.ilnext and AS.ilnext denote the state transition functions for the checker (AS = Abstract State transition) and the non-checker semantics (CS = Concrete State transition). P denotes an intermediate program representation. Note that the interpretation functions are defined to return an option datatype. This is especially relevant for the abstract semantics since some state transitions may not be performed if the original state has an unknown program counter. In these cases None is returned.

```
interp_gstore gvals lvals gstore =
    match gstore with
        | INIT => Some gvals
        | VARUPD var aval store =>
        match interp_gstore gvals lvals store, interp_val gvals lvals aval with
            | Some gvals', Some val => λ x. if x = var then val else gvals' x
            | _ , _ => None
        end
        | ACUPD var acindex aval store =>
        match interp_gstore gvals lvals store, interp_val gvals lvals acindex, interp_val gvals lvals aval with
            | Some gvals', Some ind, Some val => λ x. if x = (var,ind) then val else gvals' x
            | _ , _ , _ => None
        end
        | AVUPD var varindex aval store => ...
        match interp_gstore gvals lvals store, interp_val gvals lvals aval with
            | Some gvals', Some val => λ x. if x = (var,varindex) then val else gvals' x
            | _ , _ => None
        end
    end

with interp_lstore gvals lvals lstore = ...

with interp_pc gvals lvals av =
    match av with
        | LOCKNOWN pc => Some pc
        | LOCKUNKNOWN av pc1 pc2 =>
        match interp_val gvals lvals av with
            | Some val => Some ( if val = 1 then val pc2 else pc1)
            | _ => None
        end
    end.

with interp_output gvals lvals output aoutp =
    match aoutp with
        | NIL => Some NIL
        | CONS av arestlist =>
        match interp_val gvals lvals av with
            | Some val =>
            match interp_output gvals lvals qrestlist with
                | Some rlist => Some (CONS val rlist)
                | _ => None
            end
            | _ => None
        end
        | UNDEFINED => Some output
    end.
```

108   Figure 5.42: Abstract IL State Interpretation Helper Functions

```
with interp_val gvals lvals av =
    match av with
        | ABSCONST val => Some val
        | ABSPLUS av1 av2 =>
        match interp_val gvals lvals av1, interp_val gvals lvals av2 with
            | Some v1, Some v2 => Some (v1 + v2)
            | _ , _ => None
        end
        ...
        | VARGET (var: global variable) store => (interp_gstore gvals lvals store) var
        | VARGET (var: local variable) store => (interp_lstore gvals lvals store) var
        ...
    end.
```

Figure 5.43: Abstract IL Value Interpretation

```
interp_ilstate gvals lvals output ast =
    let (aoutp,pid,gstore,(rpid,raddr,rvar,lstore)::stack,apc) := ast in
    match
        interp_output gvals lvals output aoutp,
        interp_gstore gvals lvals gstore,
        interp_lstore gvals lvals lstore,
        interp_pc gvals lvals apc
    with
        | Some outp, Some gvals', Some lvals', Some pc =>
            Some (outp,pid,gvals',(rpid,raddr,rvar,lvals')::stack,pc)
        | _ , _ , _ , _ => None
    end.
```

Figure 5.44: Abstract IL State Interpretation

```
Lemma ilabstract_correct :
∀ gvals lvals output . ∀ P ast s ast' s'.
    interp_ilstate gvals lvals output ast = Some s ⟶
    CS.ilnext P s = s' ⟶
    AS.ilnext P ast = Some ast' ⟶
    interp_ilstate gvals lvals output ast' = Some s'
```

Figure 5.45: Correctness of Checker Semantics (IL)

Lemma tlabstract_correct :
∀ mvals rvals output . ∀ P ast s ast' s' n.
   interp_tlstate mvals rvals output ast = Some s $\longrightarrow$
   CS.tlnextn P s n = s' $\longrightarrow$
   AS.tlnextn P ast n = Some ast' $\longrightarrow$
   interp_tlstate mvals rvals output ast' = Some s'

Figure 5.46: Correctness of Checker Semantics (MIPS)

Lemma checker_correct : ∀ MemMap Vars PCRel P_{IL} P_{MIPS} s_{IL} s_{MIPS} n.
   checker MemMap Vars PCRel P_{IL} P_{MIPS} (get_pc s_{IL}) (get_pc' s_{MIPS}) n $\longrightarrow$
   Varmap_properties MemMap Vars P_{IL} P_{MIPS} $\longrightarrow$
   H = createsimulation MemMap Vars PCRel $\longrightarrow$
   H (is,ts) $\longrightarrow$
   H (CS.ilnext P_{IL} s_{IL},CS.tlnextn P_{MIPS} s_{MIPS} n)

Figure 5.47: Correctness of the checker Checker Predicate

Figure 5.46 shows the lemma stating correctness of the abstract MIPS semantics. P is a piece of MIPS code. The lemma makes use of the interp_tlstate function for interpreting abstract MIPS states. It is very similar to the correctness lemma for the intermediate language. The only major difference is the extra n argument since we deal with state transition functions CS.tlnextn and AS.tlnextn that perform n consecutive steps.

In both cases the proof is done via an induction on the abstract state representations and further case distinctions reflecting the inductive nature the interpretation functions are defined upon.

Proving the Checker Predicates Correct

Figure 5.47 shows our correctness lemma for our checker predicate that can handle primitive and array variables, arithmetic expressions, and branches: checker. The compiler provided information: MemMap, Vars, PCRel, a procedure in intermediate language P_{IL} and MIPS P_{MIPS} form as well as two program counters from the states s_{IL}, s_{MIPS} and the number of steps taken in the MIPS language n serve as parameters to the checker. The theorem says that if the checker is content, the *variable mapping* properties are fulfilled (injectivity, alignment), and the state correspondence captured in the simulation relation H as created by createsimulation holds for the two states before the step, than the state correspondence holds after the step, too. The proof is done by unfolding the checker definition. The main step of the proof is the rewriting of the computation and comparison of the abstract states by their concrete counterparts within the checker predicate. This is done by using the checker semantics correctness proofs.

Using the Correctness Proof

The established correctness proof allows us to reduce a step correctness lemma of the following form:

H (is,ts) $\longrightarrow$
H (CS.ilnext P_{IL} s_{IL},CS.tlnextn P_{MIPS} s_{MIPS} n)

to the following subgoals via an implication rule:

1. checker MemMap Vars PCRel P_{IL} P_{MIPS} (get_pc s_{IL}) (get_pc' s_{MIPS}) n

2. Varmap_properties MemMap Vars P_{IL} P_{MIPS}

3. H = createsimulation MemMap Vars PCRel

The first goal can be computed in a fast way by evaluating the checker predicate with the Coq tactic *vm_compute*. The properties of the variable mapping are proved once and for all for a procedure. Most of this is done by our injectivity checker. The last subgoal is true by construction.

Discussion

We have defined and proved a checker predicate correct with respect to the original semantics for a large subset of our intermediate language and MIPS code. All interesting cases such as arithmetic instructions and branches are covered. The proof is entirely carried out in Coq and consists of several hundred lines of proof code. The most important step within this proof is the correctness of the abstract semantics. The size of this proof alone comprises a few hundred lines of Coq proof code. When counting proof code lines, most lines comprise a single application of a tactic.

We have implemented more specialized checkers. Their correctness is ensured by similar lemmata, but the proofs are much shorter.

6 Verifying System Abstractions

This chapter presents the application of the certifying translations approach to system abstractions. Most parts are based on work done together with Ina Schaefer.

In this application scenario, we consider transformations of transition systems. This means a transition system is transformed into another transition system. We want to ensure that each translation run done by a translation tool is done correctly. The translation tool investigated in this case study conducts abstractions of transition systems. Like for code generation from compilers, we regard the input – the original system – and the output – the translated, usually abstracted system – and verify for each run of our translation tool that the translation has been done correctly. Correctness of system translations in the context of system abstractions means the preservation of distinct properties during the translation process. Typical transformations done by our translation tool comprise abstractions, e.g. the following operations:

- We omit some parts of the input systems.

- We replace variable domains by more abstract ones in the considered systems.

Both transformations reduce the complexity of the original systems, for example the size of its description is reduced.

Like for code generation in compilers, the verification of system abstractions is based on a distinct formalized semantics and on our *Generic Correctness Criterion* introduced in Chapter 4. In contrast to code generation in compilers, we use a shallow embedding of the transition systems in the theorem prover. For this reason, the systems' state transition functions are formalized directly in the theorem prover syntax. No explicit syntax representation of systems themselves is required at any point in the transformation and verification process.

The overall structure of our approach is depicted in Figure 6.1. For verifying a system abstraction, the translation tool is given a concrete system and a property to hold in both systems. As output an abstract system is produced. During the abstraction process a proof script is generated capturing the actual proof that the abstraction preserves the considered property of the systems. Proof script and system representations are passed to the theorem prover. The theorem prover serves as certificate checker and decides whether the abstraction is regarded as correct. The property is generally represented using temporal logics. For some transformations, the representation of the property is instantiated in a way such that it is general enough to hold for a larger class of systems with different domains.

The need for system abstractions arises in model checking properties of large systems. Size of systems is a limitation to model checking. Keeping the size of the state space

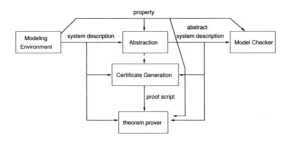

Figure 6.1: Our Certifying System Abstractions Infrastructure

that needs to be examined small is an important goal to make model checking feasible. When systems are to big to be model checked directly, they may be passed through an abstraction tool to make them smaller. In the Figure 6.1, such an application scenario is shown: after abstraction, the resulting system is fed to a model checker and the model checker decides whether the given property holds for the system or not. Our certifying system abstractions approach guarantees that such abstractions are done correctly. Thus, we can be sure that the properties verified by a trusted model checker hold for the original system, too.

The correctness criteria which have to be fulfilled to prove such transformations correct are based on simulation between abstract and concrete systems. They depend upon the property that shall be preserved. The preservation of the property has to be encoded into our *Generic Correctness Property* by instantiating state correspondence and step correctness predicates appropriately. Note that this property is the only semantical correctness issue that we require to be preserved during the system translation. It is therefore the fundamental basis of our correctness criterion for system abstractions. Unlike in compilers, this property may change for each translation run depending on both, the user provided property and system! Thus, we may have different abstractions for the same system for different properties.

The work presented in this chapter is a contribution to the EVAS [1] project [ASSV07] aimed at developing and verifying adaptive embedded systems in an automotive area. Most of the work covered in this chapter has been published in 2007 [BSPH07b, BSPH07a].

In the remainder of this chapter we introduce the class of systems we are discussing: synchronous adaptive systems (SAS) in Section 6.1. Section 6.2 elaborates on system properties and the issue when to regard an abstraction as correct. In Section 6.3 we discuss the actual task of proving the correctness of a system abstraction. Some theorem prover related issues are presented, too.

---

[1] *Entwicklungsmethodik Verifizierbarer Adaptiver eingebetteter Systeme*

114

$$SASmodulestate = val_1 \times \; ... \; \times val_n$$

$$SASstate = SASmodulestate_1 \times \; ... \; \times SASmodulestate_m$$

Figure 6.2: SAS State Definitions

6.1 SAS Transition Systems

In the context of system abstractions, we regard abstractions on synchronous adaptive systems (SAS). These were introduced in 2006 by Schaefer and Poetzsch-Heffter [SPH06] and used in the EVAS project. In this section, we present the semantics of SAS transition systems in a formalization close to the one used in our theorem provers. It is based on inductive definitions. The original work [SPH06] gives a declarative formalization. We do not have a syntax definition of SAS transition systems and use a shallow embedding of the semantics into the theorem prover.

The smallest structural construction element of a SAS transition system is a module. A module can itself be regarded as a deterministic system that reacts to some input. Thus, it performs a certain task. The algorithm this system uses may change. In fact each time the module is invoked the actual algorithm to perform the invoked task is selected. This selection is called the *adaptation*. The functionalism that chooses the actual algorithm is called *adaptation aspect*. The algorithms performing the task the module is designed for are called *configurations*. In terms of adaptive systems, these algorithms realize the *functional behavior* of the module. The adaptation aspect chooses the configuration by evaluating *configuration guards*. Variables in a module may be classified as input, output, local or adaptive variables. Note that the configuration guards may only depend on the adaptive variables in order to have a clean syntactic separation between functional and adaptive behavior.

A SAS system is composed from a set of modules that are interconnected with their input and output variables. The system is synchronous in a way that all modules perform a single step at the same time without influencing each other. Data may be interchanged between them between two steps.

In the theorem prover, we create for each distinct system its own state datatype following the state pattern shown in Figure 6.2. SAS transition systems have a modular structure. The part of a state corresponding to such a module is called a module's substate. It is defined in the first line of the figure (called *SASmodulestate*). It is a tuple consisting of values. For each variable that is used inside, a module there is a corresponding value component. States for complete systems are tuples consisting of the sub-states from its modules. Each module's sub-state has its own type depending on the number of variables used inside the module. We refer to them as *SASmodulestate$_i$* to explicitly mention the type of the ith component or simply *SASmodulestate* if this distinction is not important. To achieve an operational semantics for SAS transition systems, we need a state transition function. We define parts of state transition functions working on sub-states dedicated to single modules. This is shown in Figure 6.3. The signatures of the functions realizing the *configurations* of a distinct module and the *configuration guards*

configuration$_1$next :: *SASmodulestate* $\Rightarrow$ *SASmodulestate*

...

configuration$_n$next :: *SASmodulestate* $\Rightarrow$ *SASmodulestate*

guard$_1$ :: *SASmodulestate* $\Rightarrow$ *bool*

...

guard$_n$ :: *SASmodulestate* $\Rightarrow$ *bool*

adaptationnext :: *SASmodulestate* $\Rightarrow$ *SASmodulestate*

nextmodulestate$_i$ :: *SASmodulestate* $\Rightarrow$ *SASmodulestate*
nextmodulestate$_i$ s =
    let s' = adaptationnext s in
        if guard$_1$ s' then configuration$_1$next s'
        else if guard$_2$ s' then configuration$_2$next s'
        ...
        else if guard$_n$ s' then configuration$_n$next s'
        else error

Figure 6.3: SAS Semantics (Module)

handleInteraction :: *SASstate* $\Rightarrow$ *SASstate*

nextstate :: *SASstate* $\Rightarrow$ *SASstate*
nextstate s =
    let $(s_1,...,s_m)$ = handleinteraction s in
        (nextmodulestate$_1$ s_1,...,nextmodulestate$_m$ s_m)

Figure 6.4: SAS Semantics (System)

are shown. Their functionality is formalized in the theorem prover's object logic. The function determining the adaptation behavior is specified in the object logic of the theorem prover, too. The formalization of the function computing the succeeding state part for a module is shown: The adaptation behavior is evaluated first. Depending on that the guards determine the next configuration. This configuration is used for computing the parts of the state that are not part of the *adaptation aspect*. Variables accessed by adaptationnext function and by the *configurations* should be disjunct.

Figure 6.4 shows the state transition function for a complete system. A special function handling the interaction of the different modules is formalized in the theorem prover. When encountering a state transition this function is evaluated first and works on the input and output variables of the modules. After the module interaction is done the transition functions working on the sub-states belonging to the different modules are evaluated – the corresponding parts of the complete SAS state are altered.

Figure 6.5 shows the definition of SAS transition systems. A SAS transition system

The transition system induced by a SAS model is defined as
$K = (\Sigma, \Sigma_0, \text{nextstate})$ where

- Σ: is the set of all SAS states
- Σ_0: is the set of initial SAS states
- nextstate: is the SAS state transition function.

Figure 6.5: Definition of SAS Transition Systems

is a deterministic state transition system. It is defined as a tuple consisting of a set of states, a set of initial states and the state transition function.

Discussion of our SAS Formalization

Since we deal with systems defined via state transition functions, we have altered the semantics definition for SAS system given in 2006 by Schaefer and Poetzsch-Heffter [SPH06] to a more computable form. All aspects of the original system definition have been preserved. We do not make a syntactical distinction between the different kinds of variables (input, output, adaption, local) in our definition of SAS systems in order to keep the definitions small. One could, however, imagine some kind of semantic analysis as known from compiler construction that does such checks for our systems.

The set Σ is defined in the definition from Figure 6.5 inductively, thereby covering all reachable states a system can encounter:

- $\Sigma_0 \subseteq \Sigma$
- $x \in \Sigma \xrightarrow{\text{nextstate}} x \in \Sigma$

6.2 Correctness of Abstractions

In this section, we present and discuss our notion of correctness for system abstractions. We present the logic in which we describe properties of systems in Subsection 6.2.1. These shall be preserved during an abstraction run. In Subsection 6.2.2, we present our actual notion of abstraction correctness: We use an instantiation of our *Generic 1:1 Correctness Criterion* presented in Section 4.1.2. Furthermore, we discuss why this instantiation results in a valid correctness criterion ensuring the desired properties.

6.2.1 Formalizing Properties

A system abstraction is regarded as correct if the relevant properties of the transformed system are preserved. In this section, we present the nature of these properties.

Properties are formulated using temporal logic. Accordingly, they are defined on execution traces of systems. The following definition of an execution path of a system is suitable for use in temporal logics:

Definition 17 (Paths) *A path of a system K is defined as a sequence of states $\sigma_0 \sigma_1 \ldots$ where $\sigma_0 \in \Sigma_0$ and for all $0 \leq i$ we have $\sigma_{i+1} =$ nextstate σ_i. The set $Paths(K) = \{\sigma_0 \sigma_1 \ldots | \sigma_0 \sigma_1 \ldots$ a path of $K\}$ is the set of possible paths of K and defines the SAS semantics. Let π_j denote the suffix of path $\pi = \sigma_0 \sigma_1 \sigma_2 \ldots$ starting in state σ_j.*

In the context of this work, we define a special logic for the formalization of system properties. It is called L_{SAS}: a language for expressing properties over SAS transition systems. The following definition uses a set of variables Var. Access to variables is implemented using selectors selecting components from the tuples representing states. For convenience we write $\sigma(x)$ to access the component of Variable x holding its value in state σ. The type Val is used to denote values. L_{SAS} is a variant of the computational tree logic CTL*.

L_{SAS} formulas are built from atoms, state formulas, and path formulas. Atoms are equations on variables and values. State formulas are formulas that shall hold in a given state. They may be made up from atoms, the boolean constant true, negations of state formulas, conjunctions of state formulas, and an existentially quantified path formula meaning that there exists a path starting at the given state where the path formula holds. Path formulas are defined for traces of states. One can either express in a path formula that a given state formula shall hold in the first state of the path, the negation of a path formula shall hold, the conjunction of two path formulas shall hold, a path formula holds starting at the next state in the trace, or a state formula always holds in a trace until a second formula holds in one state.

Definition 18 (L_{SAS}) *Let $x, y \in Var$ and $v \in Val$.*

$$
\begin{aligned}
Atoms\ a &\ ::=\ x = v \mid x = y \\
StateFormula\ \varphi &\ ::=\ true \mid a \mid \neg \varphi \mid \varphi_1 \wedge \varphi_2 \mid \mathsf{E}\ \psi \\
PathFormula\ \psi &\ ::=\ \varphi \mid \neg \psi \mid \psi_1 \wedge \psi_2 \mid \mathsf{X}\ \psi \mid \psi_1\ \mathsf{U}\ \psi_2
\end{aligned}
$$

We define the other CTL* operators with the usual abbreviations as follows:

$$
\begin{aligned}
\mathsf{F}\,\psi &\ \equiv\ true\ \mathsf{U}\ \psi \\
\mathsf{G}\,\psi &\ \equiv\ \neg\,\mathsf{F}\,\neg\psi \\
\mathsf{A}\,\psi &\ \equiv\ \neg\,\mathsf{E}\,\neg\psi
\end{aligned}
$$

The subset of L_{SAS} where only the universal path quantifier A is used and negation is only applied to atoms ($\longrightarrow$ no direct use of the E quantifier in properties) is called the universal fragment AL_{SAS}. It is a variant of the ACTL* logic (cp. e.g. [CGP99]). The satisfiability of L_{SAS}-formulas over SAS models is defined as follows:

Definition 19 (Satisfaction) *Let K be a SAS transition system. For a state formula φ, $(K, \sigma) \models \varphi$ is defined inductively on the structure of φ.*

- $(K, \sigma) \models true$ *always*

- $(K, \sigma) \models (x = v)$ *iff* $\sigma(x) = v$ *and* $(K, \sigma) \models (x = y)$ *iff* $\sigma(x) = \sigma(y)$

118

- $(K, \sigma) \models \neg\varphi$ iff $(K, \sigma) \not\models \varphi$

- $(K, \sigma) \models \varphi_1 \wedge \varphi_2$ iff $(K, \sigma) \models \varphi_1$ and $(K, \sigma) \models \varphi_2$

- $(K, \sigma) \models \mathsf{E}\psi$ iff there exists a path π such that $(K, \pi) \models \psi$.

For a path formula ψ, $(K, \pi) \models \psi$ is defined inductively on the structure of ψ.

- $(K, \pi) \models \varphi$ iff $\pi = \sigma\sigma_1\sigma_2 \ldots$ and $(K, \sigma) \models \varphi$

- $(K, \pi) \models \neg\psi$ iff $(K, \pi) \not\models \psi$

- $(K, \pi) \models \psi_1 \wedge \psi_2$ iff $(K, \pi) \models \psi_1$ and $(K, \pi) \models \psi_2$

- $(K, \pi) \models \mathsf{X}\,\psi$ iff $\pi = \sigma\pi_1$ and $(K, \pi_1) \models \psi$

- $(K, \pi) \models \psi_1 \,\mathsf{U}\, \psi_2$ iff $\exists k \geq 0$ such that $(K, \pi_k) \models \psi_2$ and $\forall\, 0 \leq j \leq k\ (K, \pi_j) \models \psi_1$

Discussion

We always reason about deterministic state transition functions in our framework. Nevertheless, it is still important to distinguish between existentially quantified and universally quantified path formulas in our systems. In general, we have an infinite amount of start states resulting in an infinite number of possible execution paths.

A restrictions of atoms in (A)CTL* formulas – like in the case of AL_{SAS} to equations – is typical to the application of (A)CTL* logic. In the case of verifying system abstractions, it makes the conduction of the proofs easier. We did not encounter any case studies in the EVAS project that needed a more refined specification methodology than AL_{SAS}.

6.2.2 Property Preservation via Simulation

In this section, we present an important meta result that enables us to apply our certifying translation framework to system abstractions. We show that if the original system simulates the abstracted one and the simulation relation ensures property preservation, then the abstraction is correct with respect to the original system and the properties to be preserved during the abstraction process. In addition we describe how we instantiate our *Generic 1:1 Correctness Criterion* to achieve a criterion for use with our correctness proofs for system abstractions.

The Property Preservation Theorem

We use the following theorem proved correct and presented by Clarke, Grumberg, and Peled [CGP99].

Theorem 1 (Property Preservation on Kripke structures) *Given two Kripke structures $K = (AP', S, S_0, R, L)$ and $K' = (AP', S', S_0', R', L')$. Let $K \preceq K'$. Then for every ACTL* formula f with atomic propositions in AP', $K' \models f$ implies $K \models f$.*

It states that properties formalized in ACTL* logic are preserved under simulation. The theorem is formalized on Kripke structures, for this reason (cp. Section 3.2) the simulation has to preserve atomic propositions that are true in the states in the simulation relation.

To show that an abstract system preserves a property formulated as $A_{L_{SAS}}$ formula of a concrete system, we port the theorem to SAS transition systems by encoding SAS transition systems as Kripke structures.

The following items are necessary to define Kripke structures and apply the theorem:

1. We need to define the sets of atomic propositions AP and AP' of the Kripke structures. The properties that shall be preserved need to be formulated using these propositions.

   We use the atoms from the definition of the $A_{L_{SAS}}$ logic (cp. Definition 18) as atomic propositions. However, atoms are defined as equations on variables and constants. Variables, constants and their domains may be different in the abstract and the original system. A popular abstraction highly valuable for making systems more model-checkable is the abstraction of domains (cp. e.g. the motivating example in Section 1.1). We use the variables, constants and domains from the abstract systems to define our atomic propositions upon.

2. We define the label functions. These functions take a state and labels it to its atomic propositions. In our case, these functions have to return the set of propositions formalized on the variables, constants and domains of the abstract system. They are defined using predicates for checking an atomic proposition of a state.

3. With the help of the first two items, we map SAS transition systems to Kripke structures. To define a Kripke structure, we need a set of initial states which we already have for the SAS transition system. The set of states is also given in the SAS transition system definition. The transition relation is constructed inductively from the initial states and the state transition function.

   The set of initial states, the set of states, the transition relation, the label function and the set of atomic propositions are put together to define an appropriate Kripke structure.

To reason about different forms of atomic proposition representation – either using the variables, constants, domains from abstract or concrete system – it is useful to define an *abstraction function*. It maps an $A_{L_{SAS}}$ atom defined over the variables, constants, and domains of the concrete system to its abstract counter-part. The other way round, we define a *concretization function* that maps an $A_{L_{SAS}}$ atom defined over the variables, constants, and domains of the abstract system to a set of atoms defined upon variables, constants, and domains of the concrete system. Since the abstract systems' domains are more abstract than in the concrete system there can be more than one concrete atom corresponding to an abstract atom.

System Correctness Criterion

To prove the correctness of a system abstraction, we prove the prerequisites – the simulation – of the Theorem 1 for an original and an abstracted system. This simulation condition is formalized in a theorem prover. We end up with the *System Correctness Criterion* shown in Figure 6.6. Thus, when verifying system abstractions, we only show the simulation and the fact that it preserves atomic propositions. The conclusion that it preserves properties captured by the atomic propositions is done once and for all.

Our *System Correctness Criterion* takes several arguments:

- the state transition function of the concrete system nextstate,

- the state transition function of the abstract system nextstate',

- an initial state of the concrete system s0,

- an initial state of the abstract system s0',

- a simulation relation H – it has to be defined in a way that it ensures equality of labels, i.e. using the label functions of both systems,

- the property that shall be preserved p,

- and a concretization function $\mathcal{C}$.

The first two conditions in Figure 6.6 formalize the simulation constraints on initial states and the simulation step between two systems. These first two conditions are formalized once for all systems. The third condition requires the correctness of the concretization function and the fact that the given simulation relation indeed ensures property preservation. It uses a predicate consistency to ensure this.

consistency requires that the simulation relation ensures the following property:

- For each two states in the simulation relation, the same atomic propositions – the property p is build from – hold.

Since atomic propositions may be formalized differently using the variables, constants and domains from the original and abstracted system we use a concretization function C to map abstract propositions to $A_{L_{SAS}}$ atoms with variables, constants and domains from the concrete system. Usually an abstract proposition is mapped to a set of concrete atoms. This set might even contain an infinite number of elements. The fact that an abstract proposition holds (or does not hold) in a state from an abstract system corresponds to the fact that there is (or does not exist) a single atom from a set of concrete atoms that is true.

From the *Generic 1:1 Correctness Criterion* to the System Correctness Criterion

The presented System Correctness Criterion relates one step in the original system to one step in the abstracted system. In this subsection, we show that it can be regarded as an instance of the *Generic 1:1 Correctness Criterion*.

systemequivalence
    nextstate : (SASstate $\Rightarrow$ SASstate)
    nextstate' : (SASstate' $\Rightarrow$ SASstate')
    s0 : SASstate
    s0' : SASstate'
    H : (SASstate $\times$ SASstate' $\Rightarrow$ bool)
    p : prop
    C : concfun
    =
        H (s0,s0') $\wedge$
        $\forall$ s s'. H (s,s') $\Longrightarrow$ H (nextstate s,nextstate' s') $\wedge$
        consistency(H,p,$\mathcal{C}$)

Figure 6.6: System Correctness Criterion

This involves that we deal with the following differences in the formalization of the two criteria:

- In the formulation at hand, the simulation relation H is passed as an argument instead of the existential quantified simulation relation of the *Generic 1:1 Correctness Criterion*.

- The simulation relation in the *Generic 1:1 Correctness Criterion* needs to fulfill a state correspondence predicate. This is in the given formalization stated as the consistency predicate. The predicate itself is constant for all notions of system correctness. It is instantiated with the concretization function $\mathcal{C}$ and a property p. Thus, it can be regarded as a special case of the state correspondence criterion.

Since we are dealing with a 1:1 step relation, there is no need for step correctness predicates. Thus, the *Generic 1:1 Correctness Criterion* is sufficient.

To show that the System Correctness Criterion for a single abstraction run (fixed property, concretization function, and simulation relation) is an instance of the *Generic 1:1 Correctness Criterion*, we show that it implies the latter. We start with the definition of the *Generic 1:1 Correctness Criterion* and its instantiation with parameters corresponding to the System Correctness Criterion: The state transition functions are instantiated appropriately, the set of initial states in a way that it only contains one pair of initial states, the state correspondence predicate has to ensure the equality of atomic propositions.

GCC1:1($next \leftarrow$ nextstate ,$next' \leftarrow$ nextstate',
    $H_0 \leftarrow$ { (s0,s0') },
    $C \leftarrow$ (λ (s,s'). atomic propositions of p are the same in s and s'))
    $\exists$ H.
        $\forall s_0\ s_0'.\ (s_0, s_0') \in H_0 \longrightarrow H(s_0, s_0') \wedge$
        $\forall s\ s'.\ H(s,s') \longrightarrow H (next(s),\ next'(s')) \wedge$

$$\forall\ s\ s'\ .\ \mathsf{H}(s,\!s') \longrightarrow C(s,s')$$

We can evaluate this to:

∃ H.

$\quad \forall\ s_0\ s_0'.\ (s_0, s_0') \in \{\ (\mathsf{s0,s0')}\ \},\ \longrightarrow \mathsf{H}(s_0, s_0')\ \wedge$
$\quad \forall\ s\ s'.\ \mathsf{H}(s,\!s') \longrightarrow \mathsf{H}\ (\mathsf{nextstate}(s),\ \mathsf{nextstate'}(s'))\ \wedge$
$\quad \forall\ s\ s'\ .\ \mathsf{H}(s,\!s') \longrightarrow$
$\qquad\quad (\lambda\ \mathsf{s\ s'.}\ \text{atomic propositions of } p \text{ are the same in s and s')}\ s\ s'$

We can give a witness for the simulation relation H and use the definition of consistency to rewrite the last line. Note that the check that atomic properties hold in the original system requires the use of the concretization function $\mathcal{C}$. Thus, the following formula is strengthened, i.e. it implies the *Generic 1:1 Correctness Criterion*:

$\quad \forall\ s_0\ s_0'.\ (s_0, s_0') \in \{\ (\mathsf{s0,s0')}\ \} \longrightarrow \mathsf{H}(s_0, s_0')\ \wedge$
$\quad \forall\ s\ s'.\ \mathsf{H}(s,\!s') \longrightarrow \mathsf{H}\ (\mathsf{nextstate}(s),\ \mathsf{nextstate'}(s'))\ \wedge$
$\quad \mathsf{consistency}(\mathsf{R},\mathsf{p},\mathcal{C})$

By keeping the state transition functions, reformalizing the initial states and introducing the simulation relation, the property that shall be preserved, and the concretization function as new parameters, we derive the System Correctness Criterion.

Discussion

We have successfully considered two approaches to carry the results of property preservation of ACTL* formula via simulation to SAS transition systems. Both approaches are described in our 2007 technical report [BSPH07a].

The approach sketched in this thesis derives its results directly from the Theorem 1. It works with a single formulation of the property to be preserved. In the approach described above further challenges may occur with the correctness of abstraction and concretization of atomic properties. This is especially true if the property that shall be preserved is described using concrete AL_{SAS} atoms. This is hidden within the consistency(R,p,$\mathcal{C}$) predicate in Figure 6.6. Since this thesis is about proving the simulation between two given systems for given semantical requirements, the proof that abstract and concrete properties correspond to each other is out of the scope of this thesis (but see [BSPH07a] on this).

Our second approach works with two different formalizations of the property to be checked: one for an abstract system and the second for the concrete system. Both property formalizations have to correspond in a way described in our 2007 technical report [BSPH07a] to each other. We prove this for every verification run. We focus on the simulation issues of our correctness proofs in this thesis. For this reason we did present the first correctness approach based on Theorem 1 – which assumes that mappings from concrete to abstract atoms are correct – rather than the second approach.

6.3 Proving Abstractions Correct

To prove an abstraction correct, we have to prove that original and abstract system fulfill the *System Correctness Criterion* shown in Figure 6.6. This requires several steps.

1. In the first step, we generate – based on the property to be preserved – a simulation relation. Each abstraction and property to be checked requires the generation of its own simulation relation. The simulation relation relates states from the concrete system with states from the abstract system. It has to ensure that atomic propositions are the same. Given a property p, a concretization function $\mathcal{C}$. Let AP' be the set of AL_{SAS} abstract atoms that occur in p. The simulation relation H(s,s') requires :

$$\forall a' \in AP'. \ a' \text{ holds in s' iff } \exists a \in \mathcal{C}(a'). \ a \text{ holds in s}$$

2. Once, we have established the simulation relation, we use it to prove the first two items of the criterion shown in Figure 6.6 correct. The proof that initial states are in the relation is usually quite simple: it can be done by using a few lines of proof code. As in certifying code generation, proving the simulation step correct is slightly more complex. We either generate a proof script or use a generic one. It turned out to be sufficient for many cases to select a pre-written proof script that is generic to many abstractions.

3. Finally, we have to prove that the simulation relation indeed ensures correctness of atomic propositions – thus, ensuring correctness of an abstraction.

Unlike in certifying code generation, the case distinction on possible program points does not have to occur in system abstractions. The proof of the simulation step is structured as follows:

- It starts directly with the computation of a symbolic representation of the successors of a pair of arbitrary states from original and abstracted systems. This is done by unfolding the state transition function definitions.

- Given the fact that the simulation relation holds for the two arbitrary states before the simulation relation, we derive that it always holds after the state transition steps, too.

In case of abstractions of integer domains, the proof that the simulation relation holds after a state transition of original and abstracted system breaks down to showing the equivalence of formulas containing (in-)equalities between involved variables and constants. Specialized theorem prover tactics can solve these equalities in many cases without requiring further adaptation.

As discussed in Section 6.2.2, the proof of simulation relation correctness is not directly in the scope of this thesis. However, we did conduct first experiments on proving distinct simulation relations correct and did not experience any problems.

H :: SASstate × SASstate' ⇒ bool
    H (s,s') =
    $\exists x \in \mathcal{C}$ (input value of s'). x = input value of s

Figure 6.7: Simulation Relation for the Example System

H :: SASstate ⇒ SASstate' ⇒ bool
    H A B ==
    ((B(in) = low) = (A(in) < 50)) ∧
    ((B(in) = high) = (A(in) >= 50)) ∧
    (B(conf) = A(conf))

Figure 6.8: Theorem Prover Formalization of the Simulation Relation for the Example System

A Small Example

This example is based on the system abstraction motivating example from Section 1.1. To prove that the desired property:

- input value below 50 then second configuration is chosen

is preserved during the abstraction, we have to define a concretization function which is derived from the domain abstraction undertaken:

$\mathcal{C}$(low) = { x | x < 50 }
$\mathcal{C}$(high) = { x | x >= 50 }

The property to be preserved has to be reformulated using the abstract domains:

- input value low then second configuration is chosen

The simulation relation is constructed such that it ensures: iff the variable in is below 50 in the concrete system, it has the value low in the abstract system. On the other hand, if it has a value greater or equal 50 in the concrete system, it has the value high in the abstract system. conf denotes an identifier for the chosen configuration.

The resulting simulation relation is shown in Figure 6.7. A theorem prover formalization is shown in Figure 6.8. It is sufficient to prove the desired property. Consistency of the simulation relation is given because all atomic propositions are included and are correctly related to each other. Note, that the definition of the simulation relations based on label functions is already simplified to an equation in both figures.

126

7 Evaluation

We evaluate our framework and our implementations in this chapter. The different implementations of our certifying compiler are compared in Section 7.1. The implementation of our certifying system abstraction infrastructure is evaluated in Section 7.2. In Section 7.3 we contrast the feasibility of Isabelle and Coq as certificate checkers. We present measured checking times for various case studies. We give a short evaluation of our semantical framework in Section 7.4. Section 7.5 comprises some concluding remarks and discussion of work related to this chapter.

7.1 Our Certifying Compilers

In this section we compare our two implementations of the compiler code generation phase and the implementations of the corresponding certificate generators. Certificates are generated for *Isabelle/HOL 2005* and *Coq 8.1* as theorem provers respectively. During this chapter we refer to the Isabelle version as the *first implementation*. The Coq version is referred to as the *second implementation* to emphasize on the chronological order in which we have developed them.

It should also be noted that of course one can only use Isabelle certificates and formalizations with Isabelle as certificate checker and Coq certificates and formalizations only with Coq as certificate checker.

The Languages, Compilation, and Certificate Generation

Both implementations use a subset of the intermediate language presented in Section 5.1 and generate MIPS code (cp. Section 5.2). The intermediate language subset used in the *second implementation* is almost complete. We do, however, realize the statement that calls a procedure with a non fixed number of arguments with several statements each taking a fixed number of arguments. In the *first implementation* we did not consider procedure calls at all. However, since we regard code generation for procedures independently from each other in the *second implementation* the proving overhead for this additional feature is not very big.

The code generation algorithm used in both versions is essentially described in Section 5.3 and is very similar for both implementations.

Certificate generation as well as generation of theorem prover representations is very close to the procurement described in Section 5.5 and relies on the same bits of compiler provided information in both implementations. Generated program representations are equally human readable. Since the Isabelle implementation was first, the separation between certificate generation and compiler is not so clear as in the *second implementation*. This, however, has nothing to do with the used theorem prover.

The code size for generating the theorem prover representations of the intermediate language and MIPS programs comprises less than 100 lines of ML code in both implementations. A small code size is crucial, because this is the only part of our compiler and certificate generator that belongs to the trusted computing base!

The part that generates representations for the compiler provided information is also of comparable size in both implementations. It consists of less than 100 lines of ML code, too.

The actual proof script generator comprises less than 1000 lines of ML code in both implementations. It is slightly larger in the *second implementation* than in the *first implementation*. This is due to the greater subset of the intermediate language that is used. Due to ML's pattern matching ability in function definitions the ML programming language allows a very compact encoding of the proof script generator.

Coq formalizations that work with our *second implementation* are presented in Appendix A.

7.2 Verification of System Abstractions

The checking process in our system abstractions case study is implemented using Isabelle/HOL as theorem prover. Isabelle/HOL is used for both: to formalize systems and check the correctness proofs.

In our system abstractions case study we regard synchronous adaptive systems that are specified as transition systems at the time the abstractions are performed. During the development of an adaptive synchronous system other representations are encountered, too. Originally the functionality of our adaptive systems is specified using various description mechanisms including graphical languages like Simulink. From these description languages parts of system descriptions are exported to an XML format file denoting a description of a complete system. This format serves as basis for other purposes than system abstraction and model checking as well. E.g. code generation may be done from system descriptions.

For system abstractions the XML format file is parsed into a tree-like Java object structure. Our abstractions work on this structure and modifies it.

For compatibility reasons the tool that generates the abstractions and the tool that writes the system descriptions into Isabelle/HOL theory files have been implemented in Java, too. The Isabelle system description generation is invoked before and after an abstraction. A visitor pattern generates the Isabelle code. For each node in the XML tree distinct code is omitted and composed into an Isabelle theory. In terms of code size the Isabelle representation is relatively large compared to an ML equivalent comprising several hundred lines of code that belong to the trusted computing base. The author of this thesis roughly assumes that by using an ML implementation the code size could be reduced by the factor 5.

list length	look-up time: Isabelle 2005	look-up time: Coq 8.1
500	0.41s	
1000	1.15s	
2000	3.83s	
10000	103.95s	0.01s
20000		0.02s
30000		0.03s

Figure 7.1: Look-up from Lists

7.3 Certificate Checking with Isabelle and Coq

As mentioned in the introduction, it turned out during the development of our certifying compilers that the checking of the certificates is the actual bottleneck of certifying compilation. At the beginning of this section we take a look at basic operations that have to be conducted in our generated certificates over and over again. Further on we evaluate the complete checking process for our implementations. The experiments featured in this section have been conducted on an Intel Core 2 Duo machine with 2.16 GHz using one core if not otherwise mentioned. The operating system used is Mac OS X. Isabelle 2005 is used with SML [MTH90] instead of Isabelle's ML of choice: Poly/ML [Mat05] for compatibility reasons.

7.3.1 Look-up Operations

Look-up of information from data structures turned out to be especially critical in our *first implementation*. In this subsection we examine look-ups from lists, sets, functions, and trees. These look-up operations are evaluated without a specific application context.

Look-up from Lists

The table in Figure 7.1 shows the worst case time for look-up of one element from a list for Isabelle 2005 and Coq 8.1. For creating the data from this table we used look-up operations of natural numbers from lists of natural numbers. The elements that we searched for were placed at the end of the list. For this reason they were matched last. This procurement results in a worst case look-up times. The look-ups in Coq were computed using the *vm_compute* tactic. In Isabelle we applied the rule:

$$(a \text{ mem } (x \mathrel{\#} xs)) - ((a - x) \vee (a \text{ mem } xs))$$

via Isabelle's simplifier as often as possible before simplifying the resulting term. Since the term gets bigger with each rule application, the technique does not completely scale (especially in the case comprising 10000 list elements). To overcome this we could further simplify the term after each rule application. Although this does scale it has turned out to be even slower in our examined cases.

$(\lambda x.$

    if $x = $ value$_1$ then rvalue$_1$ else

    if $x = $ value$_2$ then rvalue$_2$ else

    .

    .

    if $x < $ value$_i$ $\wedge$ $x > $ value$_j$ then rvalue$_i$+value$_i$*4

    .

    if $x = $ value$_n$ then rvalue$_m$ else defaultval $)$

Figure 7.2: Function used for Mapping Data

length of the if-cascade	look-up time: Isabelle 2005	look-up time: Coq 8.1
100	0.06s	< 0.001s
200	0.1s	< 0.001s
1000	0.61s	0.005s

Figure 7.3: Look-up from Functions

The Coq implementation is much faster due to the fact that *vm_compute* can execute the look-up function in a relatively native way. On the other hand in our Isabelle implementation we need to do a higher-order unification for each rule application.

Lists are only used in the *first implementation* for storing the program representations. In our *second implementation* we make use of lists at several points including the store of the program representations and the formalization of the *program counter relation*.

Look-up from Functions

Functions may be used to map some pieces of data to other pieces of data realizing a mapping. An exemplary schema of such a function is shown in Figure 7.2.

The table in Figure 7.3 shows the time measured for looking up values from mappings of natural numbers to boolean values in Isabelle/HOL 2005 and Coq 8.1. Like with the lists, we measure the worst case scenario with the element to be searched for at the very end of the if-cascade. The look-up scales with the size of the mapping. Coq outperforms Isabelle about the factor 100 compared to >= 10000 for look-up from lists. Isabelle has a relatively short formalization and syntax for function updates. This allows the definition of rules working directly on them without requiring an explicit function representation with the if-cascades.

In both implementations function mappings are used for the *variable mapping*. Note that we do not need a separate if-statement for each variable! As Figure 7.2 suggests, several variables may be catched by a single if-statement, if their allocation follows a certain pattern. Recall that such a pattern is mandatory for array elements (cp. Section 5.4.5)! Nevertheless, the use of such more sophisticated if-conditions may slow the look-ups down.

set size	look-up time: Isabelle 2005	look-up time: Coq 8.1
500	0.1s	< 0.001s
1000	0.2s	< 0.001s
2000	0.5s	< 0.001s

Figure 7.4: Look-up from Sets

Other uses of look-up from functions comprise the definitions of memory (in both intermediate and MIPS code) and the register set. In these cases, for verifying simulation steps the access time is usually not very critical. Access to function updates comprise only the values written during the actual step one is currently reasoning about.

Look-up from Sets

Coq has several different set formalizations. The most efficient finite set implementation in Coq is directly based on lists. Thus, there is no access time difference between lists. Isabelle/HOL has only one set implementation which works for finite sets similar to lists.

Figure 7.4 shows a table with worst case look-up times of an element in a set of natural numbers. Like with the lists, worst case means that the element to be looked up is stored at the very end of the list representation. In Isabelle the decision whether a certain element is in a set is derived faster than the decision whether it is in a list. Like with function updates, list look-ups do not work via a formalized function but use some rules that are matched on the list representation directly.

In our implementations the sets of variables are formalized as sets.

Search Trees

We also investigated search trees as store for information. These provide at least in our time complexity investigations faster accesses for searching elements.

Nevertheless, we encountered several problems resulting in the following disadvantages:

- In the Isabelle representation the examination of a node and the decision in which part of the tree a certain element is stored is much more complicated than matching rewrite rules on function update or set representations. The matching operation requires many unification steps. In the Coq case, however, we can directly write an executable function that does this examination for us, requiring no unification steps.

- People expect some kind of data structures in the semantics formalization. E.g. they expect sets instead of search trees for certain specification parts. To keep these people content one must specify the original data as a set and then convert it to a search tree. This is a very time consuming task – especially when carried out in a theorem prover's object logic. Furthermore, one must prove that operations on the search tree have equivalent effects to corresponding operations on sets or lists respectively.

In the *first implementation* we do not use search trees at all. In the *second implementation* we use them for encoding very large program representations.

Note that our time complexity investigations from Section 5.4 improve with the use of search trees. Look-ups that could be done in $O(n)$ with n being the length of some information storing structure can be done in $O(log\ n)$.

Conclusion

Lists, functions, sets, and search trees may be used as basic data structures for storing information used in formalizations in higher-order theorem provers. Performance of look-ups is crucial in certifying translation scenarios. For this reason a careful examination of the pros and cons of each structure and for each theorem prover is important before choosing a certain formalization. It turns out that developing a certifying translation infrastructure is even from the theorem prover point of view very much an engineering task.

7.3.2 Other Performance Effecting Formalization Choices

We noticed that various effects slow the certificate checking down. Some of these are hard to measure and we are not able to give comprehensive data. They comprise the following items:

- The number of definitions, lemmata and other proof objects seems to be a factor relevant to Isabelle's performance. The more proof objects are in the system, the slower the system gets. This is not just true for tactics like *simp* that build a search space using all available lemmata that are marked to contribute to the simplification process.

- The parsing of object logic terms is not linear with respect to the length of the term. Some of this is due to type inference that needs to be done during the parsing process. Even for a fully type annotated term there is no linear parsing behavior. This is especially true for Isabelle. However, in both Coq and Isabelle the size of terms is limited. A common solution is to compose large terms from sub-terms defined as independent units. Sometimes it can even be convenient to define them in other files.

7.3.3 Certificate Checking for Code Generation

In this subsection we discuss the time we have measured for checking the certificates generated during compiler code generation. We compare our different implementations.

program	no. variables	IL length	TL length	time to prove correct
fibo (100 elements)	112	13	55	762 s
fibo (200 elements)	212	13	55	1518 s
sort	46	58	261	6102 s
sort2	166	178	900	176424 s ($\approx$ 2 days)

Figure 7.5: Checking Time for the *First Implementation*

Certificate Checking in the *First Implementation*

The table in Figure 7.5 shows the time[1] it takes to prove the code generation for a piece of intermediate language code *fibo*[2] and two different pieces of intermediate language code realizing a sorting algorithm correct within the theorem prover Isabelle/HOL. It also shows the length of the original intermediate language code (IL length) as well as the length of the generated MIPS code (TL length). The time to verify a code generation run is linear to the size of the variables (counting each array element as a single variable) and the length of the piece of code. It can be seen that with doubling the amount of variables in the fibo code the verification of the code generation takes nearly twice as much time. The sorting algorithms take longer due to the processing of more and complicated instructions.

Certificate Checking in the *Second Implementation*

The table in Figure 7.6 shows the time it takes to prove the code generation of different procedures correct. It shows the number of variables occurring in the procedures plus global variables used by it (counting each array element as a single variable). The length of the original intermediate language procedure (IL length) as well as the length of the generated MIPS code (TL length). In the last three columns the time it takes to check the proofs for the three different phases is shown. The *sort* procedures sort arrays from 1000 (*sort1*) up to 5000 (*sort1c*) elements. The *arith* procedures mostly contain arithmetic operations while the *arrays* procedures perform operations on differently sized arrays. With procedures reaching several hundred lines of code the time it takes to check the proofs is increasing faster than linear. This is due to the larger data structures which have to be handled during the proof process. Accesses to these structures grow linear with code size, however, since the structures themselves are growing linear, we end up with a time that is growing quadratic. A similar argument holds for the *variable mapping* in the *first phase*. We also proclaimed in Section 5.4 quadratic time behavior in the *second phase* since each proof for a single step lemma would grow linear with the size of the procedure due to the look-up of statements, instructions, variable, memory and program counter correspondences from list like data structures. This is confirmed through this table.

---

[1]Unlike the rest of this chapter the experiments for this table have been conducted on a Sun UltraSPARC III with 900 MHz.

[2]It computes the first 100, 200 Fibonacci numbers resp. and writes them into an array.

procedure	no. variables	IL length	TL length	phase1	phase2	phase3
sort1	1008	16	67	3m 17s	5s	2s
sort1a	2008	16	67	10m 28s	5s	2s
sort1b	3008	16	67	21m 29s	5s	2s
sort1c	4008	16	67	36m 15s	5s	2s
sort1d	5008	16	67	54m 50s	5s	2s
arith1	16	177	705	2s	38s	29s
arith2	18	353	1409	2s	1m 53s	1m 51s
arrays1	2030	520	2059	10m 34s	4m 25s	4m 21s
arrays2	2030	1030	4107	10m 34s	14m 47s	9m 32s

Figure 7.6: Checking Time for the *Second Implementation*

Apart from the different machines they are implemented on the *first implementation* and the *second implementation* are hard to compare in terms of time efficiency for the following reasons:

- The *first implementation* realizes only a subset of the instructions used in the *second implementation*.

- The handling of array out of bounds exceptions is done differently (cp. Sections 5.1 and 5.4.6).

- The optimizations performed on generated code are not exactly the same.

7.3.4 Speedup using Checkers and Explicit Proof Terms

The table in Figure 7.7 shows the time measured using the checker for the injectivity proof from Section 5.6 in the first phase. In addition to this we use explicit proof terms in the third phase. It can be seen that the first phase checker speeds up the verification of the first phase issues by a factor of more than 100. As mentioned in Section 5.4 apart from the injectivity proof other things are done in the first phase, too. Moreover, the parsing of the variable mapping is part of the *first phase*, too. Thus, the actual execution of the checker is even much faster than the measured factor of >100.

Due to an artifact in the Coq implementation the processing of the explicit proof term in the *third phase* is too slow and not linear. Nevertheless, for the given examples it outperforms the linear non proof term based implementation shown in Figure 7.6.

Using the General Checker

Further speedup can be achieved by using the checker for the *second phase*. Our most general checker implementation can verify 500 lines of intermediate language code in less than seven seconds. 2000 lines of intermediate code take slightly less than one minute. The non-linear increase of checking times is due to the longer look-up times in larger

procedure	no. variables	IL length	TL length	phase1	phase2	phase3
sort1	1008	16	67	3s	5s	1s
sort1a	2008	16	67	6s	5s	1s
sort1b	3008	16	67	10s	5s	1s
sort1c	4008	16	67	15s	5s	1s
sort1d	5008	16	67	22s	5s	1s
arith1	16	177	705	1s	38s	13s
arith2	18	353	1409	1s	1m 53s	46s
arrays1	2030	520	2059	5s	4m 25s	1m 34s
arrays2	2030	1030	4107	5s	14m 47s	6m 24s

Figure 7.7: Certificate Verification Time for the *Second Implementation* with Checker usage in the *First Phase* and explicit Proof Terms

structures used for e.g. procedure representations. It can be significantly reduced if we use search trees instead of list like structures.

7.3.5 Proof Checking for System Abstractions

It turned out that proving system abstractions correct is much easier than proving code generation correct. In fact we have to provide a simulation relation, but once this is done the proof scripts are very easy and often generic to many abstractions. All our verification case studies can be checked within a few seconds using the Isabelle/HOL theorem prover.

The good performance of checking system abstraction certificates might sound strange at a first glance, but consider the following facts:

- Systems that are to be abstracted are usually much smaller than typical programs. Large systems contain a few hundred variables and their transition behavior could be encoded in a few hundred lines of code. For a program this would be rather small.

- Systems contain no complicated language elements such as arrays or procedure calls.

- We only relate systems with other systems basically described in the same language. This is much easier than to relate an intermediate language to machine code.

- We only consider abstractions where one step in the concrete system corresponds to one step in the abstract system.

Our largest example abstractions contained amongst others 39 variables with infinite domains that where abstracted. Examined system representations had up to 2600 lines of Isabelle code. In some of these scenarios, model checking was not possible without abstractions. Thus, our technique bridges a gap in the verification process between a system model representation in a modeling environment (used e.g. for code generation) and an input representation for verification tools.

7.4 Framework Evaluation

Our framework has turned out to be general enough to capture the characteristics of code generation and system abstractions.

Certifying code generation and system abstractions have shown that the most important variable part in terms of semantics of the *Generic Correctness Criteria* family is the notion state correspondence. While this part is instantiated for code generation once and for all to ensure the same output traces, it is instantiated for each abstraction in system abstractions with a different predicate to ensure preservation of different properties. However, in code generation the simulation relation based on this state correspondence predicate is instantiated differently for each code generation run, too.

The predicates ensuring step correctness are only needed in code generation and only on a very top level to ensure that no more than one single output occurs during the merging of steps. We did not make use of an $n : m$ relation between steps in our work so far. Presumably the step correctness predicates would get more important in such a setting.

7.5 Some Concluding Remarks

We have shown that the use of different proving methodologies and theorem provers can change the time to check the certificates significantly. A time factor of more than 10000 can be found in such investigations. Coq 8.1 outperforms Isabelle 2005 as certificate checker in all our case studies where we used both theorem provers.

In general higher-order theorem proving is much more costly than using a specialized tool or a first order theorem prover. However, it is far more complicated – for some cases impossible – to formalize a distinct semantics and correctness criterion within such tools. Especially the Coq community, but in recent times also the Isabelle community have spent great efforts to make their higher-order theorem provers faster.

Few comparisons of higher-order theorem provers have been done. Most notable is the work by Griffioen and Huisman [GH98, Hui01] which compares PVS with Isabelle/HOL with respect to several different aspects. Moreover, the POPLMARK challenge [ABF+05] is an initiative to investigate in how far results in todays leading programming language papers can be formalized in higher-order theorem provers. These tasks are proposed as a kind of benchmark for higher-order theorem provers.

8 Conclusion

This chapter summarizes the main achievements of this thesis and presents ideas for future work.

We have introduced a framework for certifying translations and demonstrated its feasibility for a code generation phase and for use with system abstractions. We have achieved results in formalizing semantics and notions of correct translation. The most important result of this work is the construction of the certifying code generation phase and the solving of practical theorem proving problems.

Achievements in the Semantic Framework

Our introduced semantic framework captures trace based semantics. We regard the behavior of systems at run-time as our basis for a notion of correct compilation and are thus able to verify reactive and non terminating systems. Our framework is generic with respect to concrete semantic issues and notions of correctness. These may be instantiated for concrete application scenarios. Our run-time behavior based semantic framework is more advanced than most other classical approaches in compiler verification. These rather look at a final value to be returned by a compiled program and base their notion of translation correctness upon this. We have applied our framework to two application areas: code generation for a compiler and system abstractions. Therewith we have shown that it is adaptable to different scenarios. The framework is flexible enough to deal with shallow embedding as well as deep embedding of semantics into the theorem prover. We have demonstrated that our semantic framework can be adapted to work with two different higher-order theorem provers: Isabelle/HOL and Coq.

Achievements for Compiler (Run) Verification

In the area of code generation for compilers we have implemented several versions that can handle programs of realistic size. The used intermediate language is feasible to handle programs from large subsets of today's higher level programming languages. The formalization of the MIPS machine's semantics is done in an operational way imitating the behavior of the real machine. We succeeded in overcoming the bottleneck of the time consumed for certificate checking. We have presented various ideas and their implementations which made this possible. The proof generation within the compiler is well separated from the rest of the compiler. It turned out to be relatively small and could be written in an intuitive trial and error way meaning that whenever a proof did not succeed we could easily extend the certificate generator with adding additional cases. Furthermore, the certificate generator is surprisingly easy to maintain.

We have introduced checker predicates to speed up distinct sub-tasks of certificate checking. With the help of our checker predicates we were able to achieve further important speed gains. We have introduced an abstract operational semantics for use with such checkers. This semantics is especially beneficial for representing and comparing values automatically in a checker. We have proved this abstract checker semantics correct with respect to the original semantics. Checker predicates only have to be verified once and for all and are applicable out of an ordinary proof script. They are a promising technique for using higher-order theorem provers for tasks demanding high execution speeds.

Our implementation ensures the correctness of code generation runs without the need for algorithm verification. The trusted computing base is very small comprising only very small programs generating theorem prover representations of intermediate and target language, the theorem prover environment, the underlying hardware and operating system.

To our knowledge we are the first to present a working certifying code generation phase that ensures correctness based on an explicitly formalized notion of correctness.

Achievements for System Abstractions

By porting our certifying translations framework to system abstractions, we have introduced a methodology and its prototypical implementation to verify them. Our methodology closes the verification chain between systems that are too large to be model checked directly and thus have to be simplified. To our knowledge we are the first to present a methodology based on certifying translations that allows the verification of these system simplifications for use by a model checker. The implementation turned out to work quite fast and is able to deal with a large bunch of system abstractions comprising domain abstractions and cone of influence reduction. Since systems for use in model checkers are in general much smaller than typical programs written in a higher programming language, it turned out that system checks can be performed much faster and the formalizations are smaller.

Other Achievements

We used two different theorem provers: Isabelle/HOL 2005 and Coq 8.1. Both have their strength and weaknesses in certain areas. In this thesis we have compared some features especially with respect to checking the certificates of the code generation from the compiler. It turned out that Coq has some features – like a more native way of executing function definitions – that speed certificate checking considerably up.

Future Work

Future investigations concerning the semantic framework comprise its extension to non-deterministic systems and asynchronous system specifications.

Interesting topics concerning future work on certifying compilers comprise but is not limited to the following items:

- Investigate other compiler phases as well (cp. the work done by Marek Gawkowski on this; proposed in 2005/06 [PHG05, GBPH06]).

- Extend the involved languages with additional features.

- Consider a more complicated, optimizing code generation phase. Especially interesting is a n:m relation between intermediate language and target code. Our framework should be able to handle these features.

- Investigate how we can further extend the use of preproved checkers to speed certain parts of the certificate checking up. Our current work shows that such checkers can be hard to prove correct – harder than generating a non checker based proof. However, further work has to be done to find out in which situation this extra work pays off.

- With the techniques presented in this thesis we should be able to produce a certifying compiler for a small programming language like Java Card. Such a real live proof of our methodology is an important subject of future work, too.

In system abstractions important topics for future work are the consideration of larger systems and the port of our methodology to other case studies. It would be especially interesting to look at asynchronous and non-deterministic systems in system abstractions. Further future work comprises the use of different logics for system property specification. Regardless of Isabelle/HOL's good performance in system abstractions, further investigations considering Coq for checking the certificates are an important issue, too.

Apart from compilers and system abstractions other areas where certificate checking by higher-order theorem provers might be beneficial are also of great interest to the author of this thesis.

Bibliography

[ABF⁺05] B. Aydemir, A. Bohannon, M. Fairbairn, J. Foster, B. Pierce, P. Sewell, D. Vytiniotis, G. Washburn, S. Weirich, and S. Zdancewic. Mechanized Metatheory for the Masses: The POPLMARK Challenge. Proc. of. *Theorem Proving in Higher Order Logics: 18th International Conference, TPHOLs 2005, Oxford, UK, August 22-25, 2005*. LNCS. Springer-Verlag. 2005.

[App01] A. W. Appel. Foundational proof-carrying code. In *LICS '01: Proceedings of the 16th Annual IEEE Symposium on Logic in Computer Science*, page 247. IEEE Computer Society, Washington, DC, USA, 2001.

[App03] A. W. Appel. Foundational proof-carrying code. Proc. of. *Foundations of Intrusion Tolerant Systems, 2003 [Organically Assured and Survivable Information Systems]*, pages 25–34, 2003.

[ASSV07] R. Adler, I. Schaefer, T. Schüle, and E. Vecchi. From Model-Based Design to Formal Verification of Adaptive Embedded Systems . In *9th International Conference on Formal Engineering Methods (ICFEM 2007), Boca Raton, FL*, LNCS. Springer-Verlag, November 2007.

[BBF⁺92] B. Buth, K.-H. Buth, M. Fränzle, B. von Karger, Y. Lakhnech, H. Langmaack, and M. Müller-Olm. Provably correct compiler development and implementation. In *CC '92: Proceedings of the 4th International Conference on Compiler Construction*, pages 141–155. Springer-Verlag, 1992.

[BBLS93] S. Bensalem, A. Bouajjani, C. Loiseaux, and J. Sifakis. Property preserving simulations. In *CAV '92: Proceedings of the Fourth International Workshop on Computer Aided Verification*, pages 260–273. Springer-Verlag, 1993.

[BFG⁺05] C. Barrett, Y. Fang, B. Goldberg, Y. Hu, A. Pnueli, and L. Zuck. TVOC: A Translation Validator for Optimizing Compilers. In *CAV 2005*, volume 3576 of LNCS, pages 291–295. Springer-Verlag, 2005.

[BG04] J. O. Blech and S. Glesner. A Formal Correctness Proof for Code Generation from SSA Form in Isabelle/HOL. In *Proceedings der 3. Arbeitstagung Programmiersprachen (ATPS) auf der 34. Jahrestagung der Gesellschaft für Informatik*. Lecture Notes in Informatics, September 2004.

[BG08a] J. O. Blech and B. Grégoire. Certifying Code Generation Runs with Coq: A Tool Description. In *Proceedings of the 7th Workshop on Compiler Optimization meets Compiler Verification (COCV 2008), Budapest, Hungary*, ENTCS. April 2008.

[BG08b]   J. O. Blech and B. Grégoire. Certifying code generation with Coq. In *Proceedings of the 7th Workshop on Compiler Optimization meets Compiler Verification (COCV 2008), Budapest, Hungary*, ENTCS. April 2008.

[BGG05]   J. O. Blech, L. Gesellensetter, and S. Glesner. Formal Verification of Dead Code Elimination in Isabelle/HOL. In *Proceedings of the 3rd IEEE International Conference on Software Engineering and Formal Methods*, pages 200–209. IEEE, IEEE Computer Society Press, September 2005.

[BGL05]   J. O. Blech, S. Glesner, and J. Leitner. Formal Verification of Java Code Generation from UML Models. *Proceedings of the 3rd International Fujaba Days 2005: MDD in Practice*, 2005.

[BGLM05]   J. O. Blech, S. Glesner, J. Leitner, and S. Mülling. Optimizing Code Generation from SSA Form: A Comparison Between Two Formal Correctness Proofs in Isabelle/HOL. In *Proceedings of the COCV-Workshop (Compiler Optimization meets Compiler Verification), ETAPS 2005*, pages 33–51. ENTCS. Elsevier, April 2005.

[BK95]   M. Blum and S. Kannan. Designing programs that check their work. *Journal of the ACM*, 42(1):269–291, 1995.

[Ble07]   J. O. Blech. On certifying code generation. Technical Report 366/07, University of Kaiserslautern, November 2007.

[BPH07]   J. O. Blech and A. Poetzsch-Heffter. A certifying code generation phase. In *Proceedings of the 6th Workshop on Compiler Optimization meets Compiler Verification (COCV 2007), Braga, Portugal*, ENTCS. Elsevier, March 2007.

[BS03]   S. Berghofer and M. Strecker. Extracting a formally verified, fully executable compiler from a proof assistant. In *Proc. 2nd International Workshop on Compiler Optimization Meets Compiler Verification (COCV'2003)*, pages 33–50. ENTCS. Elsevier, 2003.

[BSPH07a] J. O. Blech, I. Schaefer, and A. Poetzsch-Heffter. On translation validation for system abstractions. Technical Report 361/07, University of Kaiserslautern, July 2007.

[BSPH07b] J. O. Blech, I. Schaefer, and A. Poetzsch-Heffter. Translation validation for system abstractions. In *7th Workshop on Runtime Verification (RV'07), Vancouver, Canada*. volumne 4839 of LNCS. Springer-Verlag, March 2007.

[Cas04]   P. P. Casteran. *Interactive Theorem Proving And Program Development: Coq'Art: the Calculus of Inductive Constructions*. Springer-Verlag, 2004.

[CC77]   P. Cousot and R. Cousot. Abstract interpretation: A unified lattice model for static analysis of programs by construction or approximation of fixpoints. In *Fourth Annual ACM Symnposium on Principles of Programming Languages*, pages 238–252. ACM Press, january 1977.

[CC79]   P. Cousot and R. Cousot. Systematic design of program analysis frameworks. pages 269–282. ACM Press, January 1979.

[CGL94]   E. M. Clarke, O. Grumberg, and D. E. Long. Model checking and abstraction. *ACM Transactions on Programming Languages and Systems*, 16(5):1512–1542, September 1994.

[CGP99]   E. M. Clarke, O. Grumberg, and D. A. Peled. *Model Checking*. MIT Press, 1999.

[Chu40]   A. Church. A formulation of the simple theory of types. *Journal of Symbolic Logic*, 5:56–68, 1940.

[Dav03]   M. Dave. Compiler verification: a bibliography. *ACM SIGSOFT Software Engineering Notes*, 28(6):2–2, 2003.

[DGG97]   D. Dams, R. Gerth, and O. Grumberg. Abstract interpretation of reactive systems. *ACM Trans. Program. Lang. Syst.*, 19(2):253–291, 1997.

[DHVG02]   A. Dold, F. W. v. Henke, V. Vialard, and W. Goerigk. A Mechanically Verified Compiling Specification for a Realistic Compiler. Ulmer Informatik-Berichte 02-03, Universität Ulm, Fakultät für Informatik, 2002.

[EFT96]   H. Ebbinghaus, J. Flum, and W. Thomas. *Mathematical Logic*. Springer-Verlag, 1996.

[FMO94]   M. Fränzle and M. Müller-Olm. Towards provably correct code generation for a hard real-time programming language. In *Proceedings of the Conference on Compiler Construction*, volume 786 of LNCS. Springer-Verlag, 1994.

[GB03]   S. Glesner and J. O. Blech. Classifying and formally verifying integer constant folding. In J. Knoop and W. Zimmermann, editors, *Proceedings of the Workshop COCV 2003: Compiler Optimization meets Compiler Verification*, volume 82. ETAPS Conferences, Warsaw, Poland. Vol. 82, No. 2, ENTCS. Elsevier, April 2003.

[GB06]   S. Glesner and J. O. Blech. Coalgebraic semantics for component systems. Architecting Systems with Trustworthy Components, volume 3938 of LNCS. Springer-Verlag, May 2006.

[GBPH06]   M. J. Gawkowski, J. O. Blech, and A. Poetzsch-Heffter. Certifying Compilers based on Formal Translation Contracts. Technical Report 355-06, University of Kaiserslautern, November 2006.

[GDG+96]   W. Goerigk, A. Dold, T. Gaul, G. Goos, A. Heberle, F. von Henke, U. Homann, H. Langmaack, H. Pfeifer, H. Ruess, et al. Compiler Correctness and Implementation Verification: The Verix Approach. *Proceedings of the Poster Session of CC*, 96:96–12, 1996.

143

[GGZ04]   S. Glesner, G. Goos, and W. Zimmermann. Verifix: Konstruktion und Architektur verifizierender Uebersetzer(Verifix: Construction and Architecture of Verifying Compilers). *it- Information Technology*, 46(5):265–276, 2004.

[GH98]   W. O. D. Griffioen and M. Huisman. A comparison of PVS and Isabelle/HOL. In J. Grundy and M. Newey, editors, *Proceedings of the 11th International Conference on Theorem Proving in Higher Order Logics*, Canberra, Australia, volume 1479 of LNCS, pages 123–142. Springer-Verlag, 1998. Also available as TR CSI-R9810, University of Nijmegen.

[Gla93]   R. van Glabbeek. The Linear Time-Branching Time Spectrum II. *Proceedings of the 4th International Conference on Concurrency Theory*, pages 66–81, 1993.

[Gla01]   R. v. Glabbeek. The linear time – branching time spectrum I; the semantics of concrete, sequential processes. In J. Bergstra, A. Ponse, and S. Smolka, editors, *Handbook of Process Algebra*, chapter 1, pages 3–99. Elsevier, 2001. Available at http://boole.stanford.edu/pub/spectrum1.ps.gz.

[GLB06]   S. Glesner, J. Leitner, and J. O. Blech. Coinductive verification of program optimizations using similarity relations. In *Proceedings of the Workshop Compiler Optimizations meets Compiler Verification (COCV 2006)*. 9th European Conferences on Theory and Practice of Software (ETAPS 2006), Vienna, Austria. ENTCS. Elsevier, April 2006.

[Gre03]   B. Grégoire. Compilation des termes de preuves: un (nouveau) mariage entre Coq et Ocaml. Thése de doctorat, Université Paris 7, école Polytechnique, France, December 2003.

[GZ99]   G. Goos and W. Zimmermann. Verification of compilers. In B. Steffen and E. R. Olderog, editors, *Correct System Design*, volume 1710 of LNCS, pages 201–230. Springer-Verlag, November 1999.

[Hoa69]   C. A. R. Hoare. An axiomatic basis for computer programming. *Communications of the ACM*, 12(10):576–583, 1969.

[Hui01]   M. Huisman. *Reasoning about Java Programs in Higher Order Logic using PVS and Isabelle*. Ph.D. thesis, Katholieke Universiteit Nijmegen, 2001. IPA Dissertation Series 2001-03, ISBN 90-9014440-4.

[Jam]   James Laurus. *SPIM - A MIPS32 Simulator*.

[JR97]   B. Jacobs and J. Rutten. A tutorial on (co) algebras and (co) induction. *EATCS Bulletin*, 62(222-259):3–13, 1997.

[KM]   M. Kaufmann and J. Moore. ACL2 homepage. *See URL http://www. cs.-utexas. edu/users/moore/acl2*.

[KN06]   G. Klein and T. Nipkow. A machine-checked model for a Java-like language, virtual machine and compiler. *ACM Transactions on Programming Languages and Systems*, 28(4):619–695, 2006.

[KR88]   B. Kernighan and D. Ritchie. *The C programming language*. Prentice-Hall, 1988.

[Ler98]   X. Leroy. The OCaml Programming Language, 1998.

[Ler06a]   X. Leroy. Coinductive big-step operational semantics. In *European Symposium on Programming (ESOP 2006)*, pages 54–68, volume 3924 of LNCS. Springer-Verlag, 2006.

[Ler06b]   X. Leroy. Formal certification of a compiler back-end or: programming a compiler with a proof assistant. In *POPL '06: Conference record of the 33rd ACM SIGPLAN-SIGACT symposium on Principles of programming languages*, pages 42–54. ACM Press, New York, NY, USA, 2006.

[LJWF02]   D. Lacey, N. D. Jones, E. V. Wyk, and C. C. Frederiksen. Proving correctness of compiler optimizations by temporal logic. *ACM SIGPLAN Notices*, 37(1):283–294, January 2002.

[LMRC05]   S. Lerner, T. Millstein, E. Rice, and C. Chambers. Automated soundness proofs for dataflow analyses and transformations via local rules. In *POPL '05: Proceedings of the 32nd ACM SIGPLAN-SIGACT symposium on Principles of programming languages*, pages 364–377. ACM Press, New York, NY, USA, 2005.

[LPP05]   D. Leinenbach, W. Paul, and E. Petrova. Towards the formal verification of a C0 compiler: Code generation and implementation correctness. In *Software Engineering and Formal Methods*. IEEE, IEEE Computer Society Press, September 2005.

[Mat05]   D. Matthews. Poly/ML, 2005.

[Mil71]   R. Milner. An algebraic definition of simulation between programs. In *Proc. of IJCAI*, pages 481–489. 1971.

[MN95]   O. Müller and T. Nipkow. Combining model checking and deduction for I/O-automata. In *Tools and Algorithms for the Construction and Analysis of Systems*, volume 1019 of LNCS, pages 1–16. Springer-Verlag, 1995.

[MN97]   O. Müller and T. Nipkow. Traces of I/O automata in Isabelle/HOLCF. In M. Bidoit and M. Dauchet, editors, *TAPSOFT'97: Theory and Practice of Software Development*, volume 1214 of LNCS, pages 580–594. Springer-Verlag, 1997.

[MNOS99]   O. Müller, T. Nipkow, D. von Oheimb, and O. Slotosch. HOLCF= HOL+ LCF. *Journal of Functional Programming*, 9(02):191–223, 1999.

[MO97]   M. Müller-Olm. Modular compiler verification(a refinement-algebraic approach advocating stepwise abstraction). Volume 1283 of LNCS. Springer-Verlag, 1997.

[Moo89]   J. Moore. A mechanically verified language implementation. *Journal of Automated Reasoning*, 5(4):461–492, 1989.

[Moo96]   J. Moore. *Piton: a mechanically verified assembly-level language*. Kluwer Academic Publishers Norwell, MA, USA, 1996.

[MP67]   J. McCarthy and J. Painter. Correctness of a compiler for arithmetic expressions. In J. T. Schwartz, editor, *Proceedings Symposium in Applied Mathematics, Vol. 19, Mathematical Aspects of Computer Science*, pages 33–41. American Mathematical Society, Providence, RI, 1967.

[MTH90]   R. Milner, M. Tofte, and R. Harper. *The Definition of Standard ML*. MIT press, 1990.

[Mül98]   O. Müller. I/O Automata and Beyond: Temporal Logic and Abstractions in Isabelle. In Proc. of *Theorem Proving in Higher Order Logics*, volume 1479 of LNCS. Springer-Verlag, 1998.

[Nec97]   G. C. Necula. Proof-carrying code. ACM Symposium on Principles of Programming Languages and Systems. Paris, France, January 1997.

[Nec98]   G. C. Necula. *Compiling with Proofs*. Ph.D. thesis, 1998.

[Nec00]   G. C. Necula. Translation validation for an optimizing compiler. In *Proceedings of the ACM SIGPLAN Conference on Programming Language Design and Implementation (PLDI)*, pages 83–95. 2000.

[Nip98]   T. Nipkow. Verified lexical analysis. In J. Grundy and M. Newey, editors, *Theorem Proving in Higher Order Logics*, volume 1479 of LNCS, pages 1–15. Springer-Verlag, 1998. Invited talk.

[Nip03]   T. Nipkow. Structured Proofs in Isar/HOL. In H. Geuvers and F. Wiedijk, editors, *Types for Proofs and Programs (TYPES 2002)*, volume 2646 of LNCS, pages 259–278. Springer-Verlag, 2003.

[NL98]   G. C. Necula and P. Lee. The design and implementation of a certifying compiler. In *Proceedings of the 1998 ACM SIGPLAN Conference on Programming Language Design and Implementation (PLDI)*, pages 333–344. 1998.

[NN92]   H. Nielson and F. Nielson. *Semantics with Applications: A Formal Introduction*. J. Wiley, 1992.

[NO98]   T. Nipkow and D. von Oheimb. Javalight is type-safe –definitely. In *POPL '98: Proceedings of the 25th ACM SIGPLAN-SIGACT symposium on Principles of programming languages*, pages 161–170. ACM, New York, NY, USA, 1998.

[NPW02]   T. Nipkow, L. C. Paulson, and M. Wenzel. *Isabelle/HOL — A Proof Assistant for Higher-Order Logic*, volume 2283 of LNCS. Springer-Verlag, 2002.

[ORS92]   S. Owre, J. Rushby, and N. Shankar. PVS: A Prototype Verification System. *Proceedings of the 11th International Conference on Automated Deduction: Automated Deduction*, pages 748–752, 1992.

[Pau93]   L. C. Paulson. Isabelle: The next 700 theorem provers. *The Computing Research Repository (CoRR)*, cs.LO/9301106, 1993.

[Pau94]   L. C. Paulson. *Isabelle: A Generic Theorem Prover*, volume 828 of LNCS. Springer-Verlag, 1994.

[Pau00]   L. C. Paulson. A Fixedpoint Approach to (Co) Inductive and (Co) Datatype Definitions. *Proof, Language, and Interaction: Essays in Honour of Robin Milner*, pages 187–211, 2000.

[PH98]   D. A. Patterson and J. L. Hennessy. *Computer organization and design (2nd ed.): the hardware/software interface*. Morgan Kaufmann Publishers Inc., San Francisco, CA, USA, 1998. ISBN 1-55860-428-6.

[PHG05]   A. Poetzsch-Heffter and M. J. Gawkowski. Towards proof generating compilers. *Electronic Notes in Theoretical Computer Science*, 132(1):37–51, 2005.

[Plo81]   G. D. Plotkin. A Structural Approach to Operational Semantics. Technical Report DAIMI FN-19, University of Aarhus, 1981.

[PSS98]   A. Pnueli, M. Siegel, and E. Singerman. Translation validation. In *Proceedings of TACAS*, volume 1384 of LNCS. Springer-Verlag. 1998.

[Rin99]   M. Rinard. Credible compilation. Technical Report MIT-LCS-TR-776, MIT Laboratory for Computer Science, March 1999.

[RM99]   M. Rinard and D. Marinov. Credible compilation with pointers. In *Proceedings of the FLoC Workshop on Run-Time Result Verification*. Trento, Italy, July 1999.

[RSW01]   J. Roy, C. Sun, and C. Wu. Tutorial: Open research compiler for itanium processor family (IPF). *Proc. of the 34th Annual Int'l Symp. on Microarchitecture. New York: ACM Press*, 2001.

[Sam75]   H. Samet. *Automatically Proving the Correctness of Translations Involving Optimized Code*. Ph.D. thesis, Computer Science Department, Stanford University, 1975.

[Sam76]   H. Samet. Compiler testing via symbolic interpretation. In *ACM '76: Proceedings of the annual conference*, pages 492–497. ACM, New York, NY, USA, 1976. doi:http://doi.acm.org/10.1145/800191.805648.

[Sha00a]   N. Shankar. Combining theorem proving and model checking through symbolic analysis. In *CONCUR'00: Concurrency Theory*, State College, PA,volume 1877 of LNCS, pages 1–16. Springer-Verlag, August 2000.

[Sha00b]   N. Shankar. Symbolic analysis of transition systems. In Y. Gurevich, P. W. Kutter, M. Odersky, and L. Thiele, editors, *Abstract State Machines: Theory and Applications (ASM 2000)*, Monte Verità, Switzerland, volume 1912 of LNCS, pages 287–302. Springer-Verlag, March 2000.

[SPH06]   I. Schaefer and A. Poetzsch-Heffter. Using Abstraction in Modular Verification of Synchronous Adaptive Systems. In *Proc. of "Workshop on Trustworthy Software", Saarbrücken, Germany, May 18-19*. 2006.

[Str02]   M. Strecker. Formal verification of a Java compiler in Isabelle. In *Proc. Conference on Automated Deduction (CADE)*, volume 2392 of LNCS, pages 63–77. Springer-Verlag, 2002.

[The07]   The Coq Development Team. *The Coq Proof Assistant Reference Manual – Version 8.1*, 2007. http://coq.inria.fr.

[TL08]   J.-B. Tristan and X. Leroy. Formal Verification of Translation Validators: A Case Study on Instruction Scheduling Optimizations. In *POPL '08: Conference record of the 35rd ACM SIGPLAN-SIGACT symposium on Principles of programming languages*. ACM Press, New York, NY, USA, 2008.

[WN04]   M. Wildmoser and T. Nipkow. Certifying machine code safety: Shallow versus deep embedding. In Proc. of *Theorem Proving in Higher Order Logics*, volume 3223 of LNCS. Springer-Verlag, 2004.

[WN05]   M. Wildmoser and T. Nipkow. Asserting bytecode safety. In M. Sagiv, editor, *Proceedings of the 14th European Symposium on Programming (ESOP 2005)*, volume 3444 of LNCS, pages 326–341. Springer-Verlag, 2005.

[Zim06]   W. Zimmermann. On the Correctness of Transformations in Compiler Back-Ends. In *Leveraging Applications of Formal Methods*, volume 4313 of LNCS. Springer-Verlag, 2006.

[ZPFG02]   L. Zuck, A. Pnueli, Y. Fang, and B. Goldberg. VOC: A translation validator for optimizing compilers. In proc. of *COCV'02, Compiler Optimization Meets Compiler Verification (Satellite Event of ETAPS 2002)*, volume 65 of ENTCS, pages 1–17. Elsevier, April 2002.

[ZPFG03]   L. Zuck, A. Pnueli, Y. Fang, and B. Goldberg. VOC: A methodology for the translation validation of optimizingcompilers. *Journal of Universal Computer Science*, 9(3):223–247, March 2003.

[ZPG+05]   L. Zuck, A. Pnueli, B. Goldberg, C. Barrett, Y. Fang, and Y. Hu. Translation and Run-Time Validation of Loop Transformations. *Formal Methods in System Design*, 27(3):335–360, 2005.

A Coq Formalization of Intermediate and MIPS language

This appendix contains a Coq formalization of our intermediate language and the MIPS language.

A.1 Intermediate Language

```
Require Import BinInt.
Require Import Zbool.
Require Import Bool.
Require Import List.
Require Import BinNat.
Require Import Nnat.

Inductive operand : Type :=
  | CONST : Z − > operand
  | VAR : Z − > operand
  | LOCVAR : Z − > operand
  | ARRAYC : (Z * Z) − > operand
  | ARRAYV : (Z * Z) − > operand
  | ARRAYVL : (Z * Z) − > operand.

Inductive loperand : Type :=
  | LVAR : Z − > loperand
  | LLOCVAR : Z − > loperand
  | LARRAYC : (Z * Z) − > loperand
  | LARRAYV : (Z * Z) − > loperand
  | LARRAYVL : (Z * Z) − > loperand.

Inductive ilstatement : Type :=
  | ILPLUS : (loperand * operand * operand) − > ilstatement
  | ILMINUS : (loperand * operand * operand) − > ilstatement
  | ILMULT : (loperand * operand * operand) − > ilstatement
  | ILSLT : (loperand * operand * operand) − > ilstatement
  | ILIFNEQ : (operand * N) − > ilstatement
  | ILPRINT : operand − > ilstatement
  | ILCALL1 : (loperand * N * operand) − > ilstatement
  | ILCALL2 : (loperand * N * operand * operand) − > ilstatement
  | ILRET1 : operand − > ilstatement
  | ILEXIT : ilstatement.

Inductive ilproc : Type :=
  | ILPROC : (list Z * list ilstatement) − > ilproc.

Inductive ilprog : Type :=
  | ILPROG : (N * list ilproc) − > ilprog.

Record ilstate : Set := mkilstate
termstate : N;
 output : list Z;
 pid : N;
 globvals : (Z * Z) − > Z;
 stack : list (N*N*(bool*Z)*(Z − > Z));
 pc : N
.

Definition evaloperand (op1: operand)(globvals:(Z*Z)− >Z) (locvals: Z− >Z): Z :=
match op1 with
  | CONST a => a
  | VAR a => globvals (a,Z0)
  | LOCVAR a => locvals a
  | ARRAYC (a,b) => globvals (a,b)
```

```
  | ARRAYV (a,b) => globvals (a,globvals(b,Z0))
  | ARRAYVL (a,b) => globvals (a,locvals b)
end.

Definition Ztupeq (x: (Z * Z)) (y: (Z * Z)) : bool :=
match x with (a,b) => match y with (a',b') => (andb (Zeq_bool a a') (Zeq_bool b b')) end end.

Definition evalloperandglobvals (lop: loperand)(val:Z)(globvals:(Z*Z)- >Z) (locvals: Z- >Z): ((Z*Z) - > Z) :=
match lop with
  | LVAR a => (fun (x:(Z*Z)) => if Ztupeq x (a,Z0) then val else globvals x)
  | LLOCVAR a => globvals
  | LARRAYC (a,b) => (fun (x:(Z*Z)) => if Ztupeq x (a,b) then val else globvals x)
  | LARRAYV (a,b) => (fun (x:(Z*Z)) => if Ztupeq x (a,globvals (b,Z0)) then val else globvals x)
  | LARRAYVL (a,b) => (fun (x:(Z*Z)) => if Ztupeq x (a,locvals b) then val else globvals x)
end.

Definition evalloperandlocvals (lop: loperand)(val:Z)(globvals:(Z*Z)- >Z) (locvals: Z- >Z): (Z - > Z) :=
match lop with
  | LVAR a => locvals
  | LLOCVAR a => (fun (x:Z) => if Zeq_bool x a then val else locvals x)
  | LARRAYC (a,b) => locvals
  | LARRAYV (a,b) => locvals
  | LARRAYVL (a,b) => locvals
end.


Definition ilnext (prog: ilprog) (state: ilstate) :=
match (prog) with | ILPROG (startpid,proclist) =>
match (nth (nat_of_N state.(pid)) proclist (ILPROC (nil,nil)) ) with | ILPROC(paramnames,code) =>
match (nth (nat_of_N state.(pc)) code ILEXIT) with
  | ILPLUS (lop,op1,op2) =>
  match state.(stack) with
    | nil => mkilstate 5 state.(output) state.(pid) state.(globvals) state.(stack) state.(pc)
    | (retpid,retpc,retvar,locvals)::stack' =>
      mkilstate
        0
        state.(output)
        state.(pid)
        (evalloperandglobvals lop (Zplus (evaloperand op1 state.(globvals) locvals)
                                          (evaloperand op2 state.(globvals) locvals))
           state.(globvals) locvals)
        ((retpid,retpc,retvar,
          (evalloperandlocvals lop (Zplus
            (evaloperand op1 state.(globvals) locvals)
            (evaloperand op2 state.(globvals) locvals)) state.(globvals) locvals))::stack')
        (state.(pc)+1)
  end
  | ILMINUS (lop,op1,op2) =>
  match state.(stack) with
    | nil => mkilstate 5 state.(output) state.(pid) state.(globvals) state.(stack) state.(pc)
    | (retpid,retpc,retvar,locvals)::stack' =>
      mkilstate
        0
        state.(output)
        state.(pid)
        (evalloperandglobvals lop (Zminus (evaloperand op1 state.(globvals) locvals)
                                           (evaloperand op2 state.(globvals) locvals))
           state.(globvals) locvals)
        ((retpid,retpc,retvar,
          (evalloperandlocvals lop (Zminus
            (evaloperand op1 state.(globvals) locvals)
            (evaloperand op2 state.(globvals) locvals)) state.(globvals) locvals))::stack')
        (state.(pc)+1)
  end
  | ILMULT (lop,op1,op2) =>
  match state.(stack) with
    | nil => mkilstate 5 state.(output) state.(pid) state.(globvals) state.(stack) state.(pc)
    | (retpid,retpc,retvar,locvals)::stack' =>
      mkilstate
        0
        state.(output)
        state.(pid)
        (evalloperandglobvals lop (Zmult (evaloperand op1 state.(globvals) locvals)
                                          (evaloperand op2 state.(globvals) locvals))
           state.(globvals) locvals)
        ((retpid,retpc,retvar,
          (evalloperandlocvals lop (Zmult
            (evaloperand op1 state.(globvals) locvals)
            (evaloperand op2 state.(globvals) locvals)) state.(globvals) locvals))::stack')
        (state.(pc)+1)
  end
  | ILSLT (lop,op1,op2) =>
  match state.(stack) with
    | nil => mkilstate 5 state.(output) state.(pid) state.(globvals) state.(stack) state.(pc)
```

```
          | (retpid,retpc,retvar,locvals)::stack' =>
          mkilstate
            0
            state.(output)
            state.(pid)
            (evalloperandglobvals lop (if (Zlt_bool (evaloperand op1 state.(globvals) locvals)
                                                (evaloperand op2 state.(globvals) locvals))
                            then 1 else 0 )
              state.(globvals) locvals)
            ((retpid,retpc,retvar,
               (evalloperandlocvals lop (if (Zlt_bool
                   (evaloperand op1 state.(globvals) locvals)
                   (evaloperand op2 state.(globvals) locvals)) then 1 else 0 ) state.(globvals) locvals))::stack')
            (state.(pc)+1)
end
| ILIFNEQ (op1,t) =>
match state.(stack) with
  | nil => mkilstate 5 state.(output) state.(pid) state.(globvals) state.(stack) state.(pc)
  | (retpid,retpc,retvar,locvals)::stack' =>
    mkilstate
      0
      state.(output)
      state.(pid)
      state.(globvals)
      state.(stack)
      (if Zeq_bool (evaloperand op1 state.(globvals) locvals) Z0 then state.(pc) + 1 else t)
end
| ILPRINT (op1) =>
match state.(stack) with
  | nil => mkilstate 5 state.(output) state.(pid) state.(globvals) state.(stack) state.(pc)
  | (retpid,retpc,retvar,locvals)::stack' =>
    mkilstate
      0
      ((evaloperand op1 state.(globvals) locvals) ::state.(output))
      state.(pid)
      state.(globvals)
      state.(stack)
      (state.(pc)+1)
end
| ILCALL1 (lop,m,par1) =>
match state.(stack) with
  | nil => mkilstate 5 state.(output) state.(pid) state.(globvals) state.(stack) state.(pc)
  | (retpid,retpc,retvar,locvals)::stack' =>
    match (nth (nat_of_N m) proclist (ILPROC (nil,nil)) ) with | ILPROC(paramnames,code) =>
    match lop,par1 with
    | LVAR a,VAR b =>
      mkilstate
        3
        state.(output)
        m
        state.(globvals)
        ( (state.(pid),(state.(pc)+1)%N,(false,a),
            (fun (x : Z) => if Zeq_bool x (nth 0 paramnames (0%Z)) then state.(globvals) (b,0%Z) else (0%Z) ) )::
          (state.(stack)))
        (0%N)
    | LVAR a,LOCVAR b =>
      mkilstate
        3
        state.(output)
        m
        state.(globvals)
        ( (state.(pid),(state.(pc)+1)%N,(false,a),
            (fun (x : Z) => if Zeq_bool x (nth 0 paramnames (0%Z)) then locvals b else (0%Z) ) )::
          (state.(stack)))
        (0%N)
    | LLOCVAR a,VAR b =>
      mkilstate
        3
        state.(output)
        m
        state.(globvals)
        ( (state.(pid),(state.(pc)+1)%N,(true,a),
            (fun (x : Z) => if Zeq_bool x (nth 0 paramnames (0%Z)) then state.(globvals) (b,0%Z) else (0%Z) ) )::
          (state.(stack)))
        (0%N)
    | LLOCVAR a,LOCVAR b =>
      mkilstate
        3
        state.(output)
        m
        state.(globvals)
        ( (state.(pid),(state.(pc)+1)%N,(true,a),
            (fun (x : Z) => if Zeq_bool x (nth 0 paramnames (0%Z)) then locvals b else (0%Z) ) )::
          (state.(stack)))
```

```
          (0%N)
| _,_ => mkilstate 5 state.(output) state.(pid) state.(globvals) state.(stack) state.(pc)
     end
   end
 end
| ILCALL2 (lop,m,par1,par2) =>
match state.(stack) with
 | nil => mkilstate 5 state.(output) state.(pid) state.(globvals) state.(stack) state.(pc)
 | (retpid,retpc,retvar,locvals)::stack' =>
 match (nth (nat_of_N m) proclist (ILPROC (nil,nil)) ) with | ILPROC(paramnames,code) =>
 match lop,par1,par2 with
 | LVAR a,VAR b,VAR c =>
  mkilstate
   3
   state.(output)
   m
   state.(globvals)
   ( (state.(pid),(state.(pc)+1)%N,(false,a),
      (fun (x : Z) => if Zeq_bool x (nth 0 paramnames (0%Z)) then state.(globvals) (b,0%Z) else
              if Zeq_bool x (nth 1 paramnames (0%Z)) then state.(globvals) (c,0%Z) else (0%Z) ) )::
      (state.(stack)))
   (0%N)
 | LVAR a,LOCVAR b,VAR c =>
  mkilstate
   3
   state.(output)
   m
   state.(globvals)
   ( (state.(pid),(state.(pc)+1)%N,(false,a),
      (fun (x : Z) => if Zeq_bool x (nth 0 paramnames (0%Z)) then locvals b else
              if Zeq_bool x (nth 1 paramnames (0%Z)) then state.(globvals) (c,0%Z) else (0%Z) ) )::
      (state.(stack)))
   (0%N)
 | LLOCVAR a,VAR b,VAR c =>
  mkilstate
   3
   state.(output)
   m
   state.(globvals)
   ( (state.(pid),(state.(pc)+1)%N,(true,a),
      (fun (x : Z) => if Zeq_bool x (nth 0 paramnames (0%Z)) then state.(globvals) (b,0%Z) else
              if Zeq_bool x (nth 1 paramnames (0%Z)) then state.(globvals) (c,0%Z) else (0%Z) ) )::
      (state.(stack)))
   (0%N)
 | LLOCVAR a,LOCVAR b,VAR c =>
  mkilstate
   3
   state.(output)
   m
   state.(globvals)
   ( (state.(pid),(state.(pc)+1)%N,(true,a),
      (fun (x : Z) => if Zeq_bool x (nth 0 paramnames (0%Z)) then locvals b else
              if Zeq_bool x (nth 1 paramnames (0%Z)) then state.(globvals) (c,0%Z) else (0%Z) ) )::
      (state.(stack)))
   (0%N)
 | LVAR a,VAR b,LOCVAR c =>
  mkilstate
   3
   state.(output)
   m
   state.(globvals)
   ( (state.(pid),(state.(pc)+1)%N,(false,a),
      (fun (x : Z) => if Zeq_bool x (nth 0 paramnames (0%Z)) then state.(globvals) (b,0%Z) else
              if Zeq_bool x (nth 1 paramnames (0%Z)) then locvals c else (0%Z) ) )::
      (state.(stack)))
   (0%N)
 | LVAR a,LOCVAR b,LOCVAR c =>
  mkilstate
   3
   state.(output)
   m
   state.(globvals)
   ( (state.(pid),(state.(pc)+1)%N,(false,a),
      (fun (x : Z) => if Zeq_bool x (nth 0 paramnames (0%Z)) then locvals b else
              if Zeq_bool x (nth 1 paramnames (0%Z)) then locvals c else (0%Z) ) )::
      (state.(stack)))
   (0%N)
 | LLOCVAR a,VAR b, LOCVAR c =>
  mkilstate
   3
   state.(output)
   m
   state.(globvals)
   ( (state.(pid),(state.(pc)+1)%N,(true,a),
```

154

```
                (fun (x : Z) => if Zeq_bool x (nth 0 paramnames (0%Z)) then state.(globvals) (b,0%Z) else
                            if Zeq_bool x (nth 1 paramnames (0%Z)) then locvals c else (0%Z) ) )::
              (state.(stack)))
            (0%N)
      | LLOCVAR a,LOCVAR b, LOCVAR c =>
        mkilstate
          3
          state.(output)
          m
          state.(globvals)
          ( (state.(pid),(state.(pc)+1)%N,(true,a),
              (fun (x : Z) => if Zeq_bool x (nth 0 paramnames (0%Z)) then locvals b else
                            if Zeq_bool x (nth 1 paramnames (0%Z)) then locvals c else (0%Z) ) )::
              (state.(stack)))
            (0%N)
      | _,_ => mkilstate 5 state.(output) state.(pid) state.(globvals) state.(stack) state.(pc)
      end
    end
  end
| ILRET1 (par1) =>
  match state.(stack) with
    | nil => mkilstate 5 state.(output) state.(pid) state.(globvals) state.(stack) state.(pc)
    | (retpid,retpc,(retloc,retvar),locvals)::stack' =>
    match stack' with
    | nil => mkilstate 5 state.(output) state.(pid) state.(globvals) state.(stack) state.(pc)
    | (retpid',retpc',retvar',locvals')::stack'' =>
    match retloc,par1 with
    | true, LOCVAR a =>
      mkilstate
        4
        state.(output)
        state.(pid)
        state.(globvals)
        ((retpid',retpc',retvar',(fun (x : Z) => if Zeq_bool x retvar then locvals a else locvals' x))::stack'')
        retpc
    | false, LOCVAR a =>
      mkilstate
        4
        state.(output)
        state.(pid)
        (fun (x : Z*Z) => (if Ztupeq x (retvar,0%Z) then locvals a else state.(globvals) x))
        ((retpid',retpc',retvar',locvals')::stack'')
        retpc
    | _,_ => mkilstate 5 state.(output) state.(pid) state.(globvals) state.(stack) state.(pc)
    end
    end
  end
| ILEXIT =>
  mkilstate
    1
    state.(output)
    state.(pid)
    state.(globvals)
    state.(stack)
    (state.(pc))
end
end
end.
```

A.2 MIPS language

```
Require Import BinInt.
Require Import List.
Require Import Zbool.
Require Import BinNat.
Require Import Nnat.

Open Local Scope N_scope.

Inductive tlstatement : Type :=
```

```
| TLADD : (Z * Z * Z) − > tlstatement
| TLADDC : (Z * Z * Z) − > tlstatement
| TLADD0C : (Z * Z) − > tlstatement
| TLSUB : (Z * Z * Z) − > tlstatement
| TLSUBC : (Z * Z * Z) − > tlstatement
| TLMULT : (Z * Z * Z) − > tlstatement
| TLSLT : (Z * Z * Z) − > tlstatement
| TLSHL2 : Z − > tlstatement
| TLLOAD : (Z * Z) − > tlstatement
| TLLOADC : (Z * Z) − > tlstatement
| TLLOADCSTACK : (Z * Z) − > tlstatement (*+stackpointer*)
| TLSTORE : (Z * Z) − > tlstatement
| TLSTOREC : (Z * Z) − > tlstatement
| TLSTORECSTACK : (Z * Z) − > tlstatement (*+stackpointer*)
| TLBNEQZ : (Z * N) − > tlstatement
| TLPRINT : Z − > tlstatement
| TLCALL1 : (Z * N * Z) − > tlstatement
| TLCALL2 : (Z * N * Z * Z) − > tlstatement
| TLRET1 : Z − > tlstatement
| TLEXIT : tlstatement.

Record tlstate : Set := mktlstate
tltermstate : N;
 tloutput : list Z;
 regs : Z − > Z;
 mem : Z − > Z;
 tlpc : N
 .

Definition tlnextterm (instruction: tlstatement)  :=
match (instruction) with
  | TLADD (lop,op1,op2) => 0
  | TLADDC (lop,op1,op2) => 0
  | TLADD0C (lop,op1) => 0
  | TLSUB (lop,op1,op2) => 0
  | TLSUBC (lop,op1,op2) => 0
  | TLMULT (lop,op1,op2) => 0
  | TLSLT (lop,op1,op2) => 0
  | TLSHL2 (lop) => 0
  | TLLOAD (lop,op1) => 0
  | TLLOADC (lop,op1) => 0
  | TLLOADCSTACK (lop,op1) => 0
  | TLSTORE (lop,op1) => 0
  | TLSTOREC (lop,op1) => 0
  | TLSTORECSTACK (lop,op1) => 0
  | TLBNEQZ  (lop,t) => 0
  | TLPRINT (lop) => 0
  | TLCALL1 (lop,p,op1) => 3
  | TLCALL2 (lop,p,op1,op2) => 3
  | TLRET1 (op1) => 4
  | TLEXIT => 1
end.

Definition tlnextoutput (instruction: tlstatement) (regs: Z − > Z) :=
```

```
match (instruction) with
  | TLADD (lop,op1,op2) => nil
  | TLADDC (lop,op1,op2) => nil
  | TLADD0C (lop,op1) => nil
  | TLSUB (lop,op1,op2) => nil
  | TLSUBC (lop,op1,op2) => nil
  | TLMULT (lop,op1,op2) => nil
  | TLSLT (lop,op1,op2) => nil
  | TLSHL2 (lop) => nil
  | TLLOAD (lop,op1) => nil
  | TLLOADC (lop,op1) => nil
  | TLLOADCSTACK (lop,op1) => nil
  | TLSTORE (lop,op1) => nil
  | TLSTOREC (lop,op1) => nil
  | TLSTORECSTACK (lop,op1) => nil
  | TLBNEQZ  (lop,t) => nil
  | TLPRINT (lop) => cons (regs lop ) nil
  | TLCALL1 (lop,p,op1) => nil
  | TLCALL2 (lop,p,op1,op2) => nil
  | TLRET1 (op1) => nil
  | TLEXIT => nil
end.


Definition tlnextregs (instruction:tlstatement) (regs: Z − > Z) (mem:Z − > Z) :=
match (instruction) with
  | TLADD (lop,op1,op2) =>(fun x:Z => if Zeq_bool x lop then Zplus (regs op1) (regs op2) else regs x)
  | TLADDC (lop,op1,op2) => (fun x:Z => if Zeq_bool x lop then Zplus (regs op1)  op2 else regs x)
  | TLADD0C (lop,op1) => (fun x:Z => if Zeq_bool x lop then  op1 else regs x)
  | TLSUB (lop,op1,op2) =>  (fun x:Z => if Zeq_bool x lop then Zminus (regs op1) (regs op2) else regs x)
  | TLSUBC (lop,op1,op2) => (fun x:Z => if Zeq_bool x lop then Zminus (regs op1)  op2 else regs x)
  | TLMULT (lop,op1,op2) =>  (fun x:Z => if Zeq_bool x lop then Zmult (regs op1) (regs op2) else regs x)
  | TLSLT (lop,op1,op2) =>
     (fun x:Z => if Zeq_bool x lop then (if (Zlt_bool (regs op1) (regs op2)) then 1%Z else 0%Z) else regs x)
  | TLSHL2 (lop) => (fun x:Z => if Zeq_bool x lop then Zmult (regs lop) (Zpos (xO (xO (xH)))) else regs x)
  | TLLOAD (lop,op1) => (fun x:Z => if Zeq_bool x lop then  (mem (regs op1))   else regs x)
  | TLLOADC (lop,op1) => (fun x:Z => if Zeq_bool x lop then  (mem  op1)   else regs x)
  | TLLOADCSTACK (lop,op1) => (fun x:Z => if Zeq_bool x lop then  (mem  op1)   else regs x)
  | TLSTORE (lop,op1) => regs
  | TLSTOREC (lop,op1) => regs
  | TLSTORECSTACK (lop,op1) => regs
  | TLBNEQZ  (lop,t) => regs
  | TLPRINT (lop) => regs
  | TLCALL1 (lop,p,op1) => ... regs ... (*adaptation to system's call conventions*)
  | TLCALL2 (lop,p,op1,op2) => ... regs ... (*adaptation to system's call convention*)
  | TLRET1 (op1) => ... regs ... (*adaptation to system's call convention*)
  | TLEXIT => regs
end.

Definition tlnextmem (instruction:tlstatement) (regs: Z − > Z) (mem:Z − > Z) :=
match (instruction) with
  | TLADD (lop,op1,op2) => mem
  | TLADDC (lop,op1,op2) => mem
  | TLADD0C (lop,op1) => mem
```

```
  | TLSUB (lop,op1,op2) => mem
  | TLSUBC (lop,op1,op2) => mem
  | TLMULT (lop,op1,op2) => mem
  | TLSLT (lop,op1,op2) => mem
  | TLSHL2 (lop) => mem
  | TLLOAD (lop,op1) => mem
  | TLLOADC (lop,op1) => mem
  | TLLOADCSTACK (lop,op1) => mem
  | TLSTORE (lop,op1) => (fun x:Z => if Zeq_bool x (regs op1) then  regs lop   else  mem x)
  | TLSTOREC (lop,op1) => (fun x:Z => if Zeq_bool x op1 then  regs lop   else  mem x)
  | TLSTORECSTACK (lop,op1) => (fun x:Z => if Zeq_bool x op1 then  regs lop   else  mem x)
  | TLBNEQZ  (lop,t) => mem
  | TLPRINT (lop) => mem
  | TLCALL1 (lop,p,op1) => ... mem ... (*adaptation to calling conventions*)
  | TLCALL2 (lop,p,op1,op2) => ... mem ... (*adaptation to calling conventions*)
  | TLRET1 (op1) => ... mem ... (*adaptation to calling conventions*)
  | TLEXIT => mem
end.

Definition tlnextpc (instruction:tlstatement) (regs:Z − > Z) (tlpc:N) :=
match instruction with
  | TLADD (lop,op1,op2) => tlpc+1
  | TLADDC (lop,op1,op2) => tlpc+1
  | TLADD0C (lop,op1) => tlpc+1
  | TLSUB (lop,op1,op2) => tlpc+1
  | TLSUBC (lop,op1,op2) => tlpc+1
  | TLMULT (lop,op1,op2) => tlpc+1
  | TLSLT (lop,op1,op2) => tlpc+1
  | TLSHL2 (lop) => tlpc+1
  | TLLOAD (lop,op1) => tlpc+1
  | TLLOADC (lop,op1) => tlpc+1
  | TLLOADCSTACK (lop,op1) => tlpc+1
  | TLSTORE (lop,op1) => tlpc+1
  | TLSTOREC (lop,op1) => tlpc+1
  | TLSTORECSTACK (lop,op1) => tlpc+1
  | TLBNEQZ  (lop,t) =>  (if Zeq_bool (regs lop) Z0 then tlpc + 1 else t)
  | TLPRINT (lop) => tlpc+1
  | TLCALL1 (lop,p,op1) => tlpc+1
  | TLCALL2 (lop,p,op1,op2) => tlpc+1
  | TLRET1 (op1) => 0
  | TLEXIT => tlpc
end.


Definition tlnext  (prog: list tlstatement) (state: tlstate) :=
let
inst := (nth (nat_of_N state.(tlpc)) prog TLEXIT) in let
tlpc := state.(tlpc) in let
regs := state.(regs) in let
mem := state.(mem) in

mktlstate
   (tlnextterm inst)
   ( (state.(tloutput))++ (tlnextoutput inst regs))
```

```
    (tlnextregs inst regs mem)
    (tlnextmem inst regs mem)
    (tlnextpc inst regs tlpc).


Fixpoint tlnextn  (prog: list tlstatement) (state: tlstate) (n:nat) struct n:=
match n with
  | 0%nat => state
  | S n => tlnextn prog (tlnext prog state) n
end.
```

B Correctness Formalization in Coq

This appendix shows a Coq formalization of the top level correctness condition we put upon a code generation run for a procedure.

```
Require Import List.
Require Import NArith.
Require Import ZArith.
Require Import Bool.
Require Import ListSet.

Require Import "illang".
Require Import "tllang".

Variable P_il: ilprog.
Variable P_mips : list tlstatement.

(*For one procedure: convention: global variables have positive, local variables have negative identifiers.*)
Variable Vars: set (Z * Z).
Variable MemMap : (Z * Z) − > Z.
Variable PCrel : list (N * N).

Variable createSimRel : set (Z*Z) − > ((Z * Z) − > Z) − > (list (N * N)) − > (ilstate − > tlstate − > bool).

Variable steplength: tlstate − > (list (N * N)) − > nat.

Definition SimRel : ilstate − > tlstate − > bool :=
createSimRel Vars MemMap PCrel.


Lemma SimRelCorrect :
    forall (s_il : ilstate) (s_mips : tlstate), Is_true (SimRel s_il s_mips) − > (s_il.(output)) = (s_mips.(tloutput)).


(*For procedures with call parameters: parameters have to be universally quantified*)
Lemma sim0:
forall stack,
Is_truc
(SimRel
    (mkilstate
        0
        nil
        1
        (fun x => 0%Z)
        ((0%N,0%N,(false,0%Z),(fun (x:Z) => 0%Z))::stack)
```

```
      0)
   (mktlstate
      0
      nil
      (fun x => 0%Z)
      (fun x => 0%Z)
      0)
).


Lemma simstep:
forall s_il s_mips s'_il s'_mips,
s'_il = ilnext P_il s_il — >
s'_mips = tlnextn P_mips s_mips (steplength s_mips PCrel) — >
Is_true (SimRel s_il s_mips) — >
Is_true (SimRel s'_il s'_mips).
```

C Generation of Code Generation Certificates

In this appendix we present the templates used to generate the proof code for the second phase of our code generation. Most templates are very similar and are in fact encoded in a more compact form in our certificate generator compared to the presentation in this appendix. We omit the presentation of the most trivial templates that are very similar to other ones but rather mention how they are created in a side note.

C.1 Variable-Assignment Rules

IL:
  ASSIGN_V (a,PLUS(ARVAR (c,d),ARVAR (e,f)))
MIPS:
  -
Priority: 10
ProofCode:
evaluate succeeding IL state representation
evaluate succeeding MIPS state representation
split_goal_into_subgoals:
1. memorycorrespondence:
    assert (varvals (v, i) = mem (MemMap (v, i))) for all valid v and i
       prove that a is a valid variable
       prove that c is a valid array
       prove that e is a valid array
       prove or use that d is a valid index
         prove or use that f is a valid index
    use injectivity + assertion to rewrite variable accesses with
     memory accesses in variable store representation
    qed
2. programcounter correspondence:
    look up whether program counters correspond to each other
    qed

IL:
  ASSIGN_V (a,PLUS(ARVAR (c,d),ARCONST (e,f)))
MIPS:
  -
Priority: 10
ProofCode:
evaluate succeeding IL state representation
evaluate succeeding MIPS state representation

split_goal_into_subgoals:
1. *memorycorrespondence:*
   assert (*varvals (v, i)* = *mem (MemMap (v, i)))* for all valid v and i
      prove that a is a valid variable
      prove that c is a valid array
      prove that e is a valid array
      prove or use that d is a valid index
      prove or use that f is a valid index
   use injectivity + assertion to rewrite variable accesses with
   memory accesses in variable store representation
   qed
2. *programcounter correspondence:*
   look up whether program counters correspond to each other
   qed

IL:
  ASSIGN_V (a,PLUS(ARVAR (c,d),VAR e))
MIPS:

  -

Priority: 10
ProofCode:
evaluate succeeding IL state representation
evaluate succeeding MIPS state representation
split_goal_into_subgoals:
1. *memorycorrespondence:*
   assert (*varvals (v, i)* = *mem (MemMap (v, i)))* for all valid v and i
      prove that a is a valid variable
      prove that c is a valid array
      prove or use that d is a valid index
      prove that e is a valid variable
   use injectivity + assertion to rewrite variable accesses with
   memory accesses in variable store representation
   qed
2. *programcounter correspondence:*
   look up whether program counters correspond to each other
   qed

IL:
  ASSIGN_V (a,PLUS(ARVAR (c,d),e))
MIPS:

  -

Priority: 9
ProofCode:
evaluate succeeding IL state representation
evaluate succeeding MIPS state representation
split_goal_into_subgoals:
1. *memorycorrespondence:*
   assert (*varvals (v, i)* = *mem (MemMap (v, i)))* for all valid v and i
      prove that a is a valid variable
      prove that c is a valid array
      prove or use that d is a valid index
   use injectivity + assertion to rewrite variable accesses with

164

memory accesses in variable store representation
qed

2. programcounter correspondence:
look up whether program counters correspond to each other
qed

IL:
  ASSIGN_V (a,PLUS(ARCONST (c,d),ARVAR (e,f)))
MIPS:
  -

Priority: 10
ProofCode:
evaluate succeeding IL state representation
evaluate succeeding MIPS state representation
split_goal_into_subgoals:
1. *memorycorrespondence:*
   assert (varvals (v, i) = mem (MemMap (v, i))) for all valid v and i
      prove that a is a valid variable
      prove that c is a valid array
      prove that e is a valid array
      prove or use that d is a valid index
      prove or use that f is a valid index
   use injectivity + assertion to rewrite variable accesses with
    memory accesses in variable store representation
   qed
2. *programcounter correspondence:*
   look up whether program counters correspond to each other
   qed

IL:
  ASSIGN_V (a,PLUS(ARCONST (c,d),ARCONST (e,f)))
MIPS:
  -

Priority: 10
ProofCode:
evaluate succeeding IL state representation
evaluate succeeding MIPS state representation
split_goal_into_subgoals:
1. *memorycorrespondence:*
   assert (varvals (v, i) = mem (MemMap (v, i))) for all valid v and i
      prove that a is a valid variable
      prove that c is a valid array
      prove that c is a valid array
      prove or use that d is a valid index
      prove or use that f is a valid index
   use injectivity + assertion to rewrite variable accesses with
    memory accesses in variable store representation
   qed
2. *programcounter correspondence:*
   look up whether program counters correspond to each other
   qed

IL:
  ASSIGN_V (a,PLUS(ARCONST (c,d),VAR e))
MIPS:

-

Priority: 10
ProofCode:
evaluate succeeding IL state representation
evaluate succeeding MIPS state representation
split_goal_into_subgoals:
1. *memorycorrespondence:*
  assert (varvals (v, i) = mem (MemMap (v, i))) for all valid v and i
    prove that a is a valid variable
    prove that c is a valid array
    prove or use that d is a valid index
    prove that e is a valid variable
  use injectivity + assertion to rewrite variable accesses with
   memory accesses in variable store representation
  qed
2. *programcounter correspondence:*
  look up whether program counters correspond to each other
  qed

IL:
  ASSIGN_V (a,PLUS(ARCONST (c,d),e))
MIPS:

-

Priority: 9
ProofCode:
evaluate succeeding IL state representation
evaluate succeeding MIPS state representation
split_goal_into_subgoals:
1. *memorycorrespondence:*
  assert (varvals (v, i) = mem (MemMap (v, i))) for all valid v and i
    prove that a is a valid variable
    prove that c is a valid array
    prove or use that d is a valid index
  use injectivity + assertion to rewrite variable accesses with
   memory accesses in variable store representation
  qed
2. *programcounter correspondence:*
  look up whether program counters correspond to each other
  qed

IL:
  ASSIGN_V (a,PLUS(VAR c,ARVAR (e,f)))
MIPS:

-

Priority: 10
ProofCode:
evaluate succeeding IL state representation
evaluate succeeding MIPS state representation

split_goal_into_subgoals:
1. memorycorrespondence:
  assert (varvals (v, i) = mem (MemMap (v, i))) for all valid v and i
    prove that a is a valid variable
    prove that c is a valid variable
    prove that e is a valid array
    prove or use that f is a valid index
  use injectivity + assertion to rewrite variable accesses with
   memory accesses in variable store representation
  qed
2. programcounter correspondence:
  look up whether program counters correspond to each other
  qed

IL:
  ASSIGN_V (a,PLUS(VAR c,ARCONST (e,f)))
MIPS:

  -

Priority: 10
ProofCode:
evaluate succeeding IL state representation
evaluate succeeding MIPS state representation
split_goal_into_subgoals:
1. memorycorrespondence:
  assert (varvals (v, i) = mem (MemMap (v, i))) for all valid v and i
    prove that a is a valid variable
    prove that c is a valid variable
    prove that e is a valid array
    prove or use that f is a valid index
  use injectivity + assertion to rewrite variable accesses with
   memory accesses in variable store representation
  qed
2. programcounter correspondence:
  look up whether program counters correspond to each other
  qed

IL:
  ASSIGN_V (a,PLUS(VAR c,VAR e))
MIPS:

  -

Priority: 10
ProofCode:
evaluate succeeding IL state representation
evaluate succeeding MIPS state representation
split_goal_into_subgoals:
1. memorycorrespondence:
  assert (varvals (v, i) = mem (MemMap (v, i))) for all valid v and i
    prove that a is a valid variable
    prove that c is a valid array
    prove that e is a valid variable
  use injectivity + assertion to rewrite variable accesses with
   memory accesses in variable store representation

qed

2. *programcounter correspondence:*
   look up whether program counters correspond to each other
   qed

IL:
   ASSIGN_V (a,PLUS(VAR c,e))
MIPS:

-

Priority: 9
ProofCode:
evaluate succeeding IL state representation
evaluate succeeding MIPS state representation
split_goal_into_subgoals:
1. *memorycorrespondence:*
   assert (varvals (v, i) = mem (MemMap (v, i))) for all valid v and i
      prove that a is a valid variable
      prove that c is a valid array
   use injectivity + assertion to rewrite variable accesses with
    memory accesses in variable store representation
   qed
2. *programcounter correspondence:*
   look up whether program counters correspond to each other
   qed

IL:
   ASSIGN_V (a,PLUS(c,ARVAR (e,f)))
MIPS:

-

Priority: 10
ProofCode:
evaluate succeeding IL state representation
evaluate succeeding MIPS state representation
split_goal_into_subgoals:
1. *memorycorrespondence:*
   assert (varvals (v, i) = mem (MemMap (v, i))) for all valid v and i
      prove that a is a valid variable
      prove that e is a valid array
      prove or use that f is a valid index
   use injectivity + assertion to rewrite variable accesses with
    memory accesses in variable store representation
   qed
2. *programcounter correspondence:*
   look up whether program counters correspond to each other
   qed

IL:
   ASSIGN_V (a,PLUS(c,ARCONST (e,f)))
MIPS:

-

Priority: 10

168

ProofCode:
evaluate succeeding IL state representation
evaluate succeeding MIPS state representation
split_goal_into_subgoals:
1. memorycorrespondence:
   assert (varvals (v, i) = mem (MemMap (v, i))) for all valid v and i
      prove that a is a valid variable
      prove that e is a valid array
      prove or use that f is a valid index
   use injectivity + assertion to rewrite variable accesses with
    memory accesses in variable store representation
      qed
2. programcounter correspondence:
   look up whether program counters correspond to each other
   qed

IL:
  ASSIGN_V (a,PLUS(c,VAR e))
MIPS:
  -
Priority: 10
ProofCode:
evaluate succeeding IL state representation
evaluate succeeding MIPS state representation
split_goal_into_subgoals:
1. memorycorrespondence:
   assert (varvals (v, i) = mem (MemMap (v, i))) for all valid v and i
      prove that a is a valid variable
      prove that e is a valid variable
   use injectivity + assertion to rewrite variable accesses with
    memory accesses in variable store representation
      qed
2. programcounter correspondence:
   look up whether program counters correspond to each other
   qed

IL:
  ASSIGN_V (a,PLUS(c,e))
MIPS:
  -
Priority: 8
ProofCode:
evaluate succeeding IL state representation
evaluate succeeding MIPS state representation
split_goal_into_subgoals:
1. memorycorrespondence:
   assert (varvals (v, i) = mem (MemMap (v, i))) for all valid v and i
      prove that a is a valid variable
   use injectivity + assertion to rewrite variable accesses with
    memory accesses in variable store representation
      qed
2. programcounter correspondence:

look up whether program counters correspond to each other
qed

C.2 Array-Assignment Rule 1

IL:
  ASSIGN_AV (a,b,PLUS(ARVAR (c,d),e))
MIPS:

  -

Priority: 10
ProofCode:
evaluate succeeding IL state representation
evaluate succeeding MIPS state representation
split_goal_into_subgoals:
1. *memorycorrespondence:*
    assert (varvals (v, i) = mem (MemMap (v, i))) for all valid v and i
       prove that a is a valid array
       prove that c is a valid array
       prove or use that b is a valid index
       prove or use that d is a valid index
    use injectivity + assertion to rewrite variable accesses with
     memory accesses in variable store representation
    qed
2. *programcounter correspondence:*
    look up whether program counters correspond to each other
    qed

Further array assignment templates are constructed analogous to the primitive variable assignment templates.
Templates for the other arithmetic operators do not differ from the plus operator!

C.3 Branch-Statement Rules

Like with the assignment rules we only pick one example rule and present the goto rule. Other branch rules are the same or very similar.

IL:
  BRANCH (VAR a,target)
MIPS:

  -

Priority: 10
ProofCode:
evaluate succeeding IL state representation
evaluate succeeding MIPS state representation
split_goal_into_subgoals:
1. *memorycorrespondence:*
    qed
2. *programcounter correspondence:*

170

assert (varvals a = mem (MemMap a))
   prove that a is a valid variable
   prove that assertion holds
rewrite proof goal with assertion
case a = 1:
   look up whether program counters correspond to each other
else:
   look up whether program counters correspond to each other
qed

IL:
  GOTO (target)
MIPS:
  -
Priority: 10
ProofCode:
evaluate succeeding IL state representation
evaluate succeeding MIPS state representation
split_goal_into_subgoals:
1. memorycorrespondence:
   assert (varvals a = mem (MemMap a))
   rewrite proof goal with assumption (trivial)
   qed
2. programcounter correspondence:
     look up whether program counters correspond to each other
   qed

C.4 Procedure Call and Return Rules

We present the rules for calling a procedure with one and two arguments as well as for returning from a procedure call.

IL:
  CALL1 (ret,pid,arg)
MIPS:
  -
Priority: 10
ProofCode:
evaluate succeeding IL state representation
evaluate succeeding MIPS state representation
split_goal_into_subgoals:
1. memorycorrespondence:
   assert (varvals (v, i) = mem (MemMap (v, i))) for all valid v and i
     prove that arg is a valid variable
   use injectivity + assertion to rewrite variable accesses with
   memory accesses in variable store representation
   qed
2. programcounter correspondence:
     look up whether program counters correspond to each other (trivial)
   qed

3. check call convention correctness
     look up whether pid, ret and MIPS state fulfill the call conventions
  qed

IL:
  CALL2 (ret,pid,[arg1,arg2])
MIPS:

  -

Priority: 10
ProofCode:
evaluate succeeding IL state representation
evaluate succeeding MIPS state representation
split_goal_into_subgoals:
1. memorycorrespondence:
  assert (varvals (v, i) = mem (MemMap (v, i))) for all valid v and i
    prove that arg1 is a valid variable
    prove that arg2 is a valid variable
  use injectivity + assertion to rewrite variable accesses with
  memory accesses in variable store representation
  qed
2. programcounter correspondence:
  look up whether program counters correspond to each other (trivial)
  qed
3. check call convention correctness
    look up whether pid, ret and MIPS state fulfill the call conventions
  qed

IL:
  RET (var)
MIPS:

  -

Priority: 10
ProofCode:
evaluate succeeding IL state representation
evaluate succeeding MIPS state representation
split_goal_into_subgoals:
1. memorycorrespondence:
  assert (varvals (v, i) = mem (MemMap (v, i))) for all valid v and i
    prove that var is a valid variable
    prove that return variable assignment is valid
  use injectivity + assertion to rewrite variable accesses with
  memory accesses in variable store representation
  qed
2. programcounter correspondence:
  look up whether program counters correspond to each other (trivial)
  qed
3. check call convention correctness
    look up whether MIPS state fulfills the call conventions
  qed

C.5 Print-Statement Rules

IL:
  PRINT (var)
MIPS:
  -

Priority: 10
ProofCode:
evaluate succeeding IL state representation
evaluate succeeding MIPS state representation
split_goal_into_subgoals:
1. *memorycorrespondence:*
   assert (varvals (v, i) = mem (MemMap (v, i))) for all valid v and i
      prove that var is a valid variable
   use injectivity + assertion to rewrite variable accesses with
    memory accesses in variable store representation
   qed
2. *programcounter correspondence:*
      look up whether program counters correspond to each other (trivial)
   qed
3. *check print conventions*
   qed

Lebenslauf

Persönliche Daten

Name:	Jan Olaf Blech
Geburtsdatum:	24.01.1979
Geburtstort:	Göttingen
Familienstand:	ledig
Staatsangehörigkeit:	deutsch

Ausbildung

1985 – 1989	Besuch der Brüder-Grimm Schule in Göttingen
1989 – 1991	Besuch der Orientierungsstufe Lutherschule in Göttingen
1991 – 1998	Besuch des Theodor-Heuss Gymnasiums in Göttingen
9/1995 - 12/1995	Besuch des Truro College in Truro, England
1998	Abitur am Theodor-Heuss-Gymnasium in Göttingen
10/1999 – 03/2004	Studium der Informatik an der Universität Karlsruhe(TH) Abschluss: Diplom (Informatik)

Beruflicher Werdegang

04/2004 – 09/2005	wissenschaftlicher Mitarbeiter, Institut für Programmstrukturen und Datenorganisation Universität Karlsruhe(TH)
10/2005 – 03/2006	wissenschaftlicher Mitarbeiter, Institut für Softwaretechnik und Theoretische Informatik Technische Universität Berlin
04/2006 – 06/2008	wissenschaftlicher Mitarbeiter, Arbeitsgruppe Softwaretechnik Technische Universität Kaiserslautern
seit 07/2008	Post-Doktorand, Distributed and Complex Systems Group Laboratoire VERIMAG, Gières bei Grenoble